T.H. Green's Theory of Positive Freedom

T.H. Green's Theory of Positive Freedom

From Metaphysics to Political Theory

Ben Wempe

ia

IMPRINT ACADEMIC

Published in the UK by Imprint Academic
PO Box 200, Exeter EX5 5YX, UK

Published in the USA by Imprint Academic
Philosophy Documentation Center
PO Box 7147, Charlottesville, VA 22906-7147, USA

ISBN 0907845 584

A CIP catalogue record for this book is available from the
British Library and US Library of Congress

www.imprint-academic.com/idealists

Contents

Preface to the 2004 Edition

In October 1986 I defended my Ph.D. on T.H.Green's theory of positive freedom with a book entitled *Beyond Equality: A Study of T.H.Green's Theory of Positive Freedom*. This was based on a reading of Green's unpublished manuscripts which are deposited in Balliol College Library, Oxford. I had chosen Green by way of compromise between my own interest in Hegel and the expertise of my supervisor at the European University Institute in Florence, the late Maurice Cranston. My interest in Hegel I had picked up in the course of my training in political theory at Leiden University where I had studied with Herman van Gunsteren, who eventually also was to become a supervisor to my Ph.D. But Cranston did not see fit to supervise a dissertation on Hegel, and so we came up with the British Idealists as a subject that would meet both our interests. British Idealism seemed like a fascinating period in British intellectual history since it so sharply contrasted with the traditionally empiricist nature of British philosophy. Green struck me as the 'best of the bunch' since he was the founder of the school and hence the principal champion of a new radical message in England. The topic of positive freedom was directly connected to the discipline in which I was trained. The fact that there was a substantial collection of unpublished manuscripts only made the project more exciting. I did soon realize, however, that my topic was going to be a rather lonely adventure: a relatively eccentric subject with only a handful of fellow researchers to share my interests. But I also saw the advantages: this way at least there still was something for me to discover.

I never made much of an effort to publicize this book and neither did the publisher. For that reason, it was for a long time one of the most difficult publications to obtain in the whole world. It was not just *Beyond Equality,* but also 'Beyond Reach' (I owe this quip to Derrick Darby). I completely acquiesced in the idea that my research on Green's manuscripts would remain a one man's enterprise. After all, everyone needs some subject to delve into for a dissertation and I decided that mine was as good as any. However, in 2002 I discovered much to my surprise that the climate for Idealist studies had altered radically. Not only were there many more people working in this field than I had ever thought possible, there even was sufficient support for a conference entirely devoted to Green, which was organized at Harris Manchester College, Oxford.

In this new edition of my book I want to give wider publicity to the findings of this research project from 1986. To do a full job would require a complete re-writing of the book, which would have taken much more extended research. Instead I have chosen to bring it up to date by supplementing the account from 1986 with references to all new studies on Green which have been published since then. It is not my ambition in the course of this book to actually enter into a debate with all scholars who published on Green since I finished the research on my Ph.D. In chronological order these are Jerry Gaus, 1983; Andrew Vincent, 1986, 2000; Geoffrey Thomas, 1987; Avital Simhony, 1989, 1991a, 1991b, 1993a, 1993b, 1995; Peter Nicholson, 1990; Colin Tyler, 1997; Maria Dimova-Cookson, 2001, 2003; Matt Carter, 2003 and David Brink, 2003. To make the book up to date I have provided cross references to this rapidly growing body of literature wherever this is relevant. I also have taken out some sections which now strike me as needlessly detailed digressions. In this manner, I omitted in Chapter One a reconstruction of the background of Hegel's *Propaedeutik* and an account of the various hypotheses I ventured regarding the status of the manuscript translation of this work which is kept among Green's papers. In Chapter Two I abridged the exposition of the published account of Green's general metaphysics in *Prolegomena.*

By issuing this updated edition I intend to make the results of my research accessible to a wider audience of scholars so that it can be taken into account in new directions in the interpretation of Green's body of thought.

Acknowledgements

While this new edition has a limited ambition, there neverthe-less are a great number of people and institutions whom I want to thank. First is the Rotterdam School of Management, my present employer, which generously granted and helped to finance a year's sabbatical leave. In a practical sense this was made possible by my colleague Dr. Hans van Oosterhout who took on a substantial part of my teaching responsibilities this year. Harris Manchester College offered me for a year a hospi-table and most stimulating working environment. I am partic-ularly indebted to the Principal, Revd. Dr. Ralph Waller, whose friendly and easy-going style of management radiates into every aspect of the College life; to Dr. William Mander, who nominated me as a Visiting Research Fellow; and to Sue Killoran, by any standard the best Librarian in the world. I acknowledge once again the help I received from my colleague and flatmate in Florence, David Brew, who disinterestedly spent a considerable time correcting the English in the original book. For the present edition I could rely on the unrivalled scholarship and the critical eye of Peter Nicholson. My thanks too to Dr. Geoffrey Thomas for his comments and suggestions for revising the original book.

Annet Withagen, my partner in life, contributed by her stim-ulating enthusiasm for this project. The book is dedicated to my mother, H.P.M. Wempe-Bielars and to the memory of my father, J.A.D. Wempe.

So long as the object of political progress could be sufficiently described as the equality of all men before the law, or the removal of restraints which were equally impediments to pleasure & to noble living on the part of those affected by 'em, it did not much matter how the common good was conceived. It was enough to insist that it should really be common — the good of the greatest number. But now that equality before the law has been pretty well established in middle & western Europe; now that everyone is coming to be recognised as having a title to take part in the direction of the powers of society; further questions arise as to the end to which those powers should be directed.

. . . The difficulties which reflecting & disinterested men feel in regard to the claims of the great causes & movements that affect modern society turn on questions as to the nature of the social good which is to be sought for.

T.H. Green

Introduction

Thomas Hill Green was a nineteenth century thinker, who made an important contribution to the introduction of continental idealist philosophy in Britain. In this manner he helped to establish a school of thought known as the British Idealists, which was to become the dominant trend in British philosophy in the last three decades of that century. In this book I seek to reconstruct Green's theory of positive freedom as an integral part of his system of Idealist philosophy.

A. The Thesis of the Book

One of the more remarkable features of Green's reputation as a philosopher was that, in spite of considerable literary output during his academic career, very little of this was published during his lifetime. Apart from a lengthy *Introduction* to a new edition of Hume, which he prepared with T.H. Grose, his publications did not amount to more than a small number of essays and reviews.[1] It was not until after his early death in 1882 that any of his other works were published, including

---

[1] Green's publications during his lifetime were: a contribution for the 'Old Mortality' essay reading society entitled 'The Force of Circumstances,' which was included in a volume *Undergraduate Papers*, Oxford, 1858; a winning essay for the Chancellor's Prize in 1862 on 'An Estimate of the Value and Influence of Works of Fiction in Modern Times'; two articles for the *North British Review*: on 'The Philosophy of Aristotle,' in September 1866, and on 'Popular Philosophy in its Relation to Life,' which appeared in March 1868; the two introductions to Hume's *Treatise* and *Essays* referred to above, in 1874; a series of articles in the *Contemporary Review* concerning the work of H.Spencer and G.H.Lewes, in 1877–1881 (four articles were originally planned but the publication of the last article, which was later published in Green's collected *Works*, was abandoned because of the death of Lewes, and a rejoinder to criticism of the original series appeared in 1881); two privately published Lay Sermons; four book reviews in the late 1870s for *Academy*, a periodical issued by his former pupil Appleton; a public lecture for the Liberal Association in Leicester on *Liberal Legislation and Freedom of Contract*, published by Slatter & Rose, Oxford, in 1881; and an

those with which he acquired a place in the history of British philosophy. First of all came his influential treatise on moral philosophy, *Prolegomena to Ethics*, which was based on his professorial lectures in 1880-1882.[2] Of all his posthumous publications, *Prolegomena* was without doubt the book which corresponded best to the type of work Green himself would have published, had he lived longer. According to his own account,[3] the manuscript was complete but for some twenty or thirty pages, and it required only minor editorial amendments by his former pupil A.C. Bradley before it was printed. All of Green's other posthumously published writings were included in the edition of his *Works*, edited by another pupil, R.L.Nettleship, who also wrote a short *Memoir* of Green.[4] In addition to the writings already published during his lifetime Nettleship selected two lecture courses from Green's tutorial period: one on Kant's *Critique* complemented with notes on Kant's moral philosophy and another on Mill's *Logic*, as well as Green's professorial lectures on 'The Principles of Political Obligation and the Social Virtues,' delivered over three terms in 1879-1880.[5]

The reputation as a philosopher which Green acquired through his publications was chiefly in the field of ethical and political philosophy: his ethical theory was fully worked up in his influential and authoritative *Prolegomena*, while he made his name as a political philosopher with the lectures on Political Obligation already mentioned, which were initially published in the collected *Works*, but afterwards issued under separate cover. However, if we do not restrict ourselves to Green's published writings it is difficult to avoid the conclusion that Green viewed his philosophical task primarily as metaphysical. It is evident from his manuscripts that Green

---

extract of the forthcoming *Prolegomena* on the metaphysical foundations of his moral philosophy, in *Mind* in 1882.

[2] *Prolegomena to Ethics*, Oxford, 1883. The latest edition of this text was edited and introduced by David O. Brink, Oxford, 2003. See also by the same author *Perfectionism and the Common Good: Themes in the Philosophy of T.H.Green*, Oxford, 2003.

[3] Ms letter to Messrs. Longmans dd. 14 March 1882.

[4] *The Works of Thomas Hill Green*, ed. R.L. Nettleship, 3 vols, London, 1885-8; the modern edition is *Collected Works of T.H. Green*, ed. Peter Nicholson, reissued with two new volumes (making five in total): vol. iv is *Prolegomena to Ethics*, vol. v contains selections from Green's undergraduate essays and speeches and some of the formerly unpublished manuscripts. Bristol, 1997.

[5] This was the original title of Green's lectures according to the Balliol timetable for the academic year 1879-80.

saw an idealist position in metaphysics as a necessary starting point for his philosophy, indeed for any sound philosophy. Now, it may be argued that this is an interpretation that can also readily be grasped from his published work, notably his critical exposition on Locke and Hume and his first positive statement of his doctrine in *Prolegomena*.[6] But, in the published Green, his metaphysical doctrine was stated only in concise form, and suffers from a good deal of unresolved puzzles. His unpublished philosophical papers, on which this study draws, contain ample evidence of the powerful connection Green construed between his first principles and other realms of his philosophy, including moral and political theory.

The thesis I want to defend here is that the far-reaching and beneficial influence of Green's political doctrine, on public policy as well as in the field of political theory, was founded on a misinterpretation of his philosophical stand, since the metaphysical basis on which Green argued for his political position was largely neglected. But, as my interest in Green is primarily in his social philosophy, his metaphysics is only of importance to me in so far as it has implications for his moral and political philosophy. I shall restrict myself, in dealing with Green's system of first principles, to Green's concept of the self, which may be seen as one of the least satisfactory parts of the metaphysics set out in the introductory books of the *Prolegomena*. Green treats this subject very summarily and inadequately in the course of his discussion of the relationship between, on the one hand, the eternal consciousness, an entity the activity of which according to Green must be presupposed in order to explain the very possibility of a world of experience, and, on the other hand, the finite mind or each individual conscious subject. A reading of Green's unpublished manuscripts, however, shows that his thinking on this matter was much more concrete, and his ideas much more explicit than can be gathered from the published *Works*.

This study comprises five chapters. The first discusses Green's philosophical development and examines an important influence that went into the formation of his philosophical opinions. Chapter Two considers Green's metaphysics and describes how some of the most obvious omissions from the concise version of his metaphysical doctrine, as it is found in

---

[6] As did David O. Brink in a personal communication at the Green conference held in September 2002 at Harris Manchester College, Oxford.

his published works, may be remedied by reference to Green's unpublished material. In particular, it will be demonstrated that Green's thinking on the nature of the eternal conscious-ness and its relationship to the individual self was much more concrete than might be expected on the basis of the exposition in the *Prolegomena*. Chapter Three goes on to assess the impli-cations for Green's moral and political theory which can be drawn from this conception of the self and the related concepts examined and then develops his theory of positive freedom in the light of the metaphysical principles discussed. Chapter Four argues that Green's criticism of utilitarian social theory equally flows from metaphysical considerations and describes his view of the political relevance of his own theory. It is sug-gested that it is appropriate to consider Green's social philoso-phy as an attempt to give a consistent theoretical rendering of the socialist leanings in the later work of John Stuart Mill. In this way, Green can be viewed as the first theorist of the mod-ern welfare state, and it is this last claim which the fifth chapter investigates before finally drawing a parallel between Green's dispute with the utilitarians and a more recent discussion in political theory about the two meanings of the concept of freedom.

B. Green and the Quest for a Philosophy of Life

In order to situate Green's reverting to idealist metaphysics in a context yet wider, I will begin by pointing out which other functions Green intended his idealist metaphysics to perform. No doubt, the best introduction to this argument may be found in his essay on 'Popular Philosophy in its Relation to Life,' which more clearly than any other of his publications shows that he analysed the problems of his times in terms of the lack of what he refers to as a 'philosophy of life'.[7] In this essay Green is primarily concerned with the adverse practical effects resulting from the lack of an adequate philosophy. The 'popular philosophy' which he sought to refute in his early essay was not only wrong in its ethical prescription, but also in its whole method and metaphysical outlook. Its detrimental effects were to be found not only in relation to moral conduct, but also in the field of politics, religion and epistemology. This

---

[7]   Originally published in *The North British Review*, March 1868, reprinted in
       Works, iii, pp. 92–124.

state of affairs in British philosophy was to be remedied by a 'philosophy of life,' like Hegel's. In the absence of a more adequate theory, the functions which he ascribed to such a philosophy of life were partially fulfilled by contemplative poetry, evangelical religion, and Rousseau's conception of freedom and rights.[8]

As will appear from the second chapter of this book, this way of presenting the problem of current British philosophy runs along essentially the same lines as the argument of the introduction to his *Prolegomena*.[9] In this latter text he also referred to contemplative poetry and religious faith as important forces fostering genuine moral beliefs in an age devoid of any sound ethical philosophy. In *Prolegomena*, however, the dominance of the various sciences had taken the place of the utilitarian 'popular philosophy' of his *North British Review* article. A detailed assessment of the causes of this unsatisfactory state of the British public mind is voiced in an unpublished earlier draft of Green's essay.

> Common sense, religious feeling, & positive science — these three hold divided empire over the consciousness of our time. Each hostile to the rest, they yet make common cause against the enemy of whom, tho' he scarcely holds up his head in England, it is rumoured from Germany that his method is not strictly inductive, that he claims to know God thro' no higher revelation than his reason, & that, tho' he neither robs temples nor erects barricades, he in a way of his own turns the world upside down.
>
> A consideration of the causes & history of this 3 fold hostility may give us a clearer view of the claims & office of that form of spiritual activity which provokes it.[10]

This earlier draft of Green's essay shows the central position Hegel occupied in the remedy Green recommended for the unsatisfactory connection of popular ethical philosophy and moral conduct which he found in Britain.

Before studying Green's positive doctrine of first principles in subsequent chapters, it will be helpful to situate this quest for a more adequate philosophy of life in a wider context by considering the various ways in which he sought to employ his idealist philosophy. Green's idealist metaphysics and his reverting back to Hegel served at least four separate purposes. In addition to ethics, to which subject his *Prolegomena* was con-

---

[8] *Ibid.*, p. 118.
[9] *Prolegomena*, sect. 1.
[10] Ms. 4. White quarto size sheet of notepaper, folded in two.

fined, his idealist metaphysics were applied in the fields of politics, religion, and epistemology.

Idealism and Politics

The first manner in which Green's use of idealist first principles may be rendered intelligible is by pointing out the political ends which he sought to support. At the beginning of his academic career, English society was going through a period of unprecedented change. The industrial revolution drastically altered the traditional pattern of society. Unregulated industrialization and the demographical changes which were prompted by it caused many social evils, which in turn triggered an ever increasing volume of factory legislation.

When Green started his academic career, political and social reforms were already being introduced. As yet these reforms lacked a consistent theory to defend them. Factory laws which were then being introduced in ever increasing range and numbers were passed in spite of the dominant *laissez faire* doctrine. While Green applauded all social legislation regarding the conditions of work and sanitation, as well as the political reform of 1867, he also saw that these improvements would remain vulnerable so long as there was no convincing political theory to support them.[11] Therefore, he considered it to be his philosophical task to demonstrate the archaic nature of classical liberal political theory so as to pave the way for a better theoretical rendering of these achievements.

The relevance of this political motive for an understanding of his search for an idealistic metaphysics becomes clear when we take into account that, according to Green, classical liberal political theory was inseparably connected with a certain system of metaphysical principles. In his opinion the essential flaw in the doctrine of *laissez faire* originated from an erroneous metaphysics, as was to be found in empiricist philosophy. For this reason, any sound political philosophy to replace classical liberalism had to proceed from a metaphysical criticism of its largely implicit assumption.

Therefore, as a first part of his philosophical task, Green set out to demonstrate the correlation between metaphysics and political theory. Once this intrinsic link was established he

---

[11] A similar claim about the newly acquired democratic rights in post revolutionary Europe is made in his essay on 'Popular Philosophy'. *Works*, iii, p. 120.

could proceed to point out that the shortcomings of classical liberal political theory could only be remedied on the basis of a more adequate system of first principles.

Idealism and Religion[12]

A second task Green set his idealist metaphysics relates to the field of religion. Throughout the nineteenth century the rapid development of the natural sciences had increased the tension between scientific insight and established religious dogmas. A new science like geology suggested a far older age of the world than the 6000 years which the church had always assumed. The controversy between science and church culminated in Darwin's evolutionary biology, the findings of which were published in his *Origin of Species* in 1859. It was in the heat of the controversy which this publication aroused that Green assumed his first academic position. The conflicting claims of science and religion posed no problem to Hegel's system of philosophy, however, and Green saw that an interpretation of the world in idealistic terms would allow for a reconciliation of the conflict which seemed to frustrate religious faith as much as the settlement of scientific beliefs.

It may be pointed out that Green's concern was not so much with science itself. It was rather intended to support one of the two parties in an internal conflict between two different movements within the church. In his times the religious culture of the Church of England was deeply divided between two movements, the High Churchmen and the Low Church or Broad Church movement. With regard to the conflict between the church and the sciences, the former party simply denied all scientific claims contrary to the doctrines of the Established Church and would have preferred to classify Darwin as a heretic in the same way as the conflict with Galileo had been resolved in an earlier stage of church history. The latter party, with which Green sympathised, felt it had to somehow come

---

[12]   The religious context of Green's philosophy is also made a central element in Andrew Vincent's interpretation of Green and of the reception of Idealism in Victorian Britain in general. See especially his 'The word is Nigh Thee: The Religious Context of Idealism,' pp. 6–18 in Andrew Vincent and Raymond Plant, *Philosophy, Politics and Citizenship: the Life and Thought of the British Idealists*, Oxford, 1984; 'T.H.Green and the Religion of Citizenship' in Vincent, ed., *The Philosophy of T.H. Green*, Aldershot, 1986; and 'T.H. Green: Citizenship as Political and Metaphysical,' pp. 27–54 in David Boucher and Andrew Vincent, *British Idealism and Political Theory*, Edinburgh, 2000.

to terms with the incontrovertible evidence of the natural sciences.

Apart from the controversy between natural science and church there was an equally severe but perhaps more technical conflict about the interpretation of the scriptures. Green's own tutor Benjamin Jowett, who was a fierce adherent of Broad Church principles, had made his own position in the church very precarious by his contributing to a volume called *Essays and Reviews*. In this publication, the teachings of the so-called Heidelberger Schule, a neo-Hegelian theological school founded by F.C. Baur, were unequivocally defended. When it was issued in 1861 it met with much criticism from the Established Church. The impact of the Heidelberger Schule on liberal churchmen was an instance in which Hegel's influence was not so much a reconciliatory force. In fact, it formed part of the controversy itself. For Green the technical views on the interpretation of the scriptures neatly fitted the comprehensive philosophical scheme which he constructed on the basis of his idealist first principles. Green's appreciation of Baur, which was of course closely linked with his esteem for Hegel, is clearly seen from his correspondence with his family while he was working on the project to translate Baur's *Geschichte der Christlichen Kirche*.[13]

Idealism and Knowledge

A third constituent of the background of Green's reverting back to an Hegelian-inspired system of metaphysics is of a more theoretical nature and relates to what Green saw as the essential flaw in empiricist metaphysics itself. With his *Essay*, Locke had laid the foundation of a philosophical tradition which was to dominate British philosophy until well into the nineteenth century; but on Green's showing Locke and his successors in the empiricist tradition proceeded from an insufficiently theoretical basis to explain human experience. Carrying the premises of the *Essay* to their logical conclusion, Green

[13] According to Green's correspondence with his family he first engaged on the Baur project while on a tour in Germany in the Long vacation of 1863. He first mentions the work in a letter dd. 21.9.1863: 'I hope to have finished the translation early next year, but I may be tempted to append some essays of my own,' he wrote on that occasion. As he did not get much encouragement for his translation when he got back to Oxford after the summer the project was eventually abandoned. Selections of Green's letters to his family were copied out by Nettleship in his notebook on the Green papers.

demonstrated that Locke's doctrine implied that 'nothing is real of which anything can be said' as he summed up the essentials of his criticism of Locke.[14] He firmly believed that on empiricist principles nothing but a contradictory account of what the mind does and experiences could be given.

Idealism and Morality

A fourth point which may be introduced here to complete the inventory of functions which Green attributed to his idealist metaphysics concerns his ethical philosophy. Along with the rapid development of the natural sciences, there was a distinct tendency towards a type of ethical theory which approached the subject on the basis of the same method which had been so successfully employed in the natural sciences. Green wanted to demonstrate the impossibility of such a naturalistic ethics so as to create room for his own moral philosophy. He sought to refute the idea of a naturalistic ethics in two ways, by a direct as well as an indirect argument. First, in the introduction to his *Prolegomena*, he gave a short, but fundamental criticism of its aspirations to grasp the nature of moral conduct. The second argument was a more extended statement of his own system of first principles covering the first two books of *Prolegomena*. Green's strategy in this second refutation of naturalistic ethics was to consider the theory of human experience from which naturalistic ethics could be shown to proceed. Green's point was that his opponents tacitly assumed a philosophy of man which did not properly allow for man's capacity to form a theory explaining himself.

A criticism of current ethical theories similar to the first, direct argument against naturalistic ethics occurred in his essay on 'Popular Philosophy'. In this earlier publication Green directed the force of this argument against utilitarian ethics. Like scientific ethics, utilitarian premises did not allow for the establishment of moral norms, as opposed to actual conduct. Proceeding from the view of man as motivated by two basic drives only — desire for pleasure and aversion to pain — utilitarianism cannot properly come to prescribing norms other than those to which man *ex hypothesi* conforms.

'Popular philosophy' predated *Prolegomena* by fourteen years, and while Green employed the same argument later on

---

[14] *Prolegomena*, sect. 20; cf. *Introductions* to Hume.

in *Prolegomena* when comparing his own ethical doctrine with its utilitarian counterpart, it is nevertheless clear that it was naturalistic ethics, rather than utilitarianism, which proved the more fundamental rival by the time Green came to compose *Prolegomena*.

Green's Philosophical Development

In this chapter I will reconstruct the process by which Green came to hold his position in metaphysics and the influences which went into the formation of his philosophical opinions. In particular, I propose to consider a line of influence which was perhaps the most important single source in the process of Green's philosophical development so as to clarify his intellectual growth at least on this point. In subsequent chapters we shall investigate how this line of influence can be traced in Green's later philosophical activities.

From a reading of Green's unpublished manuscripts one may conclude that, in youth, Green was very much taken with Hegel's philosophy. In developing his own mature philosophy Green gradually moved to a more independent position. This early impact of Hegel on Green is significant both in theoretical and practical terms. Green's initial enthusiasm for Hegel was to have a lasting influence and played a decisive part in his intellectual development. On the other hand, Green saw in Hegel's philosophy a remedy against the lack of political culture which he found in English society of his own times, a state of affairs which he attributed to the absence of any sound theory of conduct. When Green started his academic career he considered Hegel a most significant example of, as he characterized it in his essay for the *North British Review*, the 'philosophy of life' which could have remedied the defects of the 'popular philosophy' he found dominating public opinion.

It must be admitted, of course, that the claim that Green was largely influenced by Hegel does not represent a new interpretation of his philosophical development. Yet opinions on this point are equivocal: as frequently as he is held to be an Hegelian, Green has been taken essentially as a follower of

Kant, and other views on the philosophical influences on Green have also been defended.[1] Generally, judgments as to the link between Green and Kant form part of an attempt to do justice to the unmistakably liberal overtones of his moral and political philosophy, which apparently are thought to be incompatible with what is seen as the authoritarian character of Hegel's philosophy. A more technical ground for support- ing the Kantian interpretation of Green is found in the fact that Hegel sublimated moral conduct in a sort of public morality, *Sittlichkeit*, which he thought to be embodied in the state, while Green, like Kant, was sufficiently serious about morality to have given it independent status. As to the alternative view, most commentaries which look upon Green as an Hegelian fail to pay attention to the actual manner in which he became acquainted with Hegel and how he worked concepts derived from Hegel into his own mature philosophy. For that reason these commentaries do not amount to more than general clas- sifications which discount the independent nature of Green's later philosophy.

As will be set out, Green's unpublished manuscripts contain ample evidence to establish how he understood Hegel. A close study of Green's reading of Hegel also provides a good intro- duction to an argument concerning the link between Green's metaphysics and his political theory which will be adduced in subsequent chapters. However, before presenting Green's unpublished material on Hegel, consideration should first be given to some misapprehensions about Green's attitude to Hegel, which, in turn, contributed to a distorted view of Green's first principles. These misapprehensions originated in recollections of Green by his contemporaries as well as contra- dictory indications which may be found in Green's own publi- cations.

---

[1]   The number of commentaries on Green, portraying him as an Hegelian is legion. Two studies, which take this line, are: A.J.M. Milne, *The Social Philoso- phy of English Idealism*, London, 1962, and A.Quinton, *Absolute Idealism*, Lon- don, 1972. Green is classified as a Kantian by John Passmore, *A Hundred Years of Philosophy*, London, 1957, p. 56. It has also been argued that Green's intellec- tual development can primarily be traced to his reading of Aristotle: A.R. Cacoullos, *Thomas Hill Green: Philosopher of Rights*, New York, 1974; C.A. Smith, *A Critical Study of T.H. Green's Theory of Political Obligation*, Ph.D. thesis, London, 1977. David Brink makes a very full and balanced assessment of the various intellectual sources, indicating Aristotle, Kant and Hegel as the three major influences on Green, Introduction to *Prolegomena*, sects xxiv and xxv.

A. Misapprehensions as to Hegel's Intellectual Influence on Green

If we restrict ourselves to published sources, it is difficult to come to a conclusive view as to Green's attitude towards Hegel. In spite of the fact that his philosophical writings in a number of respects do indeed suggest great influence from Hegel, his better-known works contain hardly any reference to Hegel. Given Green's working method of philosophical criticism this omission is remarkable. For, it was his wont to develop his own arguments on the basis of a thorough criticism of the work of preceding philosophers so as to bring out the points which he considered of permanent value and to separate them from the more questionable arguments with which they were entangled. This approach is itself reminiscent of Hegel. As he dwelled on those thinkers whom he thought merited refutation, Green's discussion of the work of predecessors may be seen as an acknowledgement of their importance.

In his main publications Green deals extensively with representatives of the British empiricist tradition as well as Immanuel Kant, in whose work this tradition is said to converge with the continental tradition of rationalist philosophy. But Hegel is notably absent in Green's better known works and while his omission in the course of a book like the *Prolegomena* may still be explained by the fact that ethics was perhaps not Hegel's strongest point, the neglect of Hegel in Green's political theory is distinctly curious. Indeed, his lectures on *Political Obligation* do not even mention Hegel. It is not surprising that such a remarkable disparity was noted by Green's first biographer, R.L.Nettleship, and many subsequent commentators.[2] Discussing the importance Green attached to Hegel's contribution to philosophy, Nettleship pointed out

> the noticeable fact that, while he regarded Hegel's system as 'the last word of philosophy', he did not occupy himself with the

---

[2]   See, for example, Green's contemporaries: D.G. Ritchie, *The Principles of State Interference*, London, 1891; and J. Muirhead, *The Service of the State*, London, 1908; and more recently: M. Richter, *The Politics of Conscience: T.H. Green and his age*, London, 1964, p. 172; J.R. Rodman, 'Introduction' in *The Political Theory of T.H. Green*, New York, 1964; H.B. Acton, 'Idealism' in Paul Edwards, ed., *The Encyclopaedia of Philosophy*, vol. 4, p. 115; W.H. Walsh, 'Thomas Hill Green' in *ibid.*, vol. 3, p. 388.

exposition of it, but with the reconsideration of the elements in Kant of which it was the development.[3]

The key to this 'noticeable fact' must first be sought in Green's intellectual development. A good source which may help us clarify how his reading of Hegel actually evolved is to be found in the recollections of two of Green's philosophical colleagues whom he knew from his youth and with whom he was in touch throughout the remainder of his life. The first was Edward Caird, who came to Balliol in October 1860 and became Master of the College in 1893 after Jowett's death. With Caird, Green was from the first in closest sympathy, alike in thought and practical aim. They were both members of the legendary 'Old Mortality' essay reading society and collaborated closely in the 1860s when both men were at the beginning of their academic career, until Caird left Oxford to take up the chair of moral philosophy in Glasgow in 1866. After this date their contact then became less frequent.[4]

The second person who was in a position to pass judgment on Green's intellectual development was his lifelong friend Henry Sidgwick. Two years his junior, Sidgwick went to Rugby with Green and remained on good terms thereafter. As Sidgwick held a fellowship at Trinity College, Cambridge, his contacts with Green were less frequent than those between Green and Caird in the early 1860s, but Sidgwick and Green were in regular contact until Green's death. There is a further difference between these colleagues of Green which will prevent us from too one-sided a view of Green's thinking on Hegel. For, Green's two colleagues in fact belonged to opposing philosophical schools. While Green and Caird largely held the same philosophical views, Sidgwick was perhaps Green's most unsparing critic, a circumstance which, however, in no way affected the mutual appreciation of each other's work.

Caird made his comment on the evolution of Green's thinking on Hegel in his preface to a memorial volume dedicated to Green:

> To Hegel he latterly stood in a somewhat doubtful relation: for while in the main he accepted his criticism of Kant, and held also

---

[3]   *Memoir*, p. lxxxv.
[4]   In his letter of condolence to Mrs. Green on the occasion of her husband's death, Caird regrets that 'I did not make more exertion of later years to keep up personal relations.' Ms letter E. Caird to Charlotte Green dd. 5 April, 1882, Balliol College Library.

that something like Hegel's Idealism must be the result of the development of Kantian philosophy rightly understood, he yet regarded the Hegelian system with a certain suspicion.[5]

According to Caird, for Green, Hegel's system would have been 'too ambitious' and 'premature'. 'It must all be done over again,' Green was reported as saying. Sidgwick's comment is equally suited to reaching a conclusive view of Green's regard for Hegel. It was made shortly before Sidgwick's own death, in the course of a lecture on Green's philosophy which was delivered on 21 May 1900 to the Oxford Philosophical Society. Facing an audience which included the chief representatives of idealism, from the then Master of Balliol downwards, Sidgwick's criticism of Green's philosophy before this forum of course amounted to something like an expedition into the lion's den. As for the intellectual relationship between Hegel and Green, Sidgwick confirmed that his friend's thinking had gradually moved away from Hegel in later years and he gave two personal reminiscences to substantiate this claim. First, Sidgwick told his audience,

> I remember writing to him after a visit to Berlin in 1870, and expressing a desire to 'get away from Hegel': he replied that it seemed to him one might as well try to 'get away from thought itself'.[6]

A second recollection to underscore the distance Green had moved from Hegel in later years was taken from the last philosophical talk Sidgwick had with his friend. On this occasion Green was reported to have said: 'I looked into Hegel the other day, and found it a strange *Wirrwarr*'; and Sidgwick continued: 'the sentence startled me; and the unexpected German word for "chaos" or "muddle" fixed it firmly in my mind'.[7] When an accurate man like Sidgwick expresses himself so emphatically, there can be little doubt as to the veracity of his testimony.

Evidence from Green's Published Writings

The conclusion about the evolution of Green's thinking on Hegel, which is suggested by these two independent and reliable sources, is confirmed if we submit Green's own publica-

[5]   A. Seth and R.B. Haldane, ed., *Essays in Philosophical Criticism*, London, 1883.
[6]   'The Philosophy of T.H.Green,' *Mind*, 10 (1901), p. 19.
[7]   *Ibid.*

tions to a close chronological examination so as to bring out the evidence on his opinion on Hegel. Such an examination shows that Green's later work, with which he was to acquire his philosophical reputation, almost entirely lacks any reference to Hegel. As was hinted at above this was particularly remarkable in Green's *Lectures on the Principles of Political Obligation*. In his characteristic manner Green developed his argument there on the basis of a critical analysis of preceding philosophy. In this way he considered in succession: Hobbes, Spinoza, Locke and Rousseau; after some account of the work of Austin he then went on to expound his own doctrine, without even mentioning Hegel.

The turn of Green's thinking on Hegel in later years, to which our attention was drawn by Caird and Sidgwick, is evident from juxtaposing three book reviews which Green contributed to *Academy* from 1877 to 1881. Not surprisingly, all three books reviewed were on themes related to the new British interest in continental philosophy. The last review Green contributed to *Academy* was devoted to a book on the reception of Kant in England.[8] Significantly, Hegel is mentioned not even once in this article. Green exclusively refers to "Neo-Kantians", while the manner in which he seeks to render the necessity of an idealist philosophy already entirely corresponds with the method of argument employed in *Prolegomena*, on which he was working at the time.

It was in the context of a review of a commentary on Hegel's philosophy of religion by Edward Caird's eldest brother John that Green aligned himself with those 'who regard (Hegel's doctrine) as the last word of philosophy.' This remark was, as we saw, cited by Nettleship in his *Memoir* and in this manner it helped to stamp Green as an Hegelian. The same book review contained a remark by Green about 'one essential aberration' in Hegel which has equally frequently been used to work out Green's eventual position on Hegel. It is reproduced here merely to complete this survey of remarks on Hegel in the published Green.

> If thought and reality are to be identified ... thought must be other than the discursive activity exhibited in our inferences and analyses, other than a particular mode of consciousness ... As little can it be the process of philosophising, though Hegel himself, by what

---

[8]   'Review of J.Watson: "Kant and his English Critics",' *Academy*, September 17 and 24, 1881; reprinted in *Works*, iii, pp. 147–58.

seems to us the one essential aberration of his doctrine, treats this process as a sort of movement of the absolute thought.[9]

Apart from this 'one essential aberration' in Hegel Green draws attention to the problem of the at best indirect relevance of Hegel for the problems people are pondering over in ordinary life. 'We are Hegelian,' as he put it in this 1880 review, 'with only a fraction of our thoughts — on the Sundays of "speculation" not the weekdays of "ordinary thought".'[10] But his changed attitude to Hegel can perhaps best be gathered from the fact that Green thinks he can sum up the 'vital truth' in Hegel in three points. Having underlined earlier in the essay 'the need . . . of a reconsideration of certain points in Hegel's doctrine' he summarizes by way of conclusion the chief innovations Hegel had contributed to philosophy as follows:

> That there is one spiritual self-conscious being, of which all that is real is the activity or expression; that we are related to this spiritual being, not merely as parts of the world which is its expression, but as partakers in some inchoate measure of self-consciousness through which it at once constitutes and distinguishes itself from the world; that this participation is the source of morality and religion; this we take to be the vital truth which Hegel had to teach.[11]

This summary of course reduces Green's opinion on Hegel to readily manageable proportions. It is hardly surprising, therefore, that this statement was also frequently quoted by scholars in their attempt to characterize Green's eventual attitude to Hegel and contributed considerably to the view which arose about Green's thinking on Hegel.[12]

A better indication for Green's opinion of Hegel in later years is to be found in a review by Green of a book on Kant, written by his fellow Idealist, Edward Caird. This article appeared in the same periodical in 1877. Remarkably enough, this review received far less attention in the investigation of Green's position on Hegel than the review referred to earlier. One of the reasons why Green was reluctant to be identified too closely with Hegel emerges from the following passage in which he observed that 'the title "Hegelian" is rather wildly thrown about nowadays and has naturally fallen into some

[9]   'Review of J. Caird, "Introduction to the Philosophy of Religion",' *Academy*, 10 July 1880, reprinted in *Works*, iii, pp. 142–3.
[10] *Ibid.*, p. 142.
[11] *Ibid.*, p. 146.
[12] See, for example, Passmore, *A Hundred Years of Philosophy*, p. 56.

disrepute.' The subtle view he took on Hegel in those days may be seen from the judgment which he passed on his fellow Idealist, Caird:

> No one who by trial and error has become aware of the difficulty of mastering, and still more of appreciating, Hegel's system, would be in a hurry either to accept the title for himself or bestow it on another. We shall not, therefore, describe Professor Caird as an Hegelian, but it is clear that he has very much made Hegel's point of view his own, and it is from this that he undertakes the exposition and examination of Kant.[13]

The difference between Green's statement in his review of John Caird and the far more subtle approach in his review of Edward Caird's book on Kant may partly be attributed to the fact that this latter review was written three years earlier and that the gradual process by which Green drifted away from Hegel, so to speak, had advanced in the meantime. But the main reason for Green's different approach seems to be that he knew Caird to be of exactly the same attitude towards Hegel. While Green considers John Caird to be too much dependent on the terminology of Hegel, Edward Caird took a far more independent view of the philosopher who initially inspired him. Indeed, at one point in the review Green wonders whether his judgment on Caird's book has not been distorted by 'the partiality of a reviewer with whose views it happens exactly to correspond'.[14]

Green's Position on Hegel in Earlier Published Writings

As we go further back to his earlier work, Green's enthusiasm for Hegel becomes ever more manifest. While the last paragraph of his *Introductions* to Hume, which appeared in 1874, still discussed Kant and Hegel on an equal footing, the highest tribute is given to Hegel in an essay for the *North British Review* in 1868, entitled 'Popular Philosophy in its Relation to Life' which we already came across at the outset of this book. It was described by his biographer as 'perhaps the most pregnant and eloquent of his writings.'[15]

For our survey of the evolution of Green's thinking on Hegel it is important to observe that, having pointed out the insuffi-

[13] 'Review of E. Caird: "The Philosophy of Kant",' *Academy*, 22 September 1877, reprinted in *Works*, iii, p. 129.
[14] *Ibid*. p. 136.
[15] *Memoir*, p. lxxiii.

ciency of all empiricist philosophy since Hume, Green presented Hegel so as to indicate the direction in which English philosophy should progress in order to remedy the 'sceptical and destructive results' of popular philosophy: 'Hitherto, except from a school of German philosophers, which did not make itself generally intelligible, no adequate theory has been forthcoming'. As a result, Green goes on to say, 'scepticism of the best men' has become the main characteristic of his times. The origin of this hardly flattering feature of his own times Green finds in the absence of an adequate social theory. This absence resulted from an inadequate system of first principles.

> Art, religion and political life have outgrown the nominalistic logic and the psychology of individual introspection; yet the only recognised formulae by which speculative man can account for them to himself, are derived from that logic and psychology.[16]

Given this state of affairs, Green thinks it inevitable that there will arise an interest for 'a philosophy like that of Hegel, of which it was the professed object to find formulae adequate to the action of reason as exhibited in nature and human society, in art and religion.'[17]

Without doubt this essay, which was published in 1868, constitutes the most obvious indication of the great impact Hegel had on Green in these earlier years. It is, at any rate, the most positive comment on Hegel which is to be found in Green's published writings. In an indirect manner Hegel also figures in a still earlier essay on Aristotle, which will be discussed in more detail later in this chapter.[18]

So far we have been tracing back in time the development of Green's thinking on Hegel, as determined from evidence in his published writings. We have concluded that Green's thinking on this point underwent a considerable change. Green started with unqualified enthusiasm for Hegel, as witnessed in earlier works such as the essay for the *North British Review*, and gradually came to a more independent position in his mature philosophy, when he saw fit to leave out Hegel altogether, as in the two main publications with which he was to earn his reputation as a philosopher. As our aim is to acquire a better understanding of Green's mature philosophy we need to seek a

[16] *Works*, iii, p. 124.
[17] *Ibid.*, p. 125.
[18] Cf. Section F.

more adequate insight into the process which led him away from Hegel to his own position. For this purpose we shall first give an account of the manner in which he actually became acquainted with Hegel's philosophy.

B. Green's Study of Hegel

It was presumably Benjamin Jowett who first acquainted Green with Hegel. Jowett was, it is true, less favourably disposed towards Hegelian philosophy in later years, but in Green's undergraduate days he 'still encouraged the ablest of his pupils in the study of Hegel.'[19] In this respect Jowett was without doubt in the best position to give an account of Green's first wrestlings with Hegel. But as both men were in Oxford almost uninterruptedly and as they communicated chiefly orally, what must have been Green's most important contact during his undergraduate years paradoxically left no direct evidence in his papers. We only have the enthusiastic accounts which Green reported to his family and some occasional remarks in Jowett's correspondence to go by.[20]

Failing Jowett's testimony the best source to inform us about Green's intellectual growth in these first years at Oxford is to be found in an unpublished recollection by his private tutor, C.S. Parker. Green became acquainted with Parker on a reading party in July 1857 and remained in contact with his former tutor until Parker left Oxford to begin a political career in 1868. His recollection of Green was drafted on the occasion of Green's *Memoir*, but it was apparently too late to be included in the text. One of Parker's most striking reminiscences of his former pupil was his special interest in 'central questions' such as 'What is knowledge, desire, will, duty, conscience? What is for man the highest good, the all embracing end?' In this Parker encouraged young Green since he thought that as these 'omnipresent problems' were better thought out, the rest would become easier. Green's 'deepest interest' in these undergraduate days was, however,

> in combining intellectual with moral and religious insights. On the intellectual side he seemed much taken by what little we knew of Hegel's *Logik*, embracing in one vast Syllogism the universe of

---

[19]   Evelyn Abbott and Lewis Campbell, *The Life and Letters of Benjamin Jowett*, 2 vols (London, 1897), I, p. 261.

[20]   Abbott and Campbell, *Life and Letters of Benjamin Jowett*, vol. I.

thought and existence. On the moral side his early training had given him a high and holy ideal with a deep sense of man's inability to realize it otherwise than through a Divine indwelling Spirit.

Thus Philosophy was to him no cold and barren speculation, but a cherished creed, a help to noblest life.[21]

To the present day reader it is perhaps difficult to visualize the approach to Hegel when he first came into fashion in England and Parker's remarks about Hegel strike us as somewhat archaic. In fact, Parker himself also points to the merely superficial knowledge he and his pupil had of Hegel's works. It is likely that, in these undergraduate years, Green's enthusiasm for Hegel far outweighed his actual knowledge of Hegel.

Given the requirements of the undergraduate curriculum, it was to be expected that, until he had taken his degree, Green was in no position to pursue his interest in Hegel in any serious manner. After he had finished the programme for the school of law and history in December 1859, he was in a better position to give shape to his real interests. Green's actual study of Hegel can be reconstructed from the College Library borrowing register of this period as well as from his remaining correspondence. The letters which he sent to his family indicate that he set out to improve his German.[22] According to the borrowing register Green started his first serious reading of Hegel in the summer of 1861 when he carried with him on a reading party to Ilkley, among other books, three volumes of Hegel's *Werke*.[23] From a letter to his family it appears that he was fully aware of the heterodox nature of his philosophical interests: 'My main occupation consists in reading German books of a kind which I fear most people would think very useless,' he wrote from his seaside resort.[24]

Two Theses Regarding Green's Understanding of Hegel

The intensive study of Hegel which was thereby initiated suggests two separate theses. The first is concerned with the role Hegel played in the general process of Green's intellectual development. The second thesis deals with the precise manner in which he understood Hegel.

[21] Ms recollection, dd. 27 September 1888.
[22] 'Since I have been back here I have done little but rub up German,' Green wrote in a letter to his family, dd. 6 January 1861, copied in Nettleship's notebook on the Green manuscripts.
[23] Balliol College Library borrowing register, 1861.
[24] 31 August 1861.

In my reading of his intellectual development Green was in an initial stage very much under the influence of Hegel's philosophy. Although he gradually came to adopt a more independent position in later years, orienting himself more on Kant as time went by, it is clear, in the opinion of the present writer, that the 'return to Kant' characterizing his mature philosophy was to an important extent structured by his early study of Hegel. In fact, it was his earlier study of Hegel which provided Green with the conceptual tools to accomplish his attempt to 'get beyond' Kant. To introduce my first thesis I will begin by presenting some empirical evidence as to the dominant role of Hegel in the formation of Green's philosophical opinions.

'An Apparently Early Essay on Hegel'

A good impression of Green's dealing with Hegel in the mid-1860s emerges from a draft essay on Hegel which was preserved among the Ms collection at Balliol College Library. Nettleship identified this manuscript as 'an apparently early essay on Hegel.' Unfortunately, only parts of this draft are preserved, but these remaining fragments make clear that at this initial stage Green is concerned with refuting what he considers misinterpretations of Hegel's work rather than attempting to expound Hegel's doctrine or even to point out why it was important.

It is now 35 years years since Hegel in the well-known words, 'whatever is real is rational, whatever is rational is real', announced the result of all preceding philosophy, the principle of all that was to follow. Throughout a life which should be to his age what the life of Socrates was to his own, in writings wh[ich] are to the philosophy of the modern world all & more than all that those of Aristotle were to the philosophy of Greece, he unfolded & enforced this truth. But, like A[ristotle], he left no successor. He articulated the message which had been forming itself for utterance in the mouths of Kant, Fichte & Schelling, & his countrymen, as if stunned by its greatness, at first wondered & applauded, then roused themselves to discuss & in discussing to mutilate it, not hitherto to apply it in its fullness. . .

Such was the natural sequel of the enunciation of a principle wh[ich] the spirit of man had been so far educated as to suggest to its own highest interpreter, but not yet to interpret for itself. The physical sciences were still immersed in matter 'in disconnection, dead and spiritless' — the political world seemed to be still dominated by arbitrary will, the religious by superstition. Thus tho'

Hegel by the method, wh[ich] tho' often subjected to the cheap ridicule of ignorance has never been exploded or superseded, reduced the facts of the world to stages in a system of thought, the facts were still too repugnant to the actual consciousness of the age for the reduction to retain its interest. The exhibition of the real as the rational & rational as real was simply the scientific form of the world, wh[ich] Xty had introduced. Yet, as the Xtian belief first attained in the Hegelian philosophy a distinct rational consciousness of itself, so this consciousness has in its turn to wait appropriation & application by mankind. The spiritual hunger was there, but not the positive knowledge of the hold on reality. The Trumpet has spoken, but there has been no armed throng to answer. The full philosophical equipment has not been found in the youth of Germany.[25]

In the same way as most of the other manuscripts left by Green it is not possible to date this document with absolute certainty. In my opinion, the most plausible dating of this document would take the '35 years' mentioned at the beginning of this quotation to refer to 1831, the year of Hegel's death. This suggestion would determine the draft as written in or around 1866, a conclusion which is consistent with the fact that there is a significant correspondence of an entire passage in this draft essay on Hegel with a passage in his essay on Aristotle, which was published in the *North British Review* in September 1866.

This completes the empirical evidence which can be presented in support of the thesis that Green was initially greatly influenced by Hegel. This assertion, it will be recalled, forms part of a wider claim regarding Green's intellectual development. In my reading of Green, his intellectual development can be characterised as a process in which he, after great initial enthusiasm, gradually distanced himself from Hegel and became more oriented towards Kant. The point I want to make, however, is that the manner in which he understood Kant and tried to 'get beyond' his philosophical stance, was decisively structured by his earlier study of Hegel. For an adequate understanding of Green's own mature philosophy it is essential, therefore, to give some account of the actual manner in which he understood Hegel.

The second thesis I want to defend here regarding Green's study of Hegel in the 1860s is that one volume in particular must have been central to his attempt at mastering Hegel's system. This was the *Philosophische Propädeutik*, a posthumous

---

[25] Ms 4: 'Two Sheets of an Apparently Early Essay on Hegel'.

edition of the lectures in preparatory philosophy Hegel delivered when he was a teacher at the Agidien Gymnasium in
Nürnberg.

There is good reason to assume that Green dealt with this
book more intensively than any other of Hegel's works. Once
again I will begin by providing purely empirical evidence supporting this specific thesis, which was suggested to me on the
basis of my investigation of Green's unpublished manuscripts. In the first place this emerges from a recollection by
A.C. Bradley, Green's pupil and editor of the *Prolegomena*. This
recollection was recorded in the Ms notebook which
Nettleship used in preparing Green's *Memoir*. It appears from
this statement, moreover, that Green particularly esteemed
the short passage on 'Philosophy of Religion' in the *Propädeutik*.

The principal evidence for the suggestion that the
Propädeutik must have occupied a central place in Green's
early study of Hegel consists in a manuscript translation of
this work which is preserved together with his other papers in
Balliol College Library.[26] This manuscript, consisting of some
220 pages, covers almost the entire *Propädeutik*. The water-
marks of the paper on which the manuscript was written range
from 1857 to 1864, a circumstance which allows for the imperative, if minimal, conclusion that the project cannot have been
undertaken before these dates. This suggestion seems also
supported by the fact that he used this textbook for his own
lectures, as appears from the references in F.H.Bradley's notes
of Green's 1867 lecture course on moral philosophy.[27]

There can be little doubt that Green, who was so taken with
Hegel in his earlier years, was also acquainted with Hegel's
main works. But since he used the *Propädeutik* for his teaching
activities, he got to know the lectures from Hegel's Nürnberg
period profoundly. It will therefore be useful for the purpose
of tracing Hegel's intellectual influence on Green if we give

---

[26]   Geoffrey Thomas (*The Moral Philosophy of T.H. Green*, Oxford, 1987, p. 47) considers the translation to be a minor document. This is certainly correct in view
of Hegel's later works. My thesis, however, is that the *Propädeutik* played a
special role in the formation of Green's philosophical opinions and is especially relevant for the metaphysical basis of his political theory and the notion
of positive freedom more in particular.

[27]   Ms 1–A–1, 'Notes of Green's lectures,' Merton College Library. This Ms is now
included in vol. v of the *Collected Works of T.H. Green*, ed. Nicholson.

some account of this textbook and consider how Green understood certain of Hegel's key terms.

C. The *Philosophische Propädeutik*[28]

Rosenkranz's edition of the *Propädeutik* was primarily intended as a textbook for contemporary philosophy teachers. It is divided into courses at three levels of instruction: lower, middle, and upper form. The lectures for the lower form comprise a course on Right, Duty and Religion. These three are to be considered as institutional expressions of the human will and it is by virtue of this common element that they can be presented as parts of a single sphere in the system of philosophy set out in the *Propädeutik*. For this reason the lectures for the lower form begin with a brief account of the theory of the will. The subject matter of the lectures is announced as 'the human will considered as a relation of the particular will to the universal will.'[29]

The lectures then focus on the process by which man dissociates himself from the chain of necessity which operates in the natural order. In a manner which was to become characteristic for all his further systematic writings, Hegel distinguishes three 'moments' in this process: animal want, pure indetermination, and rational will. The first of these pertains to the agent as part of his physical constitution; by virtue of his 'wants' a man still forms an integral part of the natural order. The second 'moment' in the process of the will is an element of 'pure indetermination': any agent can adopt any 'object' at will. In virtue of the agent's capacity for rational activity the limited nature of any particular object of will is contrasted with the universality which pertains to the will when all options are still open. The distinction between form and matter of the will which is introduced at this stage plays a central part in the rationalistic theory of the will set out in the

---

[28] Unless otherwise indicated, all the following indented quotations are from the manuscript translation of the *Propädeutik*. I shall use the following abbreviations to refer to this ms: For the lower form: 1. 'Philosophy of Right, Ethics and Philosophy of Religion'R; 1.1 'Introduction' R.I; 1.2 'Explanations of Introduction (Erläuterungen)' R.E. For the middle form: 2. 'Phenomenology of the Mind' M; 3. 'Logic' L. For the upper form: 4. 'Philosophy of the Conception' C; 5. 'Encyclopedia of the Philosophical Sciences' E. In brackets is a reference to the English translation by A.V. Miller, Hegel, *The Philosophical Propaedeutic*, Oxford, 1986.

[29] R.I 1 (Miller, p. 1).

Propädeutik. The contrast of the universal form of the will with the limited nature of its matter leads to the third and conclusive 'moment' which is to be discerned in the process of willing, i.e. when the will adopts an object adequate to its universal form:

> ... for the Will to be truly and absolutely free, that which it wills, in other words, its contents must not be anything other than itself. It must will in itself alone & and have itself for object. The pure Will thus does not will any particular content for the sake of its particular desirableness, but only that the Will as such may be free & become emancipated from all limits, in other words that the Universal Will be done.[30]

In all its brevity, the introduction to the lower form course thus outlines a rationalistic theory of the will with the distinction, characteristic to Hegel, between 'abstract' and 'real' freedom, a distinction which is set out in a form-matter scheme.[31] According to its form the will is always universal and by definition free; real freedom, however, is established only when the particular will conforms to the universal will. In other words, man realizes his potential.

Having set out this theory of the will Hegel goes on to discuss Right, Duty and Religion as three stages in the process of self-assertion of the human will: 'The more exact determinations & development arising from these common principles of the will are exhibited in the philosophies of Right, of Duty, and of Religion.'[32] In view of our intended study of Green's political theory the most interesting of these is the first section on Right. In this section Hegel enters into the mutual recognition of each other by individual agents as being essentially of the same status. According to Hegel's exposition this mutual recognition forms the eventual basis of the political order in society.

The section on Right falls — in quite an unHegelian manner — into two parts. First comes a discussion of the first principles of Right. The basis of any legal system is to be found in the

---

[30] R.I 12 (Miller, p. 4).
[31] This distinction will recur in the discussion of chapter 2 and 3, where abstract freedom is associated with freedom in the negative sense, and real freedom with freedom in the positive sense. Incidentally this distinction also plays an important role in Maria Dimova-Cookson's recent article 'A New Scheme of Positive and Negative Freedom: Reconstructing T.H. Green on Freedom,' *Political Theory*, 31 (2003), pp. 508–32.
[32] R.I 12 (Miller, p. 4).

recognition of one's fellow member of the community as a person and this principle is then applied to property rights and the right of the state to punish. Second, it is set out how these first principles are 'exhibited in the Civil Community.'[33] One of the more important statements of this section is the definition of 'Law' as 'the abstract expression of the Universal self-realized Will.'[34] In the corresponding *Explanation*, which Rosenkranz compiled from notebooks of Hegel's pupils, this is amplified as follows:

> Law is the Universal Will, so far as it is identical with it in the eye of reason. In this case it is not necessary that each individual should have declared his will and then a universal result be deduced from it. And on that account it has not taken place in actual history, that a single citizen of a people should have proposed a law and then in common council should come to an agreement with others concerning the law. Law involves the necessity of 'rightful' relations of one towards another. Legislators have not laid down arbitrary principles. These are not determinations of their particular pleasure, but they have recognised in the depth of their spirit what the truth and essence of a rightful relation is.[35]

In the section on Duties, the difference is set out between Obligation, which is based on the system of legal rules, and Duty, which originates in the moral relationships which man enters into. Whereas we saw that law was defined as 'the abstract expression of the universal self-realized will,' the realm of morality represents a more concrete expression thereof. Right and morality are depicted as two successive stages in the process of self-assertion of reason, in which they have a common basis. Reason enters into both forms of human activity. Moral relationships which exist among men differ from 'righteous' ones in that the moral agent does not look upon his fellow men merely as capable of rational activity in the same way as the agent himself, as in righteous relationships, but also as a subject in the process of self-realization. In accordance with the four basic forms of moral relationship in which man may stand with respect to others, Hegel distinguishes four types of duty: Duty to self, family, state, and

---

[33] R 1 (Miller, p. 22).
[34] R 26 (Miller, p. 33).
[35] *Ibid.*

finally a category of duties to other human beings as such: social duties.[36]

The section on *Religion*, which concludes Hegel's lectures for the lower form, is very terse. It consists of only 10 paragraphs and covers less than 2 pages in the *Propädeutik*, a fact which Rosenkranz explains as being due to Religion forming a separate part of the curriculum at Nürnberg, so that a more extensive treatment of this issue was not required in a preparatory course in philosophy.[37] Yet, this section, concise as it may be, is not without interest for a detailed study of Hegel's influence on Green. For we know from reliable sources that Green spoke highly of the fragment on the philosophy of Religion in the *Propädeutik*.[38] Moreover, Hegel's philosophy of religion is of particular interest to us since, as was explained in the Introduction, Green's turning to Hegel was to an important extent prompted by religious motives.

The section begins with the transition from morality to religion. While it is true that 'the moral law in our nature' is eventually identical with 'the eternal law of Reason,' morality is equally characterized by its continuous falling short of this standard of reason. Thus, while we are 'irresistibly bound to observe the moral law' and we equally *feel* 'intrinsically bound' by it, 'this same intuitive feeling tells us of our inadequacy, as individuals, in respect of this law.'[39] Moral activity is characterized by the distinction between 'is' and 'ought,' between what each man has in him to become and the realization of this potential. It is only in the sphere of Religion that this distinction is finally overcome. God is both the beginning and the end of Hegel's doctrine in the *Propädeutik*. It is the final conclusion which must yet be presupposed to explain the very existence of a world of experience and the possibility of human activity.

In order to trace their impact on Green's mature philosophy the most significant paragraphs of the philosophy of Religion are quoted here:

> God is the Absolute Spirit, i.e. he is pure Essence, objectifying himself, envisaging in the object nought but himself, in other

---

[36] R 40 (Miller, p. 41).
[37] K. Rosenkranz, Preface to the *Propädeutik*, pp. xvii – xviii.
[38] A.C. Bradley made a remark to this effect, which was recorded in Nettleship's Ms notebook of the Green manuscripts.
[39] R 71 (Miller, p. 52).

words, the whole process of this differentiation is a return into himself, into equation of self with self.[40]

The link which Green was to construe between this central postulate in the *Propädeutik* and his own epistemology can be seen from the following section:

> The elevation of the spirit above the sensible and finite is the negative condition of this knowledge for us, but only so far as this implies that we go out beyond the sensible and finite, relinquish it, recognize its nullity. It is this knowledge of the Absolute alone which is itself absolute and immediate cognition, and cannot have any finite things as its positive ground, in other words be proved by anything which is not itself . . .
>
> This knowledge has to be more closely determined, cease to be merely internal feeling, belief in an undefined and general being, and become Cognition. The Cognition of God does not surpass the reason, for this is the reflexion of God, is essentially knowledge of the Absolute, such cognition surpasses the understanding, i.e. the knowledge of the finite and the relative.[41]

In order to render possible the entire process of differentiation in terms of which empirical reality can be understood and interpreted some self-distinguishing entity or principle must be presupposed which cannot be described otherwise than in its own terms. As will be pointed out,[42] the theme of a self-distinguishing, self-seeking principle is central to the metaphysical foundation of Green's theory of morality. Also, the eventual unity between God and reason may have been taken from the *Propädeutik*, if we judge by the paragraphs printed above.

Phenomenology of Mind

Hegel's lectures for the lower middle form, or *Obersekunda*, are dedicated to a theme which he had already worked up three years earlier, as a private tutor at Jena, in his *Phänomenologie des Geistes*[43] by way of introduction to his system of philosophy as a whole. The Nürnberg version of this same doctrine is of course much more concise. It carries a double title: 'Phenomenology of Mind, or Philosophy of Consciousness'.[44] The introductory paragraphs set out the difference between the

---

[40]   R 76 (Miller, p. 53).
[41]   R 73, 74 (Miller, pp. 52-3).
[42]   See Chapter Two.
[43]   Bamberg, 1807.
[44]   M exordium.

philosophical and the ordinary way of thinking about experience. We are accustomed to look upon objects of experience as forming an external world, existing by itself. From the philosophical viewpoint, however, objects of experience are considered in their relationship to a cognitive subject. Consciousness, then, consists in the whole of subject-object relationships. The corollary of this view is that the properties, which are attributed to things in our everyday life experiences, can no longer be taken as exclusively pertaining to things, but must rather be assumed to exist in a particular relation between object and subject.

As to this relationship between subject and object two positions can be defended to which two opposing philosophical schools correspond. Idealism, which takes the subject as fundamental, treats the object, as a result, as a mere product of the subject. The opposite position is taken by Realism, which attributes to objects an existence separate from the subject, and where the subject is, consequently, determined by the object. The standpoint of the *Propädeutik* eliminates the one-sided nature of both views and considers human knowledge as a system of subject-object relationships. Subject and object may be considered separately for purposes of analysis, but to grasp their proper nature the two must be seen in the light of their mutual relationship. The subject forms objects, and through its objects it forms itself. The process of this development is the subject matter of the *Phenomenology of Mind*, by which term Hegel understands the 'science of the forms in which the mind manifests itself.'

The Phenomenology first considers consciousness as a complex of subject–object relationships, i.e. setting aside for the time being the question of whether these relationships originate in the subject, as Idealism claimed, or in the object, as was held by Realism. If we consider consciousness as a relationship between the Ego and its objects, then consciousness can be categorised according to the nature of its object; but as the object is also essentially determined by the subject this differentiation can equally be considered as a progressive process of self-assertion. As various sorts of objects of consciousness may be distinguished, three stages can be discerned in this process of self-assertion: 'the object positing itself vis-à-vis the Ego, the Ego which becomes its own object, and thought.' To these three moments three stages of consciousness correspond: 'consciousness in general, self-consciousness, and reason.'[45]

Consciousness

This first moment of consciousness again falls into Sensation, Perception, and Understanding. In this three stage sub-division Sensation stands for the object's being immediately presented to the self under forms of space and time. In Perception objects are further formed by the cognitive activity of the self by attributing certain sensory qualities to them. Sense perception by itself, i.e. apart from any further formative act on the part of the Understanding would not amount to more than a continuous flux of impressions. Therefore, in the third stage all sense impressions are substantiated by relating them to a conception, deriving from the third mental faculty discussed in this section. Understanding does not focus merely on the appearance of the object, as was the case in perception, but comprehends the essence of the object in a conception presented to the self. The essence of the thing has only indirectly to do with the way in which it is first presented to us in perception. At the same time a closer investigation will show that this first impression, given in perception, is indeed related to the essence of the thing. However, it is only a superficial impression thereof. The 'first impression' of perception is not so much mistaken as insufficient.

Self-Consciousness

A particular instance of the formation of the object by the subject occurs when the subject makes itself into an object. This represents a second stage of the process by which Mind manifests itself in the world. Initially, Hegel declares, self-consciousness is a 'mere form without content.' The process of its further development, then, is 'to realize its conception and to become conscious of itself.'[46] A first step in such a process of self-realization consists in the subjecting of objects whereby the distinction between object and self-consciousness is removed. The striving after unifying the external world with one's self forms the basis of the dialectical relationship

---

[45]   M 9 (Miller, p. 56).
[46]   M 23 (Miller, p. 59).

between wants and their satisfaction which succeed one another in a continuous dynamic:

> The conception of self-consciousness implies a latent difference which is not yet realized. As this latent difference advances into distinctness the self-consciousness has the feeling of ... a negation of itself, the feeling of a deficiency, a *want*.[47]

This 'contradiction' is again overcome by appropriating new objects from the external world to bring them into harmony with the self.

> The condition of desire is accordingly the presence of an external independent object, or rather the consciousness of such presence: and its activity produces satisfaction only by the sublation of the object. It is in this way alone that Self-consciousness attains the feeling of self.[48]

However, when the self thus manifests itself by subjecting the external world to itself so as to order it according to its own liking, it inevitably comes into contact with other self-conscious agents. The dialectical course of this first contact of self-conscious agents leads Hegel to one of the most crucial sections of the *Phänomenologie des Geistes*. It would appear that the argument on Dominion and Servitude, which is set out in the corresponding passage of the Nürnberg Phenomenology, is one aspect of the *Propädeutik* which had a significant impact on Green and which is therefore deserving of particular attention in the present study.

Master and Servant

According to Hegel's dialectical principle the relationship of the two individual self-conscious agents, on the occasion of their first encounter, takes the form of a life and death struggle. This struggle is settled short of slaying the defeated party only because there is established an unequal relationship of dominion and servitude in which the servant, who preferred his life to his freedom, disavows his rational being and is treated accordingly as an instrument by the master. It will appear, however, that the initial, unequal relationship of dominion and servitude is disposed of by the very dialectic which called it into existence and eventually leads to the conclusive stage of 'universal consciousness,' a stage characterized by the mutual

---

[47]   M 25 (Miller, p. 60).
[48]   M 27 (Miller, p. 60).

recognition of one's fellow as equal, on which — as was explained earlier[49] — the political order of society rests.

The passage on 'Dominion and Servitude' thus brings out the dialectical mechanism behind social and political activity. It follows from the manner in which, of his own accord, man relates to the world:

> In order to assert itself as free and obtain recognition, the self-consciousness must manifest itself to the other self-consciousness, as independent of the limits of its natural environment. This is as necessary a moment as that of the freedom of the self-consciousness in itself. The absolute equation of the ego with itself is fundamentally mediate in that the equality is established only through the sublation of the immediacy of the sensible, whereby the ego is regarded by the other ego as free and independent of sense. In this way it manifests itself as adequate to its conception, and by giving reality to the ego, necessitates its recognition.[50]

The struggle between two self-conscious subjects results in an unequal relationship of Dominion and Servitude because, of the two parties, one preferred his liberty to his life and was thus in a position to defeat the party which preferred his life to his liberty. In return for his life the servant denies his own self and becomes an instrument in the hands of the master whose needs he satisfies with his labour. At the same time, however, this forms the beginning of the master's dependence on the servant. Through the labour of the servant the one-sided dependence of the servant on the master passes into a relationship of mutual dependence between two equal selves.

In the context of the present study, this section of the *Propädeutik* is so particularly important partly because it points so explicitly to the mutual recognition of individual members of a community as a necessary precondition for all political and social order. This theme will recur in the reconstruction of the metaphysical foundation of the concept of positive freedom, which will be undertaken in the subsequent two chapters.

In the course of the development of the self from the servant to the master's equal, the *Propädeutik* employs once more the concepts of 'negative' and 'positive' freedom, in a somewhat different sense than in the context of the theory of the will. 'Negative freedom' here denotes the condition of the servant,

---

[49] See pp. 26–7; cf. pp. 118–20.
[50] M 32 (Miller, p. 61).

consisting in 'abstraction from existence in the sphere of sense,' whereas 'positive freedom' is 'identical with the universal will'.[51] The process by which the self manifests itself in the external world culminates in 'universal consciousness'.[52] The exposition of the dialectical development of the self demonstrates the way in which the social nature of any individual agent is formed by an inevitable conflict of the self with other self-conscious agents, which initially results in a one-sided dependent relationship between dominion and servitude. Subsequently, this relationship gradually develops into one of mutual dependence between two equal selves.

Having thus traced the social nature of each individual agent and the mutual recognition of each individual member of the community, little need be said of the remaining part of the Nürnberg *Phenomenology*. This is the section on Reason and, according to the function it fulfils in Hegel's system, this concluding section discusses the problem of how to cope with the difference between 'objects' which exist for various individual subjects and 'objectivity' in the sense of existing independent of any particular self-conscious mind.

Thus far we have concentrated on gathering material for a substantiated account of the influence Green underwent from his early study of the *Propädeutik* to the extent that this can be traced in his mature philosophy. The only missing element is some account of the parallel arguments in epistemology, ontology and psychology in the *Propädeutik*. As will be explained in Chapter Two, an important part of the metaphysical foundation of *Prolegomena* centres on the analogy in the argumentation in each of these three separate fields. The best way of bringing out the parallel arguments in these three different metaphysical disciplines in the *Propädeutik* is to examine the theory of mind as it was set out in the Nürnberg version of the *Encyclopaedia*, supplemented with references to the explanations which Rosenkranz added to the Introduction to the lower form lecture on the philosophies of Right, Duty, and Religion.

---

[51]   M 35, 37 (Miller, pp. 62, 63).
[52]   M 38, 39 (Miller, p. 63).

D. The Parallel Structure of Epistemology and Psychology in the *Propädeutik*

The most general description of mental activity in Hegel's Nürnberg lectures is to be found in the concept of consciousness. This is defined as a relationship of subject and object.[53] According to the nature of this relationship of subject and object the mind can be divided into a theoretical and a practical mode.[54] In theoretical relations the activities of the mind are induced by an external object which determines the Ego. In practical relationships of the mind, its determinations are created out of itself. The former condition of mind contemplates the reality as it is present to us in experience, the latter stands for the faculty of will, in the exercise of which the mind actively interferes with external reality so as to bring it into accordance with its determinations. In its theoretical mode the mind is determined by the external world, but, as the *Encyclopaedia* elucidates, this is only at the level of sense impression: 'Mind only begins from without, determines the external and then goes on to relate itself to itself, and its own modifications.'[55]

Theory of Knowledge

In accordance with the dialectical form of Hegel's system, the theoretical mode of mind divides into three specific forms: feeling, representation, and thought.[56] The first form of theoretical relationship of the mind and its environment is the mere adoption of sensuous impressions by the mind. These stimuli, induced by the outside world, form the 'rough undeveloped material'[57] from which all further theoretical activities of mind proceed. Feeling stands for:

> the simple, but yet defined affection of the individual subject, such that the sensation is not yet distinguished from its content, i.e. that which is felt, in other words, the determination which we have supposed in the subject is not distinguished from the object.[58]

---

[53] R.I 2 (Miller, p. 1).
[54] R.I 1 (Miller, p. 1).
[55] E 127 (Miller, p. 149).
[56] E 131–73 (Miller, pp. 150–60).
[57] E 133 (Miller, p. 150).
[58] E 131 (Miller, p. 150).

At this elementary level of cognitive activity, the mind is deter-mined by some object external to itself, but as yet, the mind is not aware of the distinction between itself and the determina-tion induced by the external object.

The mind's awareness of itself as separate from external objects marks the transition from feeling to a following form of theoretical consciousness, i.e. representation. By virtue of this self-distinguishing activity of mind, sense impressions lose their immediate form. The external object, inducing impres-sions upon the mind through the sense organs is presented by the mind as something separate from itself. Representation consists of three subforms:

> (1) the intelligence re-collects itself, separates itself from the con-tent of feeling, (2) it imagines the same content i.e. retains it when the object is gone, recalls and reconstructs it out of itself; and (3) it deprives the content of its immediate significance, and gives it a new significance by reconstructing it in *Memory*.[59]

The third and highest stage of theoretical activity of mind is thinking. We saw that in feeling no distinction between subject and object was yet conceived. This immediate unity was dis-solved in the self-distinguishing activity of mind which marked the stage of representation. Thinking, finally, recon-ciles subject and object in a higher unity. The precise manner in which this is achieved is explained in detail in the further sub-division. Thinking first takes the form of *Understanding* which brings the manifold, given in perception, into categories or 'thought determinations of being, which constitute the inner unity of the variety produced by intuitions and representa-tions.'[60] Understanding, in the sense of the Nürnberg *Encyclopaedia*, predominantly consists in abstracting. It distin-guishes the various attributes which constitute a particular thing and separates them from the object. The second moment which can be discerned in the thinking process is *Judgment*. It proceeds to relate the several attributes, generalized by Understanding, to objects. It is only at the stage of *Pure Think-ing* or *Reason* that the conception of the thing is recognized as such. Accordingly, the universal is no longer 'external' to the content, as in the activity of Understanding. From the view-point of Reason, contents of thought are none other than

---

[59]   E 134 (Miller, p. 150–1).
[60]   E 164 (Miller, p. 158).

thought itself. In the object, reason searches and eventually finds itself.

To recapitulate the account of theoretical consciousness. In the process of thinking various 'moments' can be identified and set out separately from one another for purposes of analysis. In the course of the process, these various moments build on one another raising the mind to an ever higher level of independence of the material which was initially derived from the external world. In its earlier stages the mind was still greatly determined by the external world which it took as its initial point of reference. As the mind became engaged in higher theoretical relationships its degree of freedom increased. We saw that the theoretical faculty of Intuition stood for an entirely passive form of cognition, which did nothing but adopt whatever impressions were made on the mind. At the level of 'pure' thinking, on the other hand, the mind rendered itself completely independent of what was initially given in intuition. Cognitive activity can thus be characterized as the advancing of the mind towards complete freedom from external reality. In the course of the cognitive process, the chief characteristic of theoretical consciousness, i.e. the determination of the self by external reality, is gradually diminished and eventually overcome in the last and highest stage of pure thought. This achievement of freedom by the mind forms the basis for the subsequent mode of mind: practical consciousness, in which it proceeds actively to interfere with this very same reality bringing it into accordance with its own determinations.

The Dialectic of Practical Consciousness

The Nürnberg *Encyclopaedia* differentiated between the theoretical and practical modes of mind as on the one hand possessed of certain inner determinations and on the other the identity of the mind with its determinations.[61] The process of willing has two component parts, i.e. the inner determinations of mind and the transition of such inner determinations into the external world by means of *Action*.[62] The important point to observe here is that, in Hegel's view, action is considered as a change of *form* only. The contents of the inner determinations of mind preceding an act of will and the determinations of

---

[61]   E 173 (Miller, pp. 160–1).
[62]   R.I 4, R.E 8, 9 (Miller, pp. 2, 10–11).

external reality resulting from it are one and the same. Action merely carries the inner determinations of mind to a higher form, as is elucidated in the following example:

> the purpose to build a house is an internal determination, the form of which consists in its being in the first instance merely a purpose: the content embraces the plan of the house. Now if in this case the form be carried into its higher condition, yet the content remains as before. The house, which according to the purpose, is to be built, and that which, according to the plan is built, is the same house.[63]

In the same way, action elevates the external activity, as it was present to the mind, when it planned the building, to a higher form:

> ... in order to build a house, the ground, stones, wood and the rest of the materials are changed in a variety of ways. The form of the external is made different from what it was. It is brought into an entirely different construction from what it was before. This change is effected relatively to an aim, namely the plan of the house, with which internal element the external is thus brought into agreement.[64]

The inner determination preceding an act of will falls into three modes: Practical Feeling, Impulse, and Will proper. The first of these practical faculties of mind recognises 'righteous' and moral conduct in an immediate manner, i.e. without the mediation of thinking. A certain course of action is considered right or wrong, good or bad, because it is simply felt to be so.[65] Feeling cannot, however, provide the basis for an adequate judgment of the 'righteous' or moral nature of these acts. Because of the subjective element 'mixed with' its contents, this level of practical consciousness remains 'impure'.[66] The second mode of practical consciousness is mediated by the self, but its position still falls short of a rational position, as man's impulse is prompted by his nature. Determined by impulse, the practical mind is not free but subject to the necessity which operates in the sphere of nature.[67] As to its contents, impulse is restricted; it does not venture beyond its limited aim. Moreover, the satisfaction of impulses is accidental in that it depends on external circumstances, not on a man's

---

[63] R.E 9 (Miller, pp. 10–11).
[64] *Ibid.*
[65] E 177, R.E 2 (Miller, pp. 161, 165).
[66] E 177 (Miller, p. 161).
[67] R.I 5 (Miller, p. 2).

rational being. In this kind of practical relationship of the mind, man does not distinguish himself from his impulse.[68] Will proper passes beyond the bounds of impulse. In order to live up to its rational nature, practical consciousness

> must elevate itself out of the immersion in the impulse, so that the particular impulses do not account as absolute, but receive their place and true value only as moments of the totality in which they are purified of subjective accidentality.[69]

Such transition beyond the bounds of impulse is accomplished by reflection. It is by virtue of this theoretical mental faculty, which the earlier sections of the Nürnberg *Encyclopaedia* showed to be unique to human beings, that the human will is rendered free of the limitations of impulse and desire. As set out in the *Erläuterungen* to the first form course:

> Reflexion compares the several impulses and their aims with the fundamental aim of being. The aims of the particular impulses are limited, but they contribute, each in its own way, to the attainment of the fundamental aim. The one is more nearly related to this aim than another. Reflexion has thus to compare the impulses, to see if they are related to the fundamental aim, and if this will be promoted by their satisfaction. In reflexion begins the transition from the lower appetitive faculty to the higher. In this event the man is no longer a merely natural essence, i.e. he stands no longer in the sphere of necessity.[70]

Will proper is thus conceived as an ulterior mental faculty to which impulses and aims are presented. By virtue of his reflective faculty a man is free to weigh alternative aims against one another. It is in this emancipation from the limited nature of the aims thus presented that the will acquires the freedom of choice, which is fundamental to it. This freedom of the will is not affected by the fact that the actual decisions taken, by means of which the will thus determines itself, may coincide with one of the motives that were presented to it.

> Altho' that a variety of motives, incentives and laws may be presented to the will, yet if the man follow them, this only takes place insofar as the will itself has appropriated them and resolved to do so.[71]

---

[68] R.E 10 (Miller, p. 11).
[69] E 179 (Miller, p. 162).
[70] R.E 11 (Miller, p. 13).
[71] R.I 7 (Miller, p. 3).

The relationship between the will and the circumstances in which it finds itself, differs essentially from the relationship between objects within the sphere of nature. In nature, 'that which is involved in the cause must of necessity follow.'[72] The realm of nature is operated by laws of necessity. Mechanical causes, for instance, 'produce purely external or mechanical effects, which are entirely conditioned by their causes so that nothing is contained in them but that which was already before in the cause.'[73] A living essence, on the other hand, when influenced by certain circumstances creates an entirely new element in its reaction to those circumstances. Indeed, such reaction of a living essence is incited by the circumstances in which it finds itself at a given moment; but independent of those particular circumstances it was already 'potentially contained' in the living essence. This observation applies *a fortiori* to self-conscious agents, which by virtue of their reason distinguish themselves from their wants and thus relate entirely freely to the several motives presented to them, as well as to possible incentives inherent in a certain circumstance. For this reason, the *Propädeutik* emphasizes, it would be an essential misrepresentation of the true nature of the will to claim that one has been led by given circumstances to take a certain decision. In truth, the will is not led by circumstances, but determines itself in view of the circumstances. An attempt to apologize for a wrong verdict of the will on these grounds is to neglect the free nature of the will. To excuse oneself in this manner is to reduce oneself to a merely natural essence.

> The relation of circumstances to my will is not that of cause, nor of my will to them that of effect. According to this relation, that which is involved in the cause must of necessity follow. But as a reflective agent I am able to pass beyond every determination, which is presented by circumstances. In so far as the man pleads that he has been led astray by circumstances, incentives &c, he thereby degrades himself to the position of a mere necessary or natural essence whilst in reality his action is always his own, not another's, not the effect of aught outside himself. Circumstances or motives have only so much dominion over the man, as he himself admits to.[74]

---

[72]   R.E 15 (Miller, p. 15).
[73]   R.E 10 (Miller, p. 11).
[74]   R.E 15 (Miller, p. 15).

The Formal Freedom of the Will

To summarize the argument on the will in the *Propädeutik* thus far: the determinate nature of the several specific motives which are represented to the will does not affect the freedom of the will, even if its verdict coincides with one of such motives, nor is this freedom dependent on the circumstances in which the will reaches its decisions. In a similar way, the freedom of the will is not affected by the determinations of a man's particular position. On the basis of this concept of will, three 'moments' in the workings of will proper may be distinguished: the will as purely indeterminate, the will determinate, and the absolutely free will.

In view of its reflective faculty the mind possesses a state of pure indeterminateness of the self. The option of choice allows for a stage in which the will is indifferent towards all possible determinations. In this stage the will is 'a mere form devoid of all content.' However, such a stage of pure indeterminateness is of itself insufficient. The possibility of choice, characterizing this stage of the will, derives its meaning from the context of the process of will in which it precedes an actual decision. Discerning a 'moment' of pure indeterminateness of the will presupposes and leads to a further stage of determination. The will is conceived as an ulterior mental faculty which decides on the basis of several motives present to it. In relation to its particular verdicts the will is universal and enduring. In relation to the will its verdicts are limited and fleeting. The will is a self-conscious unity of which each act of will is a limited expression. It cannot be identified with one of its verdicts, nor is it their total sum or aggregate. On the other hand, will is nothing apart from its acts of will. It cannot be separated from or opposed to the acts of will. Thus the first moment of pure indeterminateness already implies a further stage, in which it is determined by a particular object or purpose which is 'carried into a higher form' by means of action.

From Formal to Substantive Freedom

There is, however, a contradiction inherent in this stage of the process of willing which can best be brought out by comparison with an analogous instance in the theoretical activity of mind. According to his spiritual nature, or to be more precise: his self-distinguishing activity, a man is always free and universal from the formal point of view. In the section of theoretical consciousness it was pointed out that any content of the contemplative mind received a spiritual form. In a similar way, it can be said that the will is always universal from the formal point of view, i.e. given the possibilities which are open to it. A man may commit himself to a certain determination, but it may also be another. The determinate nature of a particular verdict does not affect the universality and freedom of the will. At the same time, however, the object determining the will at a certain point in time necessarily falls short of the universal character of the will. The contents of the will are thus an inadequate interpretation of its universal nature. The contradiction between the contents of the will and its universal form is eventually overcome in the third and highest stage of will proper, the absolutely free will.

In order to bring out how such a 'synthesis' of the two preceding moments of the will is to be brought about, we have again to recall the analogous argument applied in an earlier section of the Nürnberg *Encyclopaedia*. This argument was on the determined and therefore limited and non-universal nature of objects in space and time and the manner in which these objects were to be translated into the universality of the mind. The *Encyclopaedia* put forward the argument in a discussion of forms of perception. In the faculty of intuition objects perceived were determined by spatial and temporal conditions, which are common to every act of intuition. The determinations constituting a particular object in space and time were only to be overcome by viewing the object in a wider perspective. In that manner, former determinations can be shown to be merely relative and thereby disposed of. The bounds of a historical period lose their absolute character when seen in a wider context. At the same time, however, this wider view itself sets new boundaries. The argument of the *Propädeutik* is that this transition beyond the boundaries of a certain object in space and time can be repeated *ad infinitum* without ever dissolving the determinate nature of the object thus perceived. The only way to free such an object from its spatial and temporal determinations is to abstract from the dimensions of space and time altogether. Such abstraction is carried out in the activities of theoretical mind.

A similar argument applies to the determinations of the objects of will. Whatever such objects may be, they will always be determined and therefore limited. The only way to live up to the universal nature of the will is to abstract from particular determinations altogether. The will, in other words, must be universally determined. It must have itself as its object or, in the terminology of *Propädeutik*, 'the absolutely free will wills only itself.' From the concluding paragraphs of the introduction to the first form course it appears that this paradoxical formula should be taken to mean that the particular will should conform to the universal will. We may conclude that, according to the argument of the *Propädeutik*, it follows from the rational nature of each individual agent that his will will coincide with the universal will, i.e. the will of the community as a whole. Once this link has been made, the relationship between the system of righteous, moral and political rules can easily be ascertained. The rationale of such systems is to be found in their contribution to the common good of a community. The analysis of the human will, which the *Propädeutik* undertakes by way of introduction, serves to point out the eventual identity of the object of the absolutely free will of the individual and the common good of the community.

It is useful at this point to recall the main themes of our inquiry into the theory of the will in the *Propädeutik*. We have seen that in practical relationships the mind enters the external world. The external reality is ordered according to its inner determinations. These are carried into a higher form and objectified by means of action. In its process of development the will passes through several stages in which it becomes progressively more adequate in regard of its presupposed essence. Practical feeling already represents a practical relationship of the mind, but it is still handicapped since the inner determinations from which such action proceeds fall short of rationality. Impulse represents a higher, but still limited form of rationality, as man does not transcend the bounds of nature which belong to him immediately. Only in will proper does the mind engage in practical relations corresponding adequately to its rational nature. By virtue of its speculative faculty, the mind is able to consider the several particular impulses that are presented to it, to compare them with one another and each of them with 'the fundamental aim of its being.' In this way the mind transcends the bounds of particular impulses. However, in the lower stages of the proper will, such transition beyond the bounds of particular impulses is never complete, or rather, it is merely relative. Particular acts of will transcend their limited nature only when the individual coincides with the universal will, which views the common good of society as its end. The systems of moral and political rules, which each in their own way promote to the common good of a community, can be viewed as institutional expressions of the acts of will on the part of individual agents.

E. Insights Green Derived from the *Propädeutik*

Having given an account of the Ms translation of the *Propädeutik*, we may now draw up an inventory of the main philosophical inferences Green drew from his early study of Hegel. Perhaps the best way to do this is to consider those respects in which Green's later philosophical writings correspond to the doctrine of the *Propädeutik*. In the absence of further evidence I will take themes or points, which Green's mature philosophy shares with the manuscript translation of the *Propädeutik*, as an indication of the impact of his early study of Hegel on his own philosophical development. Given that our purpose is to throw new light on Green's political theory, we shall focus on this subject in the *Propädeutik*. As has already been indicated, the political theory in Hegel's textbook proceeded on certain metaphysical principles, notably on an analysis of the nature of the human will. The principles resulting from this metaphysical enquiry, we saw, should also be considered to give an adequate account of the social philosophy discussed in the *Propädeutik*. The points which Green's later philosophical writings have in common with this manuscript translation of Hegel's fall under two headings, i.e. more general metaphysical issues and points more specifically relating to moral and political philosophy.

Metaphysical Foundations

The most obvious point of conformity between the *Propädeutik* and Green's mature philosophy is the rationalist theory of the will. It forms an integral part of Hegel's Nürnberg lectures and Green's 'metaphysic of morals' covers an entire book of *Prolegomena*.[75] The idea that a closer investigation of the workings of the human will provides a better insight into the nature of moral and political activity is a prominent feature of the first form lecture course of the *Propädeutik*, where moral and politi-

---

[75] Book II, sects 85–183.

cal institutions are defined as expressions of the human will. In a similar manner *Prolegomena* analyses what is involved in the process of willing to proceed from such an analysis to some conclusion concerning the nature of morality. *Political Obligation*, in its turn, explicitly defines political activity as a sine qua non for moral activity, by which definition the relationship of the system of law and the will of the individual agent becomes apparent.

The theory of the will leads to a more general metaphysical theme which equally features in the *Propädeutik* as well as in Green's mature philosophy. This is the strict analogy of the argument on the nature of the human will and a more general metaphysical argument which occurs both in epistemology and ontology. In the *Propädeutik* the parallel structure of the arguments on theoretical and practical consciousness cannot fail to attract the attention of the alert reader. In a similar manner, the theory of the will in the *Prolegomena* is preceded by an analysis of what is involved in human experience. The discourse on epistemology carries ontological implications which are discussed before Green comes to a statement of his theory of the will.

The *Propädeutik* characterized theoretical consciousness as a development of the mind from a condition of subjection to the external world towards complete freedom. This liberation proceeded in three steps, i.e. intuition, perception and conception, in each of which the mind acquired a higher degree of independence. On the basis of the freedom thus acquired the mind then went on to subject the external world involving practical relationships between mind and world which, again, proceeded in three stages: practical feeling, desire, and rational will. While this architectonic structure was not followed in *Prolegomena*, the analogy of the arguments in epistemology and psychology forms an aspect of Green's mature philosophy in which he unmistakably owed an intellectual debt to the *Propädeutik*. *Prolegomena*, moreover, extended this analogy to the realm of ontology. Green touched upon this latter metaphysical science in so far as it was already implied by his epistemology. Thus, ontology is worked up in *Prolegomena* in a very concise fashion. Green only engaged in discussing ontology in thinking out the implications of his epistemological position. The *Propädeutik*, however, is even more brief on this subject. Yet one may identify some passages which are strikingly similar to Green's stipulations concerning ontology. Green's postulate of an eternal consciousness was modelled on the exposition of the philosophy of religion in the *Propädeutik*, some paragraphs of which were already quoted in the foregoing account of Hegel's textbook.

Morals and Politics

Common points of Green's mature philosophy and the manuscript translation of *Propädeutik* pertaining more specifically to moral and political theory are to be found in the distinction between 'moral duty' and 'political obligation' which follows from the distinction between the fabric of law and the system of moral rules. The distinction between these two sets of rules, both of which are considered as institutional expressions of the will, is elucidated in the explanations to the introduction of the first form course of the *Propädeutik*.[76] The most striking difference between these two forms of human activity is that moral duty involves a certain disposition from which it is performed, whereas political obligations exclusively bear upon conduct. In the lectures to the first form Right is defined as essentially negative, whereas moral duties are of a positive nature. The German origin of the correlative concepts of 'obligation' and 'duty' which are nowadays eminently associated with Green's philosophy,[77] is to be found in the related concepts of 'Schuldigkeit' and 'Pflicht'.[78]

In a similar manner the twin concepts of 'negative' and 'positive' freedom occur in various places in the Nürnberg lectures, figuring primarily in the context of the theory of the will. Paragraph 7 of the introduction to the lectures on social philosophy opposed the 'abstract freedom' of the will, a function of its faculty to choose any object of will, to the 'true and absolute' freedom which is acquired in objects of will satisfying its rational nature. These two 'moments' of the will in the process of choosing are further elucidated in the corresponding explanations.[79] Similar terminology is employed in the context of the philosophy of consciousness in the *Propädeutik* where paragraph 35 described the 'purely negative freedom' of the ser-

---

[76] R.E 22, R 32 (Miller, pp. 19, 36).
[77] A.P.d'Entrèves, *The Medieval Contribution to Political Thought*, London, 1939, p. 3.
[78] R 32 (Miller, p. 36).
[79] R.E 19–21 (Miller, pp. 30–1).

vant, who preferred his life to his freedom and was consequently reduced to an instrument in the hands of the master. This condition of man was contrasted with the 'positive freedom' pertaining to the universal consciousness in which the two self-conscious agents recognised one another as equals[80] and were in a position to identify their own good with the common good of the community. In the *Erläuterungen* 'formal freedom'[81] is contrasted with the 'absolute free will,'[82] the difference being that in the former instance a limited object is adopted as object of will, whereas in the latter the object of will is 'unlimited' or 'universal,' i.e. it has itself for object.

A further aspect of Green's mature political philosophy which is reminiscent of the *Propädeutik* is the view that the recognition of each other as equals by all members of a community alike forms the basis of a system of law constituting that community. Green worked up this point in his lectures on *Political Obligation* as a claim on the part of society to the obedience of the citizen and, conversely, a claim on the part of each individual citizen to have his rights granted to him by society.[83] In *Propädeutik*, as in Hegel's mature system of philosophy, this forms part of the dialectical development of consciousness, as was elucidated in the passage on Dominion and Servitude and the transition of this condition of man into the stage of 'universal consciousness'.[84] In the context of the first form course of *Propädeutik* this insight then occurs as one of the postulates of social philosophy. The recognition by each member of a political community of all other members as equally capable of rational activity is identified as the basis of the political and moral order. In the same manner, there is a notable similarity between the structure of the first form course on social philosophy and Green's later lectures on *Political Obligation*. Both lecture courses in social philosophy begin with an account of some fundamental principle which is derived from an analysis of the human will. From this first principle of Right, implications are drawn for a theory of property rights and a theory of the right of the state to punish transgressions. In conformity with these derivatory rights, further functions

---

[80] M 37 (Miller, p. 63).
[81] R.E 19 (Miller, p. 17).
[82] R.E 20 (Miller, p. 18).
[83] *Political Obligation*, sects 26 and 117, cf. *Prolegomena*, sect. 200.
[84] M 36–9 (Miller, pp. 62–3).

for the state are to be established.[85] In this respect the structure of the Nürnberg course conforms entirely to Hegel's later *Grundlinien*. In the same way Green begins his lectures on *Political Obligation* with an investigation of the 'true ground or justification for obedience to law,'[86] which his editor entitled 'The Grounds of Political Obligation.' After a critical review of preceding political theory Green goes on to develop this fundamental principle into a right to life and liberty. The implications of this basic right are explored in two later sections entitled 'The Right of the State in regard to Property' and 'The Right of the State to Punish'.[87]

In its exposition of moral philosophy the *Propädeutik* also puts forward a set of social virtues, and in view of Green's intensive involvement with this textbook it may be conjectured that Green's intended lecture on social virtues was also inspired by his earlier work on the *Propädeutik*. As Green's plan never materialized, it is difficult to say precisely what he had in mind with this project, but his intention of extending his professorial lectures on political theory to this realm can readily be discerned in the original announcement of his lectures in the Balliol timetable for 1879–1880. In Green's lecture notes there only remains a brief section which Nettleship entitled 'Rights and Virtues'.[88]

In order to conclude this inventory of the topics on which Green's mature philosophy would seem to result from his study of Hegel in the 1860s, a final observation should be made with regard to the criticism of utilitarianism for which Green found much useful material in the *Propädeutik*. The terminology which the author saw fit to adjust for his own philosophical purposes occurs in the discussion on moral philosophy and perhaps it is even more obvious in the corresponding *Erläuterungen*.[89] These explanations give an account of the relationship of rational activity and conduct motivated by pleasure. It may be taken as a further indication of the impact of the *Propädeutik* on Green's philosophical development that this relation is sketched in exactly the same manner in the *Propädeutik* as in the criticism of utilitarianism with which

---

[85]   R 3–21 (Miller, pp. 22–31).
[86]   *Political Obligation*, sect. 1.
[87]   *Ibid.*, sects 176 ff. and 211 ff. respectively.
[88]   *Ibid.*, sects 247 ff.
[89]   R 36 ff., R.I 20–4 (Miller, pp. 38, 18–21).

Green was to earn a good deal of his reputation as a philosopher. Both the *Propädeutik* and Green's mature philosophical position take the line that, initially and under certain circumstances, rational activity coincides with the pursuit of pleasure. There is, however, a point at which the two ways of conceiving human conduct produce different results. It is as a result of this difference that it becomes important to replace the inadequate view of 'Endaimonism'[90] with a theory which better fits the essential nature of man and his activity. The discussion of moral principles, for example, characterizes the moral agent as the 'Trieb des Menschen nach seinem besonderen Dasein' which is designed to make the external world conform with its inner determinations. Such condition is identified with 'Vergnügen' and 'Glückseligkeit,' which is translated as 'Pleasure' and 'Happiness' respectively. Similarly, it is stated that

> Reason suppresses the Indeterminateness which attends the feeling of pleasure in the contemplation of its objects, it purifies the content of the impulse from the subjective and accidental, in respect of content it teaches the knowledge of the Universal, the *essential element constituting the values of desire*, whilst irrespective of form or Intention it supplies that of the *Objective*, i.e. Action for the sake of the thing itself.

And again, in the corresponding explanation:

> *The desire of the pleasant may coincide with Reason*, i.e. both may have the same content, so that Reason *legitimates* the content. In respect of form, Impulse acts for the sake of the subjective feeling, in other words, has the pleasure of the subject for its aim. In an action for the sake of an universal object, the object itself is the aim. The desire of pleasure on the contrary is always self-regarding.[91]

Readers familiar with Green's mature philosophy will note the striking similarity of these passages with Green's own position. This will further be explained in Chapter IV which is devoted to Green's criticism of utilitarianism.

F. Green and Aristotle

In the preceding three sections of this chapter we considered a textbook which Green used in the first years of his professional career. In my reconstruction of the process of Green's intellec-

---

[90]   R 36 (Miller, p. 38).
[91]   *Ibid.* (Miller, p. 38).

tual development, this textbook was of crucial importance and we reviewed the chief conclusions which he drew from it. Before we go on in the next chapter to assess its impact on Green's further philosophical development, we still need to consider a rival interpretation on the basis of Green's reading of Aristotle. It is evident from the manuscripts that Green spent much time and energy on Aristotle. Of course, Aristotle has always occupied a special position at the University of Oxford from the very beginning to the present day and in Green's times this situation was certainly not substantially different.[92] There is evidence to suggest that, as compared to Aristotle, Hegel's influence on Green was the more influential. In order to point this out we need to introduce some biographical details about Green's treatment of Aristotle. We shall also have to make use of the manuscript of an essay on Aristotle which Green published in the *North British Review* in September 1866.[93] This essay was his sole separate publication on this philosopher.

Green's first acquaintance with Aristotle was, not unusually for a boy of middle class background, during his own education at school. In his period at Rugby we already hear of a 'tough bit of Aristotle for unseen Greek'[94] and the Examination Register of Balliol allows us to establish what Green was given to read during his undergraduate years.[95] These details do not, of course, represent anything uncommon and, given the requirement of the curriculum, it is hardly surprising that Green engaged in a considerable amount of work on Aristotle, especially during the first years of his professional career. At the end of 1861, when his work for the school of law and history came to an end, we learn from a letter to his sister Emily that he was 'busy with Aristotle and kindred subjects, being desirous to stick to them rather than to history'. Throughout his professional career he lectured on the *Ethics*. The first time he delivered a lecture on this subject was on 23 October 1863, but it turned out to be less easy going that he had thought. As he wrote to Emily: 'it is uphill work, trying to expound Aris-

---

[92] On Aristotle's influence in Oxford in Green's times, see J.H.Newman's lectures on *The Idea of a University*, ed. C.F.Harrold, London, 1947, p. 97.

[93] 'The Philosophy of Aristotle,' *North British Review*, September 1866, reprinted in *Works*, iii, pp. 46-91.

[94] Correspondence, 1852, as copied by Nettleship in his Ms notebook on the Green papers.

[95] Sections from the *Ethics* and the *Politics*.

totle to men who are only just through Moderations & void of the least tincture of philosophy.'

While his involvement with Aristotle was thus primarily guided by his professional work, Green nevertheless had a genuine interest in Aristotle, as indicated by the fact already revealed in his correspondence that he preferred Aristotle 'and kindred subjects' to history. This can also be seen from the preferences he showed in choosing a number of literary projects which he hoped would contribute towards establishing a certain academic reputation. When Jowett proposed that he should prepare an edition of *Thucydides* Green declined because he felt 'no spontaneous interest' in the work. Instead he contemplated an edition of *De Anima* which was, as he said, 'much more in my line & not half the length of *Thucydides*.'[96] A second literary project from which something of a genuine interest in Aristotle can be seen was a commentary on the *Nichomachean Ethics*. Green worked upon this project at about the same time with his friend Edward Caird and hoped 'to get every other day clear' for this purpose.[97] Initially it was intended for a new series of Greek and Latin books used in schools to be published by Macmillan, but as this project did not materialize, Green then set his sight on a publication with the University Press. In March of the same year, however, the Trustees decided to award the contract for editing the *Ethics* to someone else. Jowett then offered to find another publisher and to write a preface so that Green and Caird resolved in any case to continue. The work was finally interrupted when Green left Oxford to take on the schools commissionership in April of the following year. Green then worked all the material he had gathered with his study of Aristotle into an article which he published on the occasion of A. Grant's new edition of the *Ethics*.

These biographical details about the laborious first steps in Green's professional career are included here to introduce

[96]   Letter to his sister Emily, 23.x.1863. Nettleship conjectured that Green was disappointed with the work on closer analysis (*Memoir*, p. xl). But this does not tally with Green's comment on this work in his *North British Review* article on Aristotle which was of a later date than the intended translation of *De Anima*. In this article Green stated that *De Anima* and *Metaphysics* set out a 'more thorough and therefore truer idealism than Aristotle's earlier writings' (*Works*, iii, p. 62). Be that as it may, the project was nevertheless abandoned with only a translation of parts of the work accomplished. The Ms of this translation is preserved in the collection at Balliol (Ms 16).

[97]   Letter to his family 22.i.1864.

some statements from his correspondence which would be difficult to appreciate without reference to the circumstances in which they were written. When the University Press decided not to assign the editing of the *Ethics* to Green, his reaction in a letter to his father shows that he was well aware of the unorthodox nature of his interpretation of Aristotle: 'I am not sorry,' he wrote, 'to have a little more freedom in the mode of doing the work than one would have had in doing it for the University Press.'[98] The same awareness of his heterodox views on Aristotle appears from an earlier comment when he still expected to publish with the University Press. In this letter he already anticipated the hostile reception he was likely to get with his commentary since, as he wrote,

> the Ethics is a book which everyone supposes himself to know & about which there are certain traditional views, upon which I am pretty sure to stumble.[99]

Unfortunately, Green was to find out that his suspicions were not without foundation. The opinions about his article on Aristotle were unsparing. And the reason for this soon emerges when we turn to the text: throughout the essay Green seems engaged in philosophical problems of a much later date which he attempts to read into Aristotle and now that we know about the insights he had just gathered from the *Propädeutik* at that time, the particular nature of Green's reading of Aristotle becomes more intelligible.

Green's Re-interpretation of Aristotle

A reading of Green's essay shows that his primary aim was to establish a theory of knowledge, which will be found to coincide in the main with his later epistemology in *Prolegomena*. Green thought that, to the perceptive reader, this theory of knowledge could be seen to be anticipated in Aristotle's writings — especially in those writings which were, in Green's opinion, largely neglected. However, when taking account of the enterprise Green sought to undertake with his essay, one may wonder why he went to the trouble of making this latter, derivative point. It is possible that he thought to win over opponents by linking his theory with certain aspects in the lesser known works of an authoritative philosopher. How-

[98]   4.viii.1864.
[99]   22.i.1864.

ever, it would seem that this detour did not do a great deal to dispose Oxford in favour of the philosophical opinions he sought to defend. Rather, he became noted for his unorthodox interpretation of Aristotle in which very few of his contemporaries saw any point.

Green refuted the view that knowledge is given in sense experience, as was defended by certain philosophical schools. He held that if anything substantial was given in sense, i.e. independent of thought, the latter was thereby made altogether redundant as a source of knowledge. 'Give sensation this first inch, and it takes an ell,'[100] as he epitomised this conclusion in his review article. In Green's understanding, empiricist theory viewed thought essentially as a process of abstraction. It assumed, in other words, that all properties which are discerned in external things are already contained in the first sensuous impression; but if this were a correct description, thought would become a process producing ever more meagre representations of reality. Rather than leading us towards the real nature of things, thought would lead us away from it.

The view of thought Green sought to defend is more in line with everyday life experience and scientific practice. Such a more realistic view of the process of thinking would take thinking as beginning with the emptiest of abstractions, the prediction of being, which would then gradually be 'filled in' by thinking activity. On this view knowledge results from a series of judgments by the cognitive subject. On the basis of a series of consistent judgments the subject forms a conception of the external thing it has under consideration – or, if we are to consider the cognitive process as a whole, a conception of the world. Subsequent judgments are fitted into such a conception of the world and may lead to a farther refining thereof. To the extent that judgments cannot be related to an existing conception they may be rejected or, if there is a certain persistence in the contradiction between judgments and existing conceptions, this may lead to a revision of these conceptions. In this way what initially appeared to contradict the result of previous interpretative activity of thought may yet translate it to a higher plane. On this basis, knowledge clearly becomes a product of the cognitive subject. In every judgment on the part of the subject relations are attributed to the object and, as the

[100] *Works*, iii, p. 61.

cognitive process proceeds, objects of knowledge are further determined.

As a subordinate purpose of his essay, Green tries to point out the beginnings of such a theory of knowledge (which is in my view clearly of a much more recent date), in Aristotle's writings. Moreover, Green used the theory of knowledge outlined here as a critical tool to refute certain other aspects of Aristotle. Green's argument was that there were two inconsistent theories of knowledge to be discerned in Aristotle. First was an empiricist theory which starts from the 'sensible thing' to proceed from this assumption to derive all knowledge. The second theory, which followed the lines set out above, looks upon thought as a continuous process of interpretation of sensuous impulses from which all knowledge originates. It must be taken as one of the ironies of intellectual history, Green suggested, that it was precisely the erroneous theory with which Aristotle was to be associated by his scholastic interpreters and it was, at any rate, this view of Aristotle which still dominated philosophical opinions in Green's days, while the other — in Green's opinion, truer — theory of knowledge in Aristotle was largely neglected.

It will be clear that the theory of knowledge Green defended was not without certain definite implications for other branches of metaphysical inquiry. For, proceeding from the idea of knowledge as formed by the cognitive agent, is not the corollary of this view that every individual conscious agent merely builds his own world of experience? What, in other words, is the objective status of the conceptions individual agents form about the world? What, indeed, is the guarantee that there is such a thing as an objective world?

In order to avoid any such disrupting consequences of his idealistic position in epistemology Green therefore had to assume some primary subject. In the same way as, in the individual process of thought, the cognitive self must be presupposed from the first and most elementary stage on, a primary subject must be assumed in order to explain the possibility of an objective world of fact, i.e. independent of our cognitive activity. In the universe of properties attributed by individual agents, the presupposition of a primary self

> is the thread on which all hang, for it is the expression of the activity of thought which creates them all . . . As, according to the Hegelian dictum, God without the world would be no God, so

'pure thought,' of which being is the reflex, as thought about nothing, is no thought.[101]

In the same section the theory of the self, which Green was to develop analogous to his views on the eternal consciousness, is also anticipated.

Having elaborated his theory of knowledge, and having set out its ontological implications, Green admitted frankly that what he had in mind was a distinct interpretation of Aristotle:

> In the latter statements, it must be confessed that we are going far beyond our record as expounders of Aristotle. We are so combining his isolated formulae as to extract a meaning from them which he did not extract himself. It is just from his failure to recognise the identity of the 'being as being' . . . with 'thought as thought' that his shortcomings arise.[102]

And again, towards the end of the essay he admits that 'we are saying here for Aristotle . . . what he did not say for himself.'[103]

G. Conclusion

As to Green's philosophical interest in Aristotle we may thus conclude that perhaps Nettleship was not so far off the mark after all when he conjectured that 'if he had been free to choose, he would not have spent upon Aristotle so much of his force as a teacher.'[104] However, when Nettleship, in the same passage, remarks about Green's lectures on the *Ethics* that, while he put his strength into these lectures, 'he did not do this by using the book as a peg on which to hang disquisitions on modern questions' we must conclude that this may have been true for Green's later lectures, which Nettleship himself attended; but there seems to be room for doubt whether this can fairly be said of his earlier essay on Aristotle. A reading of this essay seems conclusive as to Green's involvement in altogether different problems, the origin of which we can explain through our knowledge about his study of Hegel which he undertook in the early 1860s. In a similar manner, he commented on Hegel in the 1867 lecture course attended by F.H. Bradley, that 'In Aristotle, we have much the same doctrine.'[105] This comment may also be interpreted as an indication that, for Green,

---

[101] *Ibid.*, p. 80.
[102] *Ibid.*, pp. 80–1.
[103] *Ibid.*, p. 83.
[104] *Memoir*, p. lxxi.
[105] *Works*, vol. v, p. 173.

Aristotle and Hegel were not quite as far apart as we would presently think. As a final point it may be said that Green's interest in Hegel does not of course exclude his dealing with Aristotle. As a matter of fact, Aristotle was very dear to Hegel, although his lectures on ancient Greek philosophy would have bewildered an Oxford audience in the 1860s as much as did Green's essay for the *North British Review*.

There is yet another persistent misunderstanding as to the somewhat idiosyncratic interpretation of Aristotle, particularly in connection with his article on this subject. It is said that what was taken to be a youthful indiscretion of Green haunted him for a long time and that it hindered his academic career a great deal. This claim is often substantiated by a reference to Green's application for a chair of philosophy at St. Andrews for which he competed in 1864, but which he failed to get, supposedly because of his unorthodox essay on Aristotle.[106]

However, a simple dating of the two events shows that, whatever else may have been the objections to the young Oxonion on the part of the St. Andrews selectors, it cannot have been an article which was only written two years later. This obvious fact did not, however, prevent Melvin Richter, in his biography of Green entitled *The Politics of Conscience*, from uncritically reproducing this very account from Jowett's *Life and Letters*.[107]

---

[106] See Abbott and Campbell, *The Life and Letters of Benjamin Jowett*, I, p. 341.
[107] p. 92.

Chapter II

'Certain Primary Problems...'

T.H. Green has traditionally been known for his moral and political theory. Yet, a reading of Green's unpublished manuscripts would suggest a somewhat different view of his philosophical activities. There are at least two principal revisions to be made in the reputation as a philosopher Green acquired through his published writings. These revisions are concerned with the systematic nature of his philosophy and the central part played by metaphysics in his thinking. His unpublished manuscripts make it clear that Green construed moral and political theory as forming part of a comprehensive system of philosophy which was constructed on the basis of certain idealist first principles. With a view to reconstructing this system of philosophy the present chapter will seek to give some account of its metaphysical basis. By way of introduction to such an account I will begin by considering some of the reasons explaining the discrepancy between Green's traditional reputation as a moral and political philosopher and the attention he actually paid to metaphysical inquiry.

One rather obvious reason explaining why Green's first principles remained unknown for so long is simply that much of his metaphysic was never published. The only positive statement of his first principles which was ever published is to be found in the two introductory books of his treatise on moral philosophy, *Prolegomena to Ethics*. In fact, these introductory books were merely intended as a broad survey of 'some metaphysical and psychological questions preliminary to moral philosophy,'[1] as his corresponding professorial lectures on the subject were announced. Another significant factor underlying the neglect of Green's idealist first principles has to do

---

[1]   Balliol College roster, October, 1878.

with the manner in which his published metaphysics was presented. In the introduction to his *Prolegomena*, for example, Green described metaphysics as 'the most difficult and least plausible part of his philosophy.'[2] A.C. Bradley, the editor of the posthumously published *Prolegomena*, added a little extra with his statement that 'readers unaccustomed to metaphysical and psychological discussions' would best turn immediately to the final two books, which contained Green's actual moral philosophy, as the substantive argument could equally be gathered without reference to his metaphysics.[3] Needless to say, these comments did little to encourage readers of Green's *Prolegomena* in the study of his first principles. But the main reason which may be pointed out to account for the neglect of Green's doctrine of first principles is that, in the form in which it was published, his metaphysical system was perhaps less than satisfactory. To the extent it was framed in a positive doctrine, Green's metaphysics formed the most frequently criticised aspect of his entire theoretical system. His critics, from Sidgwick on, found it obscure and incoherent.[4] As a consequence, there was a general tendency to consider his ethical theory as a separate and independent province of philosophy.[5]

As it stands, Green's published metaphysics suffers from several shortcomings. In any event, it is insufficiently specific. Perhaps the most unfortunate omission of his account of first principles in *Prolegomena* is that Green failed to make clear the intrinsic link he construed between metaphysics and ethical philosophy. Therefore it was not only unclear to the general public what Green's metaphysics was about, its importance will easily have eluded the readers of *Prolegomena*. In this chapter I propose to supplement the published version of

---

[2]   *Prolegomena*, sect. 2.
[3]   *Ibid.*, Preface, p. vi.
[4]   Sidgwick, 'The Philosophy of T.H.Green,' pp. 19, 25–6.
[5]   The tendency to separate moral and political philosophy from its foundation in idealist metaphysics was further fuelled by the 'refutation of idealism' which marked the establishment of Realism in the first quarter of the twentieth century. See also Section F. On the whole, idealist metaphysics and logic were the first to be discredited and in this sense it would seem perfectly intelligible that certain theorists, while clearly adhering to Green's social teachings, saw fit to consider his social doctrine independently of his idealist metaphysics. In the heat of the anti-German sentiments after World War I idealist metaphysics was even explicitly rejected by men who otherwise reckoned themselves to be faithful disciples of Green. See, for a classic example, L.T. Hobhouse, *The Metaphysical Theory of the State*, London, 1918.

Green's metaphysics by drawing from his unpublished manuscripts. Through the notes of Green's tutorial and professorial lectures on this subject we can provide a more explicit account of his system of first principles than would have been possible on the basis of his publications. The chapter is structured as follows. I shall begin by giving some account of Green's doctrine of first principles as it is to be found in the introductory books of *Prolegomena*, identifying some major shortcomings in his doctrine (Sections A to E). I shall then discuss the principal criticisms which they have provoked (Section F). Drawing on the unpublished manuscripts we may go on subsequently to demonstrate how some of these criticisms can be dismissed, especially those which accuse Green of insufficiently determining his concept of the eternal consciousness (Section G). On the basis of a fuller statement of Green's views on this point a theory of the self can then be elaborated along the lines of the doctrine of the self-assertion of reason, with which Green became acquainted from the study he made of the *Propädeutik*.

A. The Function of Idealist Metaphysics in Green's Moral Philosophy

When Green died he left the manuscript of *Prolegomena* virtually complete; apart from certain minor editorial amendments it was otherwise ready for the press. Of all his posthumous publications, *Prolegomena* corresponded best to the type of work Green would have published, had he lived longer. By contrast with other manuscript lecture notes which were included in the collected *Works*, we do not need to make the caveat that Green's text was not intended for publication.

To situate this book in its context we need to point to the impressive results which the exact sciences had recently accomplished. In view of these developments, attempts were made to apply the same sort of method as had been so successfully employed in the field of exact science to man and human conduct. By submitting moral conduct to this scientific method, an attempt was made to remedy the notoriously elusive character of traditional normative moral philosophy. The result was a 'scientific theory of morals' in which man was essentially considered as a phenomenon in the same way as other phenomena in the world of nature. Moral conduct could then be explained in terms of a physical theory of conscience.

In the wake of this new trend towards scientific ethics, Green felt obliged to create room for his own work by demonstrating this rival approach to the problem of morality to be vacuous. It was Green's customary method to give as strong a statement as possible of the point of view that he sought to refute, before proceeding actually to refute it. In the context of such a case for natural ethics, Green considered that a good deal of the traditional questions posed by moral philosophy seemed to have lost their significance. With its clear-cut image, he suggested, the new scientific ethics formed an attractive alternative to the more traditional approach. Even if it is admitted that this scientific ethics leaves 'certain primary problems untouched,' this would seem to be only a minor defect in view of the sound results which the new approach had already produced.

Of course, the beginnings of a scientific theory of morals long predated Green's times. But it was around the time Green started his academic career that a new specific element had been added to the idea of a scientific ethics which made the thesis more plausible than ever. This was the doctrine of hereditary transmission which formed part of Darwin's evolutionary biology. Whereas earlier versions of the 'scientific theory of man' were rendered less convincing because they had to assume that human consciousness arose from animal feelings and appetites within the course of each individual's development, the notion of hereditary transmission allowed for this process to be extended over an infinite number of generations. Obviously, the plausibility of the argument was thus enhanced enormously and Green felt an even greater need to refute such a doctrine of scientific ethics.

To refute the pretensions of this rival approach to the problem of morality Green in fact developed two separate lines of argument. One direct and fundamental criticism of this new branch of natural science was delivered in the course of the introduction itself. Green observed there that if man was to be considered merely as a product of natural forces any prescriptive aspects of moral philosophy could be immediately discarded. For, morality at least presupposes the possibility that man could act in a manner different from his actual conduct. It presupposes, in other words, a certain independence of 'natural forces' and the scientific theory of morality does not allow for this. It follows, *ex hypothesi*, that no moral activity is possible, far less a theory thereof.[6]

'Can There Be a Natural Science of Man?'

While this seems sufficiently powerful an argument to dismiss the case of natural ethics, Green apparently saw the need further to consolidate his position by providing yet an alternative argument. In addition to the direct attack on the claims and pretensions of naturalistic ethics, he also developed a longer, indirect attack. This argument proceeded in two stages: before refuting natural ethics itself, Green focussed on the theory of man underlying this conception of morality so as to cut away from under its feet its very foundation. He observed that moral claims occupy a middle position somewhere in between purely 'objective' matters of fact, on the one hand, and purely subjective preferences, or 'matters of taste,' on the other. The corollary of this special position of moral claims is that in principle it is possible to convince others of certain ethical norms by stating reasons to support them. Owing to this characteristic position of ethics, halfway between objective and subjective, rational agents may conceivably continue to disagree about some moral norm or other. On the other hand, as distinguished from purely subjective preferences on the part of an individual, moral norms are open to argumentation. By this very feature of morality it is possible to convince others of the validity of some specific moral norm or position.

Given this specific, non-factual nature of morality, Green saw that it would be pointless to organise a direct dispute between the two competing definitions of morality. Without agreement as to a number of basic assumptions such a dispute would necessarily result in a frontal clash of two opposing conceptions of morality. In view of the impossibility of a direct confrontation, Green sought to establish the required agreement as to basic assumptions by entering an analysis of human knowledge. The first stage in Green's argument, then, was to consider the question 'Can there be a natural science of man?,' and it was under this significant title that the first sections of

---

[6]   *Prolegomena*, sects 7, 8.

his forthcoming *Prolegomena* were published in *Mind* in 1882.[7] When this question had to be answered in the negative, as he thought he could easily demonstrate, he expected to be in a better position to show that the scientific method does not provide an appropriate basis for a theory of morality.

The Self-Distinguishing Principle

The core of Green's argument against a natural science of man will be described in the following analysis as his 'self-distinguishing principle' in consciousness. On this principle, thinking must be seen as something essentially different from animal feeling. It follows, for Green, that the former could in no way be derived from the latter. On this view, any 'natural history of ethics' was therefore left without a connecting mechanism to allow consciousness to develop out of animal feeling. The missing link in all arguments for a scientific theory of man was the presupposition of an entity or agency which had an element of identity with the self-conscious individual agent. Green's primary conclusion, then, was that in order to explain the development of man's self-conscious activity out of animal feeling, some spiritual agency must be presupposed to render such evolution possible. Thought could not originate from anything but itself and the genesis of our thinking could only be explained by positing the existence of an ideal entity which realizes itself in our thinking.[8]

In the light of Green's controversy with naturalistic ethics his involvement with metaphysics of knowledge and nature becomes intelligible. Green's dealing with questions of 'pure' metaphysics was prompted by an attempt to avoid the seemingly pointless dispute as to which of the two rival theories was truer to the nature of morality. Green rightly saw that such a debate would be futile unless there was agreement on a number of basic points. In order to avoid such an irresolvable, direct debate on the nature of moral activity Green wanted to take the argument one step further back and sought to point out that on the principles of naturalistic ethics human knowledge could not be accounted for. It is clear to Green that if he could show anything to this effect, naturalistic ethics would be

---

[7]   This article, which roughly covers Book I of *Prolegomena*, is also mentioned in a draft letter to Longmans and Co, dated 11 March, 1882, about the possible publication of *Prolegomena*.

[8]   *Prolegomena*, sects 15, 16; cf. 52–4.

left in a potentially awkward position since, as it claimed to be a theory, it could easily be shown to take human knowledge for granted. Once it is shown that knowledge cannot be accounted for on naturalist principles, this conclusion at the same time seems to exclude the possibility of a scientific *theory* of ethics.[9]

This, then, is a brief description of the strategy with which Green seeks to criticise naturalistic ethics. He works his way around the problem of defining morality by first undertaking an analysis of human knowledge. Since this constitutes a less controversial topic than the question as to the definition of morality, a theory of knowledge would seem to be a suitable subject for a preliminary discussion so as to agree upon certain common assumptions. In our turn, we shall find grounds for questioning the position which Green developed in his controversy with the adherents of a scientific theory of morals. On analysis, Green's position will be found to centre on postulates which perhaps received less critical attention than was invested in his own analysis of the tacit assumptions of naturalistic ethics, the inconsistency of which he brought to the fore so unsparingly. These assumptions, at all events, seem less than fully thought out by Green and in order to bring them out clearly it is useful to consider the manner in which they were postulated. This will be undertaken in a following paragraph, dealing with Green's method of argument. However, before entering the details of Green's doctrine of metaphysics, it will be helpful to give some account of the structure of Green's argument in his moral treatise so as to bring out the task Green set to idealist metaphysics in the context of his theory of morality.

B. The Structure of Green's Argument
in *Prolegomena*

The mere fact that in a book on moral philosophy of 400 pages more than 150 pages deal with questions of metaphysics is of course remarkable. In order to point out the function of metaphysics in Green's argument in ethical philosophy it will be expedient to begin by analysing the structure of the argument in his *Prolegomena*. This comprises four books: moral philosophy proper forms the subject of Book III and is preceded by a

---

[9] *Ibid.*, sect. 8.

book on epistemology and what Bradley presented as the 'metaphysic of nature'; and a second book setting out his theory of the will, or metaphysic of morals. The third book containing moral philosophy proper is followed by a final book on 'the practical value of moral philosophy,' which compares his own theory and Sidgwick's utilitarian ethics on this point.

The three transitions connecting these parts of the treatise may be viewed as three fundamental *nexi* in Green's argumentation. No doubt the most self-evident of these is the last *nexus*: in the earlier books a theory of morality is worked up which is then applied to questions of practical conduct in the concluding book. Having argued in the speculative and theoretical parts that his doctrine is more adequate to the nature of morality than any of its contemporary competitors, Green seeks to point out in this final book that his doctrine also offers better practical guidance for moral conduct.

To determine the part played by metaphysics in Green's argumentation we must concentrate on the first two *nexi* of his argument. The thesis Green seeks to defend in his moral philosophy proper is that there is a gradual substantiation of some moral ideal to be discerned in human history. His mode of argument on this point falls into two separate lines of argument. On the one hand, he holds that the ethical activity and ethical judgments, which people actually hold, can only be understood on the assumption of some moral ideal which is gradually manifesting itself in the history of mankind.[10] On the other hand, he finds this assumption confirmed in the actual course of human history: analysis of earlier ages shows an unmistakable moral progress.[11]

The structure of Green's argument is best elucidated by pointing out what purpose Green thinks to achieve in this manner. This may be summarised as follows. With regard to the nature of morality Green finds himself faced with a dilemma. On the one hand, he cannot proceed entirely on an *a priori* argument. For, carried to its logical extreme, an *a priori*, rationalist argument would not leave room for individual moral autonomy. In order to remedy this defect Green develops a second line of argument. Whereas the first argument establishes the conditions required for morality to be possible, the second line of argument takes for granted the fact of moral-

[10] *Prolegomena*, sects 199–205.
[11] *Ibid.*, sects 206–45.

ity: individual agents actually hold moral judgments, perhaps not always and continuously, but the actual practice of human interaction shows that people are capable of a specific category of judgments, upon which they are able to act and which are commonly classified as moral judgments and action. Proceeding from this 'fact of morality,' Green seeks to work up an independent criterion by which to define morality so as to avoid the extreme implications of a consequent rationalism.

On the other hand, Green employs his rationalist line of argument to remedy any unsound consequences of a purely empiricist theory of ethics. The moral judgments that are actually held by individual agents do not by themselves provide a sufficient basis for a theory of morality. On such a basis the concept of morality would be reduced to something purely subjective; moral conduct would become entirely dependent on the moral intuitions people actually hold. Moreover, such an intuitive basis could not provide a criterion to settle any conflicts between moral claims.

With the construction of two lines of argument which mutually reinforce one another, Green intends to develop a middle way to lead him in between the two extremes to which he would be carried by each of the single origins mentioned. His rationalist line of argument provides him with a criterion to correct the casuistry of contingent moral claims, while, on the other hand, his appeal to the moral judgments people actually cherish, allows for an escape from a purely *a priori* ethics with all the problems inherent in such an approach to morality.

The Formative Principle in Practical Reason

In order further to substantiate his argument on the development of the moral ideal he seeks to support this postulate with an analysis of human willing. One of his assumptions is that the formation of the moral ideal, as it operates in human history, essentially corresponds to the way in which individual preferences are constituted. Green intends to judge the conduct of individual agents by a standard derived from the general structure of human willing. According to this point of view it can be determined from the structure of the will what preferences, or 'objects of will,' would be adequate to the will in the same way as a doctor can understand the working of a healthy organ from diagnosing a diseased one.

Green construes the formation of individual preferences as a continuous process in which all sorts of 'objects of desire' are being presented to the agent. Such a flux of contingent desires originates in man's animal organism. From this material the agent will form a practical conception of a set of goals which are to be realised through his activity. Consistency is the criterion on the basis of which the 'multitude' of desires is synthetised into a practical conception: desires which mutually exdude each other cannot form part of the same practical conception.

The *nexus* between moral philosophy proper and metaphysics of morals consists in the fact that the analysis of the will in its process of choosing, which Green undertakes in Book II of *Prolegomena*, provides him with a model which can be discerned in individual character as much as in the development of norms which are accepted as binding in a given society. On the basis of the consistency criterion governing the formation of a practical conception by an individual agent, Green's argument goes, it can also be seen why and in what way individual agents eventually cannot but will things which contribute to the common good.

Such a development consists in the ever increasing rationalisation of an individual's practical conception which is brought about by the formative activity of reason operating on a matter which consists of contingent desires. In the same way as an individual practical conception will display an ever greater degree of rationality, agents will eventually come to share a conception of common good. The argument concerning an ever increasing rationalisation in human willing is therefore central to Green's argument in moral theory. Green is well aware, however, that the presupposition of such a principle being operative in human willing does not allow for empirical proof. For that purpose, human will, in its empirical manifestations, seems far too arbitrary. It is in order to support this central part of his argument with something better than a mere postulate that Green turns to an analysis of human knowledge.

A Teleological Interpretation of Theoretical Reason

In the same way as the formative activity of reason can be seen in the constitution of man's practical conception, Green asserts that there is also a teleological principle to be discerned in theoretical reason. It will be recalled from the exposition of the

Propädeutik that man relates to the external world either through the practical or theoretical mode of mind. By pointing out the essential analogy between these two modes of mind Green seeks to make plausible that there is indeed an essential similarity between these two processes. This constitutes a *nexus* with which the *Prolegomena* begins. In the absence of a logically compulsive proof of the formative activity of reason in human willing and the consequent eventual harmony between the various practical conceptions of individual members of a society, Green believes that the formative activity of reason is best made evident in the constitution of human experience.

Having pointed out the expository strategy in the *Prolegomena* and the function of Green's general metaphysics in his ethical theory we may now go on to a more detailed analysis of Green's theory of human knowledge.

C. Metaphysics of Knowledge

The working method of *Prolegomena* has some features which are undeniably characteristic of Green. For he developed a particular liking for voicing his numerous stipulations as rhetorical questions. Most of these conform to the logical formula that, in view of the particular nature of the problem under consideration, there is only one solution thinkable. Now, of course, such an argument merely signifies that Green himself cannot think of any other explanation but the hypothesis which he himself supports and which, for that reason, must be taken to be *implied* in the very possibility of the events or phenomena he is considering. Green seems to be taking this type of proof as logically compulsive, but if so, he overlooks the difficulty of setting up the original premise, i.e. of being sure that only if what he spells out as the conditions of our knowledge were true should we have the experience we have. It will be evident that Green's position here is always open to falsification by suggesting an alternative explanation, but in *Prolegomena* the obvious weakness of this scheme of reasoning is blurred by the rhetorical form in which Green presents most of his stipulations. Green, in a fashion which will be found to recur on several occasions in *Prolegomena*, first formulates a provisional question, from which a general conclusion is drawn. This is, in turn, voiced as a rhetorical question and it is not until Green has thus brought in the tacit assumptions, which form the framework of his entire moral enquiry, that he finally formulates the question from which his investigation of first principles proceeds. He first asks whether we can express

> our idea of matter of fact … except as an idea of a relation which is always the same between the same objects; or our idea of an object except as that which is always the same in the same relations?[12]

But the greatest step in his scheme of reasoning is taken with the following tentative question, which immediately follows:

> And does not each expression imply the idea of a world as a single and eternal system of related elements, which may be related with endless diversity but must *be* related still?[13]

At this stage it is not difficult for Green to come to his concluding question:

> If we may properly call the consciousness which yields this idea 'understanding', are we not entitled to say that understanding is the source of there being for us an objective world, that it is the principle of objectivity?[14]

Even if we waive the objection to Green's definition of matters of fact, it must be observed that he does not provide anything like a proof of our knowledge implying a 'single and unalterable system of relations.' Nor is there any ground for his attributing eternal status to it.

Green's notion of an eternal system of terms in relation forms an integral part of a more general argument which may be termed a theory of the formative activity of thought. Green sought to render the essentials of this doctrine by pointing out two intuitive insights which he hoped would immediately appeal to his readers. The first was an investigation of what was involved in the distinction between appearance and reality which, as Green pointed out, is implied even in the simplest judgments of everyday life experience. The second theme with which he sought to convey his theory of human experience was an elaboration of the difference between change and consciousness of change.

The Formative Principle in Human Experience: Appearance and Reality

In order to render plausible his doctrine of an eternal system of terms-in-relation Green set out to inquire what was involved

---

[12]   *Ibid.*, sect. 14.
[13]   *Ibid.*
[14]   *Ibid.*

in the distinction between appearance and reality.[15] The theory of perception which he developed in the course of this investigation represents an important elaboration of Hegel's philosophy of mind in the *Propädeutik*. Furthermore, his findings are in keeping with everyday life experience. Everyone knows from his own experience cases of creative misunderstandings. A strong point in Green's epistemological stand which emerges from such cases is that these misunderstandings always involve a constructive or synthetic element. This is, at any rate, the way in which Green explains the otherwise unaccountable observation that if we misperceive some object of knowledge, we nevertheless perceive *something*. If there were no constructive activity of mind going into the constitution of knowledge we would expect a misunderstanding of reality to result in a complete void or chaos of impressions instead of an object or conception. Green's point is, however, that in making perceptual mistakes we always take one particular object for another. *Prolegomena* mentions the example of an engine driver who 'sees a signal wrong,' which on Green's principles can be reduced to mistaking one set of relations for another.[16] This example from everyday life clearly illustrates the synthetic activity of mind in the constitution of human experience.

Two analogies may here be set out. First, there is a remarkable analogy between misperception and misapprehension which may be explained, on Green's principles, from the fact that perception and conception are both forms of mental activity in which the mind attempts to fix the eternal reality in thought-determinations. As a second point, it may be noted that the theory of thinking which results from Green's views on perception and conception bears characteristics similar to the structure of scientific discovery.[17] A new scientific conception also results from newly collected data which can no longer be explained on the basis of the existing scientific theory. Such friction will give rise to a new viewpoint comprehending

[15] *Ibid.*, sects 12–18. This scheme is also dwelled upon in Green's tutorial lectures on logic from the 1874–75 academic year, which Nettleship included in *Works*, ii, pp. 158 ff., as 'The Logic of the Formal Logicians.' This is somewhat misleading, however, since in contrast with what might be expected from this title, Green is primarily concerned with setting out his own position, as against that of formal logicians such as Sir William Hamilton and H.L.Mansel.
[16] *Prolegomena*, sect. 12; cf. *Works*, ii, p. 177.
[17] This analogy is worked out in greater detail in Ms 6a.

both the former theory and the findings which were initially found to contradict it.

The distinction between appearance and reality served as an introduction to his theory of experience, and in order to come to a full understanding of the intrinsic link between Green's metaphysics of knowledge and his moral doctrine we now need to come to terms with this central notion in Green's thinking.

The Self-Distinguishing Principle in Human Experience: Change and Consciousness of Change

It was around the notion of experience that Green's discussion with the empiricists evolved. Empiricist philosophy proceeded on the view that man can look straight to the facts. For empiricism, experience is simply a series of mental conditions in which the subject finds itself over time. On this view none but a passive role is attributed to the mind which simply experiences the situation as it is determined by certain conditions. According to this point of view there is no essential difference between the experience of man and, for example, a plant. On empiricist premises man reacts to external stimuli, in the same way as plants. In Green's view, however, there is an essential difference between the two kinds of 'experience'. In *Prolegomena* this is illustrated by the distinction between change and consciousness of change, or, as he formulates it in another passage, the difference between 'a mere series of related events' and consciousness thereof.[18]

Green's point in the dispute with empiricism is that human experience must always be of the latter kind. Moreover, he emphasizes that the difference between consciousness of a series of events and each of the individual events which make up the series is absolute and fundamental. Consciousness cannot be reduced to anything other than itself nor can it be identified with any of the events of which consciousness is formed. Consciousness therefore cannot reside in any of the events which make up the series since it must somehow be continuously present throughout the occurrence of the series. Due to the fact that the two thus belong to two entirely different categories, consciousness can never derive from any of the events of which it is conscious, as, in fact, is done by empiricist psy-

---

[18]   *Prolegomena*, sects 15–16.

chology and the numerous 'natural histories of ethics' which were attempted in Green's days. Green's argument brought out that all these attempts were based upon the same premises.[19] By the same token, Green refutes the suggestion that consciousness could be shown to derive from previous events. For, this suggestion merely throws the question back to an earlier stage, as long as it does not account for the question how such a previous event could exist without consciousness. As this question cannot satisfactorily be answered, Green sees fit to conclude that experience as consciousness of events cannot be explained except on the supposition of some conscious activity or other. As consciousness and any thing or event unrelated to self-conscious thought belong to two fundamentally different categories and as this difference is absolute and insurmountable, consciousness cannot be explained in terms of any thing or event unrelated to consciousness.

Anticipating the criticism of Green's published moral doctrine, it will be helpful if we consider an aspect of his terminology. Although Green does not show himself to be aware of it, the notion of 'series' in itself already forms part of the ordering activity of consciousness. And in view of this observation, it becomes somewhat inconsequential when Green uses the phrase 'mere series' to describe the state of things before or, at all events, unrelated to consciousness. This terminology seems inconsistent with the fundamental thesis that order can only exist for some consciousness or other. On this premise 'mere series' must be taken as a contradiction in terms since a 'series' already implies a summary notion of coherence of events ordered in series. As a matter of fact one may wonder whether on Green's principles he can legitimately speak of 'mere' events.[20]

D. The Teleological Principle in Reality

Thus far we have mainly considered Green's analysis of the cognitive activity of man. As a result of this analysis the central position of consciousness in the constitution of experience was brought to the fore. In order to explain the genesis and growth of knowledge at all, some form of permanent consciousness must be presupposed. It follows from such an epistemological

---

[19] *Ibid.*, sects 48–50.
[20] *Ibid.*, sect. 16.

position that human knowledge, which is thus constituted, does not reach beyond the experience of each individual self-conscious agent. On the basis of epistemology alone there is nothing to guarantee that our knowledge is anything more than a subjective illusion. The objective reality — that is, as it exists independent of the cognitive activity of any *particular* self-conscious mind — which is presupposed in the distinction between appearance and reality requires something beyond the consciousness of the individual cognitive agents.

In order to establish the conditions of an objective order of nature — 'objective' once again in the sense explained — Green proceeds to inquire what exactly is involved in the order of nature. For that purpose he recalls the Kantian dictum that 'understanding makes nature,' while drawing at once attention to the fundamental sense in which Kant qualified this statement: '"Macht zwar der Verstand die Natur, aber er schafft sie nicht." The understanding "makes" nature, but out of a material which it does not make.'[21] However, Green makes it clear from the very outset that Kant's metaphysics cannot be more than a starting point, especially in view of his untenable stand as to some world of things-in-themselves. And, while Kant's epistemology is still of great use to later thinkers, the absence of any ontology, which follows from his view of an unknowable thing-in-itself, must be taken to be as unsatisfactory as the notion of the sheer given from which empiricist philosophy proceeded.

In order to make room for an exposition of his own standpoint in this matter Green thinks it necessary to settle the misleading question 'what is the real?'[22] This question is misleading in so far as it suggests that there is something like the unreal which could be distinguished from the real. This, on Green's premises, would be an impossibility, a literal contradiction in terms. Everything existing belongs to the real. Things may not be fully known and our judgments may be mistaken; but, as is more evident from the manuscripts than from the text of *Prolegomena*, such a mistake must be seen as an 'inchoate truth'[23] rather than unreal.

Having dismissed the question 'What is the real?' as improperly stated, Green suggests what he thinks is a more

---

[21]   *Ibid.*, sect. 11.
[22]   *Ibid.*, sects 22–4.
[23]   Ms 10a.

sensible question: 'What is implied in there being a nature of things?'[24] The answer to this question is closely connected to the question whether a conception of nature as a single all-inclusive system of relations can subsist by itself, whether or not, as Green says, it needs 'something else' to render it possible.

> To suppose that this 'something else', if nature were found unthinkable without it, is related to those conditions, of which the relation to each other forms the system of nature, in the same way in which these are related to each other, would no doubt be in contradiction with our account of this system as one and all-inclusive. It could not therefore be held to be related to them as, for instance, an invariable antecedent to an invariable sequent, or as one body to another outside it. But there would be no contradiction in admitting a principle which renders all relations possible, and is itself determined by none of them . . .[25]

As we saw, the notion of a principle which renders a system of relations possible without itself being conditioned by any of the relations constituting such a system, is but an instance of a recurring theme in Green's philosophy. In the context of the passage quoted above it is employed in an attempt to explain the objective order of things, independent of the cognitive activity of any particular self-conscious agent, but an analogous argument is adduced to explain the formative activity of each particular intelligence in the constitution of experience. In the same manner the notion of an entity which renders possible but which is yet not itself determined by any of the acts which issue from it, is central to his philosophy of character.[26]

Green reduces the question as to the conditions of a system of terms-in-relation to the more elementary question as to the nature of a relation itself and the 'existence of many-in-one' which it involves. And he explains

> a plurality of things cannot of themselves unite in one relation, nor can a single thing of itself bring itself into a multitude of relations . . . Their common being is not something into which their several existences disappear. On the contrary, if they did not survive in their singleness, there could be no relation between them — nothing but a blank featureless identity.[27]

---

[24] *Prolegomena*, sect. 27.
[25] *Ibid*.
[26] The analogous argument in epistemology is developed in Green's doctrine of free cause, *Prolegomena*, Book I, Chapter 3.
[27] *Prolegomena*, sect. 28.

On the basis of this conclusion Green thinks he can legitimately conclude that if relations enter into the constitution of
reality, there must be some synthesising activity which com-
bines manifold things 'without effacing their severalty'.[28]
Having demonstrated in his epistemology the formative activity of some self-conscious agency in the constitution of knowledge, Green goes on to point out that 'the same or an
analogous action is necessary to account for any relation whatever — for a relation between material atoms as much as any
other.'[29] In fact, as we shall see, this stipulation commits Green
to the view that relations can exist only *for* some self-conscious
agency or other and thereby the extension of Green's argument in epistemology to his ontology is concluded.[30]

Truth and Omniscience

It is in the context of the formative activity of thought in the
constitution of reality that Green introduces the doctrine of
omniscience. This doctrine will be found to feature promi-
nently in his philosophy of character as well as in his metaphysics of knowledge and nature.

> The illusive appearance, as opposed to the reality, of any event is
> what *that* event really is not; but at the same time it really is some-
> thing. It is real, not indeed with the particular reality which the
> subject of the illusion ascribes to it, but with a reality which a
> superior intelligence might understand.[31]

Green's next step is then to discuss a more appropriate question than the futile inquiry as to 'what is the real?' A more
expedient strategy to establish a criterion of truth may be
found in the following statement:

> How do we decide whether any particular event or object is really
> what it seems to be, or whether our belief about it is true? — the
> answer must be that we do so by testing the unalterableness of the
> qualities which we ascribe to it, or which form its apparent
> nature.[32]

---

[28] *Ibid.*
[29] *Ibid.*, sect. 29.
[30] Cf. *ibid.*, sect. 51. In Green's tutorial lectures on logic this assertion is explicitly
      made: *Works*, ii, p. 176.
[31] *Prolegomena*, sect. 23. This assertion is substantiated in 'The Logic of the For-
      mal Logicians.'
[32] *Prolegomena*, sect. 24.

So, after a long detour, Green eventually offers here his crite-rion of truth: unalterability of relations. But this leaves essen-tially unexplained how finite agents can benefit from the knowledge of such an eternal and unalterable system of rela-tions in their judgments as to what is relatively more and what is less appropriate to the truth, which distinction corresponds to the 'real' and the 'apparent' in everyday life judgments. According to Green, the view that 'whatever anything really is it is unalterably' underlies the simplest judgments of everyday life experience as much as the most advanced scientific quest for laws of universal change. To some extent Green seems to recognize the difficulty of his position when he states that the 'unalterableness' criterion applies to the relations between appearance and its conditions.[33] Again, an element of Green's omniscience argument is touched upon when he states that

> The complete determination of an event it may be impossible for our intelligence to arrive at. There may always remain unascertained conditions which may render the relation between appearance and such conditions of it as we know, liable to change.[34]

Notwithstanding this limited nature of our understanding, according to Green's argument, all inquiry into the real nature of things presupposes such an eternal and unalterable system of relations, by reference to which we can judge our own con-ception of the world.

The Concept of Relation in Green

In his investigation of what is involved in 'there being a nature of things'[35] there occurs a relatively sudden transposition of the key of Green's argument. Whereas he had been consider-ing the implications of his epistemology for his theory of real-ity it seems as if he somehow abandons the train of the argument springing from an analysis of the conditions of knowledge and makes a fresh start. For, in the course of his ontological argument, he appeals to the reader's common sense and urges him to reflect on the concept of relation.[36]

The question of 'there being a nature of things,' we saw, was made dependent on the question whether the conception of

[33] *Ibid.*, sect. 25.
[34] *Ibid.*, sect. 26.
[35] *Ibid.*, sect. 27.
[36] *Ibid.*, sect. 28.

nature as a single all-inclusive system of relations can stand by itself, in other words, whether it needs any further assumption to make it feasible. No sooner is this rendering of the problem stated than Green realizes the contradiction in terms involved in asking whether a conception of nature can be on its own if, according to a more general feature of his theoretical system, conceptions cannot exist except in some form of consciousness or other. Having recognised the difficulty, Green attempts to work his way around the problem by analysing one of the central notions in his metaphysical argument, i.e. the notion of 'relation'.

A little misleading as it is such a familiar notion, Green says, it involves 'all the mystery . . . of the existence of many in one.'[37] In the same way as in his epistemology, Green argues that the only 'combining agency' to produce unity in diversity is intelligence. Green's ontology is thus open to a similar criticism to that made against his epistemology, i.e. of assuming his suggested solution to a problem to be the only one without providing anything of substance to allow a critical examination of this postulate, which thus remains yet another unreasoned assumption of his thinking. Again, Green seems to make an even more arbitrary deduction in the following statement:

> Either then we must deny the reality of relations altogether and treat them as fictions of our combining intelligence; or we must hold that, being the product of our combining intelligence, they are yet 'empirically real' on the ground that our intelligence is a factor in the real of experience; or if we suppose them to be real otherwise than merely as for us . . . we must recognise as the condition of this reality the action of some unifying principle analogous to that of our understanding.[38]

The first option logically results in a position to which, in Green's opinion, a philosophy like Locke's necessarily leads. The corollary of such a position is that 'nothing is real of which anything can be said,' as he epitomized the result of Locke's *Essay*, when carried to its logical outcome.[39] For this reason, if one, like Locke, sticks to the distinction between 'the real' and 'the work of the mind' this more or less automatically leads to the notion of a thing-in-itself on which the ordering intellect has no hold. This ostensibly extreme conclusion follows from

---

[37] *Ibid.*
[38] *Ibid.*, sect. 29.
[39] *Ibid.*, sect. 20; cf. 30.

the consideration that the activity of the mind in the constitution of relations cannot be denied (on Green's principles). In this sense, and on the basis of all these premises, Locke's starting point logically leads to Kant's theory of a reality of things-in-themselves, unknowable for the human intellect.

The Relationship of Knowledge and 'Nature'

In earlier paragraphs of *Prolegomena* Green takes proper account of the possibility that the unity of experience and unity in nature, if indeed there is one, may derive from different sources. He observes that in such a case, it still must be explained how the two nevertheless seem to correspond.[40] It may be noted in passing that this precaution is rather superficial. For, if indeed the unity of experience of each individual self-conscious agent did not correspond to the unity pervading nature there could be no such thing as a common experience and hence communication between different agents would be inexplicable. Nor would there be any ground to assume an objective world of fact. However, close analysis of the section on ontology can show Green to extend this very reasoning from knowledge to nature. Let us consider how he actually proceeds.

While he uses the two terms synonymously in the rest of *Prolegomena*, he distinguishes knowledge and experience throughout the paragraph under consideration. The former is presented as derived from the latter:

> ... the derivation of knowledge from an experience of unalterably related phenomena is its derivation from objects unalterably related in consciousness . . . The question then arises how a succession of feelings becomes such a relation of objects in consciousness.[41]

However, if a relation of objects existed or could be known to exist otherwise than for consciousness, one might wonder how it could be known at all. What possible means could there be of establishing whether the two actually correspond? At this point Green states, characteristically, that the only explanation which he can give is that there must be an identity between relations in knowledge and relations constituting objective nature. But, as will be apparent from what we have

[40]   *Ibid.*, sect. 19.
[41]   *Ibid.*, sect. 31.

already seen, it had not yet been established as a matter of fact that relations also went into the constitution of nature. Green, in other words, tries to argue from his conclusion of the analysis of the conditions of knowledge to an analogous conclusion about objective reality. For two objects to be in relation there must be some permanent agency or entity in which this relation can exist. Here Green makes use of the fact that 'object,' 'subject' and 'relation' can linguistically be employed separately from one another, whereas according to his own principles such separation is not conceivable.[42]

So far in this chapter we have considered a number of themes central to Green's philosophy of theoretical reason. Green's published statement of his system of first principles provided us with sufficient evidence as to how he construed the relationship between epistemology and ontology. Green's investigation of human experience aimed at demonstrating that all knowledge consists in properties attributed to objects by the mind. These attributes were essentialy thought-relationships between objects. We saw furthermore that Green's idealistic epistemology centred on the assertion of a spiritual or synthetic principle in the constitution of knowledge. It is only due to its discerning activity that there is a world to be known *for us*. The conclusion of Green's epistemology impacts on his theory of reality. For, on the hypothesis that knowledge is constituted by the synthetising activity of our understanding, what becomes of the independent status of the object known? In its unqualified sense Green's conclusion seemed to raise doubts as to the possibility of an intelligible world independent of our cognitive activity. It was with a view to remedying this disturbing conclusion that Green worked out the concept of an eternal consciousness, constituting a world of knowable facts which are nevertheless independent of the cognitive activity of individual self-conscious agents.

The Doctrine of an Eternal Consciousness in Prolegomena

Having considered the central issues of Green's philosophy of theoretical reason, we are now in a better position to understand Green's stipulation of an eternal consciousness producing a single, unalterable and eternal system of thought-relations. This notion must be seen as the imagined outcome of

---

[42]   See, for example, sects 9, 28, 32, 62–5.

the process of human understanding. It is the ideal condition of all possible knowledge acquired, all thought-determinations realized. The history of thought shows a continuous process towards a more complete understanding, which from Green's point of view is the same as the more complete determination of the cosmos of experience by thought-relations. While Green's train of thought on this point can be made intelligible by pointing to the function his stipulation had to perform, it does not follow that the conditions which he discerned form the only possible explanation for an objective world of fact.

Apart from this point of meta-criticism we may wonder to what extent Green succeeds in showing that the theory he espouses is sufficient for the task for which it is designed. In particular, as regards the question of the implications for an objective world of fact, which may be drawn from the analysis of the cognitive activity of each individual agent, we identified a serious flaw in the exposition of *Prolegomena*. As was explained, Green extended his argument in epistemology to ontology. In a following section we shall go on to consider the consequences for the metaphysical doctrine of *Prolegomena*.

Another question which suggests itself with regard to Green's ontology is as to the qualification 'unalterable'. This seems prompted by the consideration that what must be taken as an integral part of our experience, i.e. the distinction between appearance and reality, presupposes a certain criterion or standard to distinguish them by. When writing the manuscript of *Prolegomena* Green apparently thought such a standard is only to be found in an unalterable order by reference to which the validity of our temporary conceptions can be judged. A little reflection will show that Green's idea is not up to the task it is meant for. For even if such a perfect understanding could ever be reached it is difficult to see how it could possibly relate to our common understanding. Moreover, the achievement of such insight seems to leave little, if any, room for misunderstanding characterizing the cognitive activity of individual self-conscious agents. Nor would further progress in knowledge be possible on that account.

Green must have intended the notion of unalterability of the eternal order of relations as an implicit presupposition underlying any judgment as to what is real and what is apparent.

Textual analysis of *Prolegomena* confirms this.[43] If the unalterability of the system of relations is not more than a presupposition it will at once be clear that such an 'unalterable order' cannot serve as a standard by which to judge everyday life conceptions.

As to the theme of an unalterable eternal order two observations can therefore be made. First, the criterion of the unalterability of the system of relations is introduced as a *deus ex machina* since the link between this stipulation and the cognitive process, as instanced in each individual self-conscious agent, is not further illuminated in Green's analysis. Moreover, on closer examination this link turns out to be quite inadequate for Green's purpose. Second, it must be noted that *Propädeutik* provided a criterion which would have been more suited to perform this task, i.e. the coherence criterion of truth. Green's unpublished lecture notes make it clear that at an earlier stage Green did, in fact, espouse this doctrine.[44] And, in the opinion of the present writer, it would have better fitted the general argument of *Prolegomena*. For reasons about which one can only speculate, he later propounds the unalterability criterion which also found its way into *Prolegomena*.

The postulate of an unalterable system of terms-in-relation makes Green's metaphysics of knowledge and nature into an essentially closed system. There always remains the possibility that when everything has become known, or to stick to Green's metaphor, when the entire 'cosmos of experience' has been determined by thought-relations the whole system will be falsified or when this possibility is denied — as, after all, every possible thought-determination has been realized — the system becomes completely *a priori*. The coherence criterion, on the other hand, offers a more powerful principle. It produces an essentially open system which can always be adapted to new impressions or thought determinations issuing from the cognitive mind. Such an adaptation raises the

[43]   See for example *ibid.*, sect. 25: ' ... the conviction here illustrated, that whatever anything is really it is unalterably, regulates equally our most primitive and our most developed judgments of reality.'

[44]   There is ample evidence in the manuscripts to confirm this. See for example Ms 10a on the formative activity of thought; Ms 14:4 on the 'false abstraction of thought from things' (Green's phrase) which will be quoted in Section G. The doctrine equally readily emerges from Green's discussion on the nominalist-realist controversy in Ms 6a, see especially pp. 28 and 30 where he considers an objection to the effect that subsequent conceptions of the same thing may be mutually exclusive, as can be shown from the history of the physical sciences.

synthesis of the preceding impressions to a higher level. Furthermore, the coherence criterion is much more in line with the doctrine of formative activity of thought which Green espoused in his earlier unpublished manuscripts.[45]

Before proceeding to a further elaboration of Green's doctrine of an eternally complete agent by drawing from his unpublished manuscripts, I will briefly consider the summary comments on this subject which are to be found in his published metaphysics. Having derived in the first chapter the activity of some eternal teleological principle, Green concludes his pure metaphysics with two short chapters on the relationship of such an eternal consciousness to the finite consciousness to sharpen his theory and to bring out the significance of his doctrine of first principles for his moral philosophy. Unfortunately, the title which Green's editor assigned to the second chapter seems to promise more than Green is actually offering. According to Bradley's title, it purports to deal with 'The Relation of Man, as Intelligence, to the Spiritual Principle in Nature'. In fact, in addition to the postulate of an eternal consciousness, which resulted from his preceding ontological inquiry, the chapter merely records Green's opinion that the growth of human knowledge, both at the level of individual agents and for humanity at large, can only be explained on the hypothesis that our knowledge is gradually communicated to us, or reproduced in us. Apart from this further elaboration of Green's central thesis on the role of thinking activity in knowledge and in reality, the second chapter is largely devoted to the problem of the place of time in Green's metaphysical outlook of the world, to which we shall now turn.

E. Teleology, Time and Eternity

In Green's opinion, the chief problem following from the view that reality is a teleological system is as to the place of time within the system as a whole. A teleological process can only be fully understood when regarded from two points of view, which cannot be reduced to a single perspective. Regarding the particular phases in the development of any organic body, we may speak of its life history as a temporal process; but regarding all these particular modes in view of the end to

---

[45] See the manuscripts mentioned in the previous note, especially Ms 10a.

which they are organic, its essential being may be regarded as in some sense transcending the temporal process. This conclusion about the seemingly paradoxical nature of the teleological process in general also applies to the cognitive process which, as Green established in the preceding chapter of *Prolegomena*, could only be understood in teleological terms. Our conscious experience is, on the one hand, 'an order of events in time consisting in modifications of our sensibility.' On the other hand it is equally characterized as:

> a consciousness of those events — a consciousness of them as a related series, and as determined in their relations to each other by relation to something else, which is from the first conceived as other than the modifications of our sensibility . . .[46]

These events are not ordered in time, i.e. there is no before or after in the act of consciousness itself. As was also pointed out in the preceding chapter of *Prolegomena*, 'a consciousness of related events, as related, cannot consist in those events.'[47]

Green's point is perhaps best summarized by saying that while there is succession in the series of events of which man is conscious, this succession cannot be in the consciousness itself. In view of its function as a permanent principle rendering possible human experience, consciousness must somehow be taken to transcend the temporal process. This seemingly paradoxical relationship of temporal and non-temporal elements in the cognitive process cannot be dismissed by saying that the consciousness of a series of events is *simultaneous* with the series. In a series of events in time the individual events cannot be present simultaneously; the first event already belongs to the past when the second is present, and so on. There is succession in the events of which we are conscious, but our consciousness is not itself a succession in time. In seeking to understand our consciousness we thus have to take account of two opposite points of view. On the one hand, consciousness has an obviously temporal aspect, as is clearly seen from the learning process, for instance. On the other hand, this temporal character of the growth of our knowledge does not affect the essentially non-temporal character of consciousness, which Green is to work out as an element of identity of the finite and the eternal consciousness.

---

[46] *Prolegomena*, sect. 55.
[47] *Ibid.*

The most explicit statement of Green's doctrine of the relationship between man and the eternal consciousness is provided when Green, in an attempt to explain the seemingly paradoxical relationship of the temporal and the non-temporal elements in the cognitive process, sees fit to phrase his doctrine, as he admits, 'in a bald dogmatic way.'[48] 'It will be found,' Green announces on this occasion,

> that this apparent state of the case can only be explained by supposing that in the growth of our experience, in the process of our learning to know the world, an animal organism, which has its history in time, gradually becomes the vehicle of an eternally complete consciousness. What we call our mental history is not a history of this consciousness, which in itself can have no history, but a history of the process by which the animal organism becomes its vehicle.[49]

Green's presentation of his argument may be taken to suggest that this provisional statement is still to be supported by further evidence, but *Prolegomena* does not provide anything to substantiate Green's thesis. The only manner in which he seeks to render it plausible is by pointing out that this same difficulty concerning the relationship between the temporal and the non-temporal element in knowledge attaches to 'any case of an end gradually realizing itself through a certain organism.'[50]

Human Intelligence as a 'Free Cause'

The concluding chapter of his 'pure' metaphysics expounds Green's doctrine of 'free causality.' This doctrine may be said to form the *nexus* between Green's investigation of theoretical reason and his examination of practical reason which covers the second book of *Prolegomena*. The concluding chapter on the principles of 'pure' metaphysics aims at showing the free causality involved in human intelligence and once this doctrine is rendered plausible for the theoretical mode of mind, the second book goes on to work out an analogous doctrine for the human activity called willing.

It will be recalled that the starting point of Green's 'pure' metaphysics was a series of questions — in which we discerned some rhetorical features — intended to expose the

[48]   *Ibid.*, sect. 68.
[49]   *Ibid.*, sect. 67.
[50]   *Ibid.*, sect. 68.

insufficiency of naturalistic ethics. His main argument against this rival school in moral philosophy was that, on their premises, no freedom would be possible. If man is seen as a mere product of natural forces, he also lacks the capacity to distance himself from his actual behaviour, which is the pre-condition of all moral activity. In the first part of his metaphysics of knowledge and nature Green, as it were, created room for a 'truer' theory of morality by disentangling and refuting the premises of a theory which denies the possibility of freedom. In terms of the series of questions from which the volume proceeds, the first part of his pure metaphysics shows extensively that a natural theory of man, which can be shown to underlie natural ethics, simply does not allow for man's setting up a theory explaining himself. Further to this conclusion, the final chapter of the first book of *Prolegomena* gives a positive statement of the freedom involved in human intelligence by setting out his doctrine of free causality.

The argument of a free cause in human intelligence forms the apex of his metaphysics of knowledge and nature. Green reproduced the argument concerning free causality in human intelligence to support an analogous claim of free causality in human volition. He set out his doctrine through a brief assessment of the concept of cause in its ordinary meaning as it is operative *within* the system of terms-in-relation figuring in Green's stipulative definition of 'nature'.[51] In this sense cause must be seen as an 'assemblage of conditions'[52] or an invariable antecedent. Cause is distinct from its effect, however much the effect may depend on the cause. In the case of the relationship between the eternal consciousness and the cosmos of possible experience as a whole, this system is defined as single and all-inclusive.[53] As Green sets out this difference:

> There is nothing to qualify the determined world *as a whole* but that inner determination of all contained in it by mutual relation, which is due to the action of the unifying principle; nor anything to qualify the unifying principle but this very action, with the self-distinction necessary to it.[54]

---

[51] Green uses the term 'nature' as a system of intelligible relations or 'cosmos of possible experience.' *Prolegomena*, sect. 8.

[52] *Prolegomena*, sect. 75.

[53] *Ibid.*, sect. 76.

[54] *Ibid.*

It is in this sense that Green claims that the teleological principle in nature is an instance of free causality. It is capable of determining the order of nature, just as in the case of a cause within the system of nature. But it differs from natural causality in that it is itself not determined by its 'effects'.

There are, however, two reasons why this enterprise is somewhat less than satisfactory. First, as was pointed out above, the point of a number of arguments in Green's pure metaphysics only emerges when they are considered in the light of the analogous argument which he seeks to defend in his metaphysics of morals so that it cannot be said to be as logically compulsive as Green would have hoped. Green's pure metaphysics is not quite so independent of the postulates with which he structures his metaphysics of morals as he wants us to believe. It would seem that Green has difficulty holding up his epistemology and his theory of reality without the support of his theory of willing, rather than the other way round.[55]

Even if this criticism is waived it may be observed, as a second point, that, by itself, drawing an analogy does not amount to a proof. Reasoning by analogy is valid only when it is in some way or other made clear that it is a *valid* analogy, i.e. that the context from which the analogy is taken conforms in all relevant senses to the case under consideration about which one seeks to demonstrate something. For this reason Green's analogy between knowledge and willing presupposes a prior inquiry to establish whether these two human activities correspond in all relevant senses necessary to be able to transpose the insights derived from one investigation to another.

F. Green's General Metaphysics and Its Critics

Ever since *Prolegomena* was issued in 1883, its first two books on metaphysics have puzzled students of his moral philosophy. In the form in which it was published, Green's treatise cannot be said to be exactly an accessible text. No wonder, then, that, being Green's final academic product, *Prolegomena* prompted a good deal of speculation as to Green's meaning.[56]

[55] This seems in line with the conclusion by Maria Dimova-Cookson, *T.H.Green's Moral and Political Philosophy: A Phenomenological Perspective*, Basingstoke, 2001, Chapter 1.

[56] And this debate still goes on. See, for example, Colin Tyler, *Thomas Hill Green (1836–1882) and the Philosophical Foundations of Politics*, Lewiston, 1997, who sets out to show that 'Green's epistemology is far more coherent and plausible

In my opinion, however, many of its idiosyncracies can be made intelligible when considered against the background of his intellectual development. Parallel to the process sketched in the previous chapter which gradually led him away from Hegel, Green can be seen to move away from the more logical rationalism which characterized his earlier work to the equilibrium in which he tried to balance his rationalist leanings by an appeal to the fact that people are actually capable of moral judgment and conduct.

As was set out earlier in the analysis of the structure of Green's argument in *Prolegomena*, this equilibrium position is central to his mature doctrine of morality. In my reading of his intellectual development Green gradually came to adopt a less logical and less straightforward position because he realised that his earlier rationalism was inconsistent with certain intuitive views about the nature of morality. Roughly speaking it may be said that to elaborate the rationalist thesis logically, thus fixing *a priori* the contents of the moral good, would be incompatible with the requirement of moral autonomy.

Once he grasped the impossibility of a logical rationalist ethics, this prompted him to revise the stringent rationalism of his earlier period in order to work up a more balanced, dualist position in which he sought to play off against each other the extreme and unsound consequences of an empiricist and a rationalist ethics, respectively.

Taking into account these 'grounded speculations' concerning Green's intellectual development, much of the otherwise confusing turnings and twistings of Green's argument in *Prolegomena* can be made intelligible. For, part of his argumentation still originates in the more logical version of his rationalism which can also be seen in his earlier work. When considering the text apart from the perspective of Green's intellectual development, it is difficult to avoid the conclusion that Green attempted simultaneously to uphold two positions

---

than has commonly been supposed'. This is largely shown by disentangling the general metaphysics from the concept of eternal consciousness and its religious connotations (p. 11). On the other hand, Maria Dimova-Cookson argues that 'Green's philosophical originality is to be found in [his metaphysics of the will], not in [his epistemology] . . . much of this originality has not been brought to light precisely because his epistemology contains philosophical statements that contradict the more powerful insights of his theory of the will . . . his epistemology fails to fulfil its initial task as it gives either wrong, or strongly one-sided accounts of Green's own philosophy' (p. 24).

which mutually exclude one another. This in fact is the criticism Green's contemporary Henry Sidgwick levelled against Green's general metaphysics, as will be discussed in the following section.

So far in this chapter we have explored the structure of Green's argument in 'pure' metaphysics as it was set out in *Prolegomena*. The function of the various kinds of metaphysical inquiry performed in Green's moral philosophy was elucidated. The argument of *Prolegomena* can be analysed in terms of a hierarchical order of chains of reasoning, each of which provides a link which was missing in the subsequent chain. In this way we found that Green's theory of the will provided a central element of his ethical doctrine itself, while the theory of the will was in turn supported by a theory of knowledge. In order to substantiate this field of inquiry Green was obliged to make certain statements concerning reality itself. It was in this context that Green introduced his concept of an eternal consciousness. The problems concerning this conception of Green's which we just noted, can be enlarged upon by drawing from his unpublished manuscripts, as shall be undertaken in the concluding section of the present chapter. But before turning to the unpublished manuscripts we shall briefly consider the major criticisms which this central postulate of Green's evoked.

Criticisms of Green's General Metaphysics

The criticisms Green's idealism has encountered since *Prolegomena* was issued in 1883 may be divided into internal and external criticisms, i.e. by successors in the idealist tradition and by those who argued from an altogether different philosophical position. To the latter category belong men such as G.E. Moore and Bertrand Russell who shortly after the turn of the century developed their criticisms of idealism, effectively ending the brief period in which the school of Green formed the dominant philosophy in Britain. However, their 'refutation of idealism' is so far distant from Green's position that it would be difficult to include their arguments in this survey of the criticisms of Green's metaphysics. On the other hand, in discussing the criticisms that were being voiced by Green's idealist successors we run the risk of becoming involved in a highly technical discussion. For this reason I shall restrict myself here, in discussing the objections raised by Green's contemporaries, to a thinker who occupied a halfway position between internal and external criticism. This was Henry Sidgwick, whom we have already encountered in the previous chapter and who may count as a good representative of the various criticisms which were held against Green around the turn of the century.[57] On the one hand, Sidgwick did not share Green's views and had a sufficiently independent position to hold a generally critical attitude towards Green; on the other hand, he was familiar enough with Green's metaphysical views to make his criticism relevant for our present purpose.

Sidgwick may be said to have voiced his criticism of Green's metaphysics literally in the lion's den — in a speech for the Oxford Philosophical Society in 1900, in front of an audience predominantly consisting of pupils of Green. His thesis was that a fundamental incoherence was to be found in Green's supposition of an eternal consciousness in that Green could be shown to require it to perform various mutually exclusive functions. According to Sidgwick, it was impossible that the eternal consciousness acted as a source of relationships constituting the intelligible world and was yet absolutely independent of it. These two mutually exclusive notions he labelled 'Spiritualist' and 'Idealistic' respectively, the former being characterized by a fundamental distinction between the mind and its ideas; the latter connoting the conception of reality which suppresses such distinction in favour of the view that the universe is essentially thought or thinking activity.[58] Sidgwick makes clear two things: first, that such combination of idealism and spiritualism cannot be defended and, second,

---

[57] One of the remarkable details about Green and Sidgwick is that the two men, who went to Rugby together and were lifelong friends, were both successful in establishing a philosophical school. Green counts as the founder of Oxford Idealism whereas Sidgwick established a philosophical school of his own at Cambridge where he was a fellow of Trinity and from 1883 Professor of moral philosophy. Sidgwick worked out a variant of utilitarianism, usually classified as universalistic utilitarianism. Apart from Sidgwick's personal acquaintance with Green, there is a further reason which makes his criticism of Green's general metaphysics especially relevant. While Sidgwick is rightly described as a utilitarian, his views differ considerably from the views of earlier generations of utilitarian theorists. With regard to Sidgwick's criticism of Green's general metaphysics it is significant to point out Sidgwick's rejection of the Empiricist epistemology underlying classical Benthamite utilitarianism, which was made explicit and subsequently developed by J.S. Mill. As to his theory of knowledge Sidgwick was thus in line with Green rather than with earlier utilitarians.

[58] 'The Philosophy of T.H. Green,' p. 20.

that Green, in the introductory books of *Prolegomena*, does not succeed in simultaneously upholding these two positions.[59]

The 'Refutation of Idealism'

Following its refutation by Realism in the beginning of the twentieth century the interest in Green's metaphysics gradually faded, although its impact on British philosophy continued in the sense that for a considerable period of time no little attention was devoted to refuting 'the school of Green'.[60] These criticisms of Green's idealism were further nurtured by the general anti-German climate after the First World War. Together with the earlier philosophical criticisms, these anti-German sentiments help to explain the rise of a group of social theorists who, while they were clearly inspired by Green's social views and adopted his notion of positive liberty, nevertheless explicitly rejected the idealist first principles from which Green proceeded.

No doubt, the most striking rejection of metaphysics as a basis for social theory is to be found in the work of a man who has been characterized as the 'paradigm case' of positive liberalism, L.T. Hobhouse.[61] This social theorist went so far as to suggest a direct connection between Hegelian theory of the state and the 1917 air raids on London.

It was not until 1934 that the first significant comment on Green was formulated which again went to the trouble of considering his metaphysics. This was in a volume designed to rework and rehabilitate Green's moral doctrine.[62] Lamont argued that there were two distinct arguments to support Green's assumption of a spiritual principle in man and nature. The first argument establishes the inseparability of subject and object, the second stipulates that matter and form are inseparable. Lamont's thesis is that whereas usually the first type of argument is taken to represent Green's position in metaphysics, it is in fact the second line of argument which is fundamental. Possible inconsistencies in his doctrine are due to arguments of the first kind. On this latter interpretation of Green, he claims, the deduction of an eternal consciousness

[59] *Ibid.*, pp. 23–4.
[60] Cf. R.G. Collingwood, *An Autobiography*, Oxford, 1939, p. 15.
[61] David Nicholls, 'Positive Liberty, 1880–1914,' *American Political Science Review*, 56 (1962), p. 117.
[62] W.D. Lamont, *Introduction to Green's Moral Philosophy*, London, 1934.

becomes 'an illegitimate and worthless addition to Green's system,' whereas on the other interpretation it must be taken as 'an essential feature.'[63]

But it is difficult to see how anything like the presupposition of an eternal consciousness would be necessitated if matter and form were simply held to be correlative without further ado. As I understand Green, the two correlates matter and form are inseparable in so far as elements are 'kept together' by the combining activity of consciousness.[64] Green in fact discerned a number of concrete instances in human experience, which he held were only appropriately to be grasped in dyadic terms, i.e. as pairs of inseparable units. It was this observation that led Green to deduce the combining activity of some self-conscious agency as a necessary condition. Green's dyadic concept of a many-in-one, to be found in as commonplace a thing as abstract properties, presupposes the combining activity of some consciousness. Therefore, on the assumption that our experience is determined by an external world existing independent of any cognitive activity, the need for any further postulate such as Green's eternal consciousness would seem to disappear.

The Revival of Idealist Studies in the 1960s

After one of the conceptual innovations central to Green's social philosophy, the idea of positive freedom, had been challenged in the 1950s,[65] there was a marked revival in the interest in Green's work in the course of the 1960s. Significantly, in this period a renewed attempt was undertaken to come to a statement of Green's social philosophy independent of its metaphysical basis by A.J.M. Milne. In his opinion, idealist metaphysics had justifiably been abandoned after the Realists' attack in the beginning of the twentieth century, but Milne thought that there was still a case to be made for 'the social philosophy of English idealism' which he attempted in a volume bearing that very title.

---

[63]   Ibid., p. 181.
[64]   Cf. Prolegomena, sects 28, 29, 62.
[65]   Cf. Chapter Five of the present book. Two major publications mark this criticism of Green's concept of positive freedom: Maurice Cranston, Freedom: A New Analysis, London, 1953; and Isaiah Berlin's inaugural address to the University of Oxford, 'Two Concepts of Liberty,' published in Four Essays on Liberty, Oxford, 1969.

Milne's thesis was all the more interesting since — in spite of his claim — he *did* engage in a metaphysical discussion with Green, on the very subject of his doctrine of an eternal consciousness. In the same way as Lamont, he argued that the presupposition of an eternal consciousness constituted a redundant element in Green's metaphysical doctrine. According to Milne, Green insufficiently distinguished two points in his attempt to create room for an objective order of experience while maintaining with Kant the claim of a subjective element in it. These two points he identified as, on the one hand, the assumption that knowledge presupposes something existent independent of it and, on the other hand, the question whether we know this independent reality as it is apart from our cognitive activity. Milne pointed out that the adoption of the former point does not necessarily lead to the second. The assertion that reality must be independent of our knowledge of it, to which Milne refers as the 'public character of facts,' does not imply that our knowledge is of reality itself, i.e. as it is apart from the way we know it.

> What is required for facts to have a public character is not that they should be the same, whether or not they are known, but only that they should be the same for all who know them.[66]

Milne's position on this point closely resembles what Kant had to say about the thing-in-itself and he concludes that the doctrine, which in the present book was indicated as 'the formative activity of thought' is quite compatible with the public character of facts. Consequently he considers as a superfluous addition to Green's epistemology the presupposition of an eternal consciousness to render possible nature as a system of intelligible relations. Nor has this entity any real significance for Green's moral theory, according to Milne.

Apart from Milne's work the revival of interest in English idealism in the 1960s was further marked by the publication of an intellectual biography of Green and his times by Melvin Richter.[67] This scholar drew attention to Green's widespread influence and the remarkable speed with which he managed to establish a philosophical school, which had few, if any, precedents in the English tradition. This relatively sudden rise of English Hegelianism is chiefly explained by reference to the

---

[66] *The Social Philosophy of English Idealism.*, London, 1962, p. 96.
[67] *The Politics of Conscience: T.H. Green and His Age.*

crisis of religious faith triggered by the challenges of recent scientific discoveries. It was, according to Richter, with a view to providing a shelter for religious opinions which no scientific discovery would be able to shake, that German *a priori* philosophy found such ready access in England in the second half of the nineteenth century. As he adduces religion as an independent explanatory variable of the profound impact Green had on his contemporaries, Richter has no need for metaphysics to occupy an independent place in Green's philosophy and his treatment of this subject matter is consequently somewhat lacking in imagination. He suggests that the concept of an eternal consciousness in Green is the translation into philosophical terms of a theological notion, i.e. of a personal God. With the help of a reference to Lamont's commentary he points out that starting from a theory of internal relations as a central element of his argument concerning knowledge, Green would logically be expected to come up with a purely immanentist view of the eternal consciousness. The fact that Green nevertheless emphasizes the 'non-naturalness' of the spiritual principle he discerned in knowledge and nature must — according to a suggestion by Lamont, which Richter approvingly quotes — be attributed to some early influences as a result of which Green looked upon God as a transcendent creative mind.[68] Seen in this light Green's equivocal treatment of the eternal consciousness becomes simply a reflection of his inability to make up his mind about a strictly theological issue, i.e. between a pantheist and a theist theology.

G. Green's Doctrine of the Self-assertion of Reason in his Unpublished Lectures

The brief inventory of commentaries on Green's general metaphysics makes it clear that his postulate of an eternal consciousness puzzled generations of students. Two fundamental objections arose relating to this conception of Green's: first, we saw that Green failed to make his meaning clear and, second, to the extent that his doctrine was intelligible, it was found to be inconsistent in the sense that the functions which Green attributed to this entity could not be ascribed to it.

In this section I propose to draw on his unpublished lecture notes so as to place the notion of an eternal consciousness in

---

[68]   *Ibid.*, pp. 183–4.

the context in which Green construed it. Such a fuller statement of Green's first principles will help us in straightening
out some of the twistings and turnings in Green's metaphysical doctrine which remain somewhat obscure in *Prolegomena*.

Manuscript 11

The more Hegelian traits which Green displays in his doctrine
of the self-assertion of reason can occasionally still be traced in
the text of *Prolegomena*.[69] It appears much more clearly from his
earlier manuscripts that this doctrine is central to his metaphysical views and may serve here to structure a number of
arguments which occur separately in his published writings,
or emerge from the body of criticism in which he was engaged
in the major part of his publications. In the same way as Hegel,
Green proceeded from the view that reason manifested itself
in the world and that our experience and the events of the
world were to be understood in the light of this process.

A logical, as opposed to a historical, categorization of the
various stages in which the self-assertion of reason takes place
can be found in a manuscript which cannot be dated precisely
for it is to be found in a series of loose folios on the history of
Greek philosophy which were for that reason put together
with manuscript notebook 11, which deals with this same subject. Green is prompted to draw up a scheme of his own in
order to provide himself with a critical tool to evaluate the
speculations of Plato. To this end he sets out to distinguish, on
the one hand, 'things as they are in themselves or for God or for
thought,' and, on the other, things 'as they are for us, who are
subject to necessary delusions'.[70] From the substitution for
'things-in-themselves' by things as they are conceived by God
— or even simply by things conceived without specifying any
subject — the influence of the idea that relations can only exist
for some consciousness or other already clearly emerges. In
this earlier manuscript the same view prompts Green to identify 'things-in-themselves' with 'things as conceived by God'.
For Green, the notion of a Kantian 'Ding-an-sich' was literally
— and figuratively — inconceivable.

On the basis of this distinction Green proceeds to categorise
the objective order, i.e. in intelligible reality as it is, independ-

---

[69] See especially Book III, Chapter 3.
[70] Ms 11, loose sheets, p. 15 (my numbering).

ent of our cognitive activity. This classification corresponds to the different stages of the process of the self-assertion of reason. On Green's premises, the objective order falls into three divisions, the first two of which are again parted in two subdivisions.

> The universe, as it exists for thought, or the system of ideas divides itself into certain spheres of ideas:
> 1. Ideas of inorganic matter
>   a. mechanical
>   b. chemical
> 2. Ideas of organic matter
>   a. self-moving — vegetable life
>   b. self-feeling — animal life
> 3. Ideas of Reason[71]

Green argues that in the first two categories of ideas thought is unconscious of itself. Consequently, he construes a fundamental opposition between these two spheres and the self-consciousness characterizing the third sphere which comprises human cognition and volition. This distinction between self-consciousness and the world of nature which logically precedes it, will develop into a fundamental opposition between nature and spirit, as was seen in the earlier discussion of *Prolegomena*.

Ideas of a lower order are functional to those of a higher order: 'The ideas of the lower sphere [are] carried on into the higher; but as such in it take a new character, as part of a new system.' Mechanical relations are functional to organic matter whereas the type of relations constituting organic matter are, in turn, functional to consciousness, which is first established in animal life, which again goes into the constitution of self-consciousness. The important point here is that lower forms of relations lose their distinct character and are included in the organic relationship of the higher order.

While Green does not extend the hierarchy of types of ideas beyond the level of self-conscious thought it may nevertheless be seen that it logically results in a system of eternal relations, as it exists for an eternal consciousness.[72] As such the scheme which Green provided in this early manuscript underlies his argument concerning appearance and reality with which he

---

[71]   *Ibid.*
[72]   In *Prolegomena* Green refers to this order of relations as a 'cosmos of possible experience,' see e.g. sect. 51.

sought to render plausible the metaphysical doctrine of *Prolegomena*. Manuscript 11 does not give a criterion by reference to which appearance may be distinguished from reality, but it does offer an explanation of the manner in which misapprehensions of reality come about. Inadequate conceptions, or conceptions short of the full nature of things arise from the limitations which are imposed upon each individual self-conscious agent by his animal nature, as opposed to the perfect conception of God. The above-mentioned categorisation of ideas, Green explains, represents

> the view of the process of the universe, as taken from outside; but we in virtue of [our] material & animal nature are stages *in* the process. In so far as we are animals, we cannot view animal life in its reality, i.e. as a system of ideas relative to a higher idea.
>
> Thus our bodily nature is one thing to us, who are liable to be deluded by it . . . another thing to God, to whom as the subject of all ideas it is necessarily related.[73]

This earlier manuscript provides us with a version of the doctrine of self-assertion of reason set out from the logical point of view. Alongside its historical manifestation the assertion of reason may be seen in the categorization of different categories of ideas, according as they involve (self)-consciousness. Anticipating his later assumption of the self-distinguishing consciousness we already see Green's stipulation that material objects can only exist before some self-conscious agency. It follows that, on Green's principles, a fuller knowledge of the nature of a thing can only consist in discerning more relations as they exist in the Divine consciousness.

Manuscript 14

The fundamental separation of ideas according to the different stages in the process of the self-assertion of reason to which they relate is not just an occasional thought of Green's earlier days. It was a theme with which he was deeply concerned, and it can be found to recur in his manuscripts as may be demonstrated in two further citations. In the first place we find the ordering of different stages in the process of the self-assertion of reason in the notes of what must have been a relatively early course on modern philosophy. This manuscript was initially labelled 'Notes of lectures on Kant's Critique of Pure Reason'

---

[73] Ms 11, loose sheets, p. 15.

by Charlotte Green, who also assigned its present number: 14. In his inventory of the manuscripts, Nettleship identified four sections dealing with different subject-matters, apart from the 50 pages on Kant. Like the manuscript quoted above it is hard to determine precisely when this lecture was delivered, but Nettleship conjectured that the material gathered under this number was, according to a note in his hand, 'all very old.' The first section which Nettleship identified as the 'beginning of [a] course on Modern Philosophy,' includes a fundamental criticism of the 'method of "false psychology"'. In this section a full statement of the order of different stages in the process of self-assertion of reason occurs when Green attempts to put his criticism of 'false psychology' into a wider context. Green's argument is that such a view of man and his activities wholly neglects the fundamental distinction between man and nature, between self-conscious agency and lower stages in the process of the self-assertion of reason. The chief implication of this distinction, he points out, is that

> While all other things are both individual & universal for man, man is both individual & universal for himself.[74]

No sooner is this inference drawn than Green develops his division between inorganic matter, organic matter, and self-conscious agency which we already saw from the other manuscript quoted just now:

> Any stick or stone is a centre of relations wide as the universe, it is so however for us, not for itself. It does not gather up its relations into consciousness. Its relations, its universality, are external to it. Its function is wholly relative to other things.
>
> [It is] otherwise with an organic body. It is dependent on relations to other things . . . thro' which ultimately it is related to the universe of things. But these relations result in an internal constitution — a relation of parts to a whole different from the sum of its parts. It is a unity constituted by a multiplicity of parts, each different from the other & the whole. It is an end to itself. Consider the parts — their end is the maintenance of the life of the one body as a whole which they [compose].
>
> Consider the one body as a whole — its end is the maintenance in their several functions of the parts which in their totality constitute it. But the organic body even in its highest form, as animal organism, tho' an end in itself does not *know* itself. Thus to the animals sensations are merely such. Not knowing themselves, not being objects to themselves, they don't impart their own permanence to

---

[74]   Ms 14:1 p. 6 (my numbering).

their feelings, so as to transform them from feelings to felt things, which are there for thought when actual feeling is over . . .

But man is self-conscious. He knows his own life. This life [is] like everything else, a manifold in unity.

It is a life of individuals, but each of these is what he is in virtue to all others: that which he has in common with others, his universality, constitutes his individuality. Again, it is a succession of individual acts & states, but of these in virtue of the unity of consciousness each qualifies the other. They are what they are as individual states in virtue of the universality.[75]

Green provided this scheme of the different stages in the process of self-assertion of reason in an attempt to place his criticism of 'false psychology' into a wider context. This criticism gravitated on the outlook on man and his activities from which empiricist philosophy proceeded. In the same manner this view of man formed part of the premises of psychologists like Herbert Spencer and G.H.Lewes which he sought to refute in his series of articles for the *Contemporary Review*, written in 1877–81.[76]

Manuscript 10a

We shall continue to reconstruct Green's doctrine of the self-assertion of reason from a further manuscript, which shows that, while reference to this notion becomes less apparent in later manuscripts, there is no doubt that Green still espoused this doctrine in the late 1860s. This appears from the inclusion of a lengthy explanation in a course on the history of moral philosophy dating back to this period. These lecture notes may be dated with greater certainty than most of the other manuscripts on the basis of a list of the names of his students which Green noted on the back cover of the notebook. The names of Green's audience, which included both Bernard Bosanquet and Liddell, shows that the course must have been delivered in the academic year 1867–1868. Charlotte Green initially assigned the title 'Notes of lectures on Kant's moral philosophy,' but this earlier designation was revised on the occasion of Nettleship's investigation of the manuscripts. Next to an essay on Kant the notebook contains a general essay on moral philosophy, discussing Hobbes, Hume, Shaftesbury, Hutcheson, and finally Kant. Another essay dealing exclu-

---

[75] *Ibid.*, pp. 6, 8.
[76] Reprinted in *Works*, i, pp. 373–541.

sively with Kant was written from the other end of the
notebook. The manner in which the two texts run into each other
in the middle of the notebook suggests that, while the general
essay was finished first, both essays were written in the same
period.

For our reconstruction of Green's doctrine of the self-assertion of reason it is important to point to a detailed statement of
the various stages which this process passes through, which
he provided to elucidate the two opposing concepts of 'nature'
and 'morality' with which he started his general lecture on
moral philosophy. He first set out to inquire into the difference
between moral philosophy and physical science, pointing out
an answer to this question would provide a 'true point of view
from which to regard [the] modern speculation on Ethics'. The
detailed account of the difference between the natural and the
moral order again confirms the earlier exposition of his views
on the structure of the self-assertion of reason.

> nature = system of sensations referred to objects. That what
> makes the sensations a system is reason.[77]

Green then went on to provide an account of the hierarchy of
ideas or types of relations, constituting different stages in the
process of the self-assertion of reason, i.e. the inorganic, the
organic and the self-conscious spheres, which again imply a
fourth sphere characterized by the activity of some eternal
conscious agency.

> A stone = certain sensations of ours — mode of consciousness —
> which reason, other mode of consciousness, combines in a thing
> as their cause. But the sensations which we refer to it are not of a
> kind to make us think of it as itself sensitive.
>   Object in this case neither feels not thinks. Neither feeling nor
> reason which together constitute it, are in it.
>   An animal, in like manner = certain sensations of ours — mode
> of consciousness — which reason, other mode of consciousness,
> combines in a thing as their cause.
>   But in this case the sensations referred to [the] object are such
> that we think of the object as itself sensitive. Object, here, feels but
> does not think.
>   In the case of man, the reason which in correlation with feeling
> constitutes him — as it does [constitute the] stone or [the] horse —

---

[77] Ms 10a, annotations on the inside cover.

is also in him, forms his consciousness of this, he knows his own nature.

Nature is revealed to him not to [the] animal.[78]

'Nature,' as an intelligible system of terms-in-relation, and morality therefore have an essential common element in reason. Green's point in this manuscript, however, is that there is also a fundamental difference in the relation in which man stands to nature and his relation to morality. This very distinction, it will be recalled, was also to be found in the philosophy of mind set out in *Propädeutik*.

> If this be [a] true account of nature it would seem that [the] relation between reason and sense constitutes nature as well as [the] moral world. True, but not [the] relation between reason and sense as in us.
>
> Nature is *there* — *given*. We find it don't make it. We, that is, in our limited human personality. The reason that makes it must be communicated to us, if we are to understand it. But the natural world is made apart from this communication. [The natural world] *is there* whether we understand it or no.
>
> Not so with [the] moral world. It is by reason, as communicated to man & not otherwise that this world is constituted.[79]

Once again we find the classification in three fundamental categories of ideas as we already encountered in an earlier manuscript. An important development of Green's position, however, is that in the manuscript presently under consideration reason is seen to operate in three ways in the constitution of our cosmos of experience. Moreover, this manuscript contains one of the earliest statements concerning the fundamental difference between the constitution of the natural and the moral world and the different part played in these domains by theoretical and practical reason, respectively.

The three manuscripts presented here readily demonstrate Green's doctrine of the self-assertion of reason in so far as it produces a hierarchy of 'ideas of reason,' each level of which can be seen as a stage in this process. For an adequate understanding of Green's thinking on this point it must be specified that the order of 'ideas of reason,' exhibits the self-assertion of reason only from the systematic point of view. The same doctrine can also be set out in terms of its historical manifestations, i.e. an account of how the self-assertion of reason can be seen in the actual progress of human understanding of the progress of

[78] *Ibid.*
[79] *Ibid.*

the moral ideal as exhibited in the history of mankind. The latter instance is relatively well documented in *Prolegomena* and need not be enlarged upon here.[80] The former, on the other hand, may only be intuited by the perceptive reader of Green's published works.

Manuscript 4

In this connection, it is instructive to draw attention to an unpublished, explicit statement of the way in which reason manifests itself in the progress of human intellect. Green may have intended this statement as an introduction to a relatively early course on logic. He begins by discerning two correlative principles in terms of which the course of events may be explained

> The universe involves a relation of two elements, a necessary & [a] contingent. That the contingent is merely contingent is implied in the fact of its being in relation to the necessary. It is in truth that which is evermore being systematized & so becoming necessary. We may, however, abstract the necessary element from the contingent, & treat it as a system not yet applied to that which it systematizes, remembering at the same time that in its truth it implies such an application, i.e. that when thought out it is found to necessitate it.
>
> This gives the distinction between Logic or Metaphysic on the one hand & the philosophy of nature & man [Spirit] which is the true applied logic on the other.[81]

It must be observed that Green's terminology had not yet assumed its definite shape when he composed this document and in later manuscripts he draws the distinction between logic, metaphysic and the other sciences in a somewhat different manner.[82] In an alternative version of the same passage we already find an explicit statement of the argument concerning the inseparability of matter and form which was earlier identified as one of the implications of the doctrine of the self-assertion of reason.

> The same doctrine may be otherwise put thus. The universe is a system of thought. It cannot be said that Logic has to do with thought as form, the sciences with things as given matter. For all thought is such, only as thinking about some *thing* & all things are

---

[80] See *Prolegomena*, Book III, Chapter 5, 'The Origin and Development of the Moral Ideal.'

[81] Ms 4, small sheet of white stationery.

[82] 'The Logic of the Formal Logicians,' *Works*, ii, pp. 158 ff.

such only as thought *about*. 'Formal' thought is nothing without matter. We may distinguish, however, between thought when its matter *is* its own, & thought when its matter *becomes* its own: in other words between *pure* and *applied* ideas. The former may then be regarded as *formative* to the latter.

Now the *applied* ideas as resulting from a reduction of the unknown to the known partake of the infinity of the unknown. You may have one without another. No one of them is absolutely necessary to all thinking. The *pure* ideas, on the other hand, involving no assimilation by thought of that which had not previously been thought are brought by thought to all its acts, i.e. are necessarily involved in all thinking. Logic is the science of these pure or necessary ideas as involved 1. in intuition 2. in conception 3. in judgment 4. in reasoning.[83]

The sheet from which these passages are taken is part of a manuscript which was assembled by Nettleship. For this reason it is not certain that all the folios and sheets collected under this manuscript number date back to the same period. So while the 'Two sheets of an apparently early essay on Hegel', which we were able to situate in Green's undergraduate years, form part of the same manuscript, this is not conclusive as to when the sheet here under consideration was written. Although it is thus not possible to date the above quoted passages accurately we may nevertheless assume that it was one of Green's earliest statements on the subject of logic.

The Argument Concerning the 'Inseparableness' of Subject and Object

As a result of his doctrine of the correlation of matter and form, Green also refutes what he calls the 'false separation of thought from things'. In order to substantiate his point he makes clear that neither of the terms could be what it is without the other:

Things, as definite, if not constituted by thought . . . are yet what they are, as known, in virtue of action of thought [while] thought, on the other hand, as secluded from things can merely traverse a series of identical nothings.[84]

It is remarkable that Green in this and similar accounts of the central role of thinking in the constitution of an intelligible world, time and again feels obliged to make an explicit restric-

[83] Ms 4, small size sheet of white stationery.
[84] Ms 14:4, fragment on the 'false abstraction of thought from things' involved in formal logic, p. 1.

tion regarding the applicability of his argument to reality itself. His point is that even if the application of his doctrine to things-in-themselves were challenged, it is in any case incontrovertible where our knowledge about things is concerned. As may be recalled from our discussion of *Prolegomena*, this restriction was an important factor governing the presentation of his published metaphysical doctrine. Yet it would appear as if this precaution of Green's is something of a conciliatory gesture to common sense.

The distinction between the real nature of things as they are in themselves and the reality as we come to know it dates back to Kant's critical philosophy. Kant demonstrated that the essential flaw in all preceding speculative metaphysics was due to the fact that they all sought to establish what things were like apart from the formal element which, in Kant's terms, necessarily went into the formation of experience. After Kant no one can seriously pose questions as to what things are like apart from our knowing them. We can only know things under the conditions of knowledge. Thus when Green repeatedly emphasizes the provision that whatever his ontology may be, his doctrine applies in any event to his epistemology, he seems concerned with an argument which, after Kant, has lost much of its philosophic significance. Moreover, it would seem that he weakens his own monistic conclusions by continuously allowing for the possibility of his epistemology and his theory of reality being governed by two distinct principles.

Coherence as a Criterion of Truth

On Green's premises, any process of knowledge inevitably presupposes a real nature of things. Green sets out to illuminate the relationship between knowledge and the reality which it represents by considering the common sense definition of truth as 'agreement with its objects'. In his view such a description remains a meaningless assertion so long as 'objects' are simply assumed to be part of an external world, i.e. without any further account of what is involved in the existence of such an intelligible world. In his own search for a criterion of truth, so as to establish a satisfactory relationship between knowledge and reality, Green tries to spell out what he thinks adherents of the common sense definition of truth sought to establish. What John Locke was really striving for when he opposed the work of nature and the work of the mind was not to exclude the mind's operations as such from the real, but only its arbitrary operations.

> True knowledge in this or that individual no doubt consists in agreement between his thought & [the] reality of things. But true knowledge, as such, means that which is valid always & for all men. Take any body of science, this is not a state of mind in this or that individual. [The] individual's state of mind is true so far as he has attained the science. The question is whether the science or all science as true is rightly defined to be agreement of thought with [its] object; whether [the] 'reality of things' is something other than thought or reason, which thought or reason reflects rightly or wrongly . . .
>
> Even in the individual the process is not so much one by which his thought comes to agree with 'the object' — as separate from it — as one by which thought, as scientific system, comes to him.[85]

On the basis of these considerations Green suggests the following theory of knowledge:

> It would seem then that our experience must be regarded as the gradual appropriation of an intellectual order, the existence of which in completeness is [the] condition of our appropriation of it in completeness.[86]

It follows from the dual position which man occupies as a cognitive agent — forming part of the intellectual order, but necessarily labouring under the limiting conditions which his animal organism imposes on him — that no absolute criterion of truth can be given.

> Absolute truth, then, would be agreement of this order with itself. Truth for us would be this agreement so far as the order has yet been appropriated by us.
>
> Practically 'consistency' *is* our test of truth . . .
>
> A notion [is] false when it won't square with the system of notions that form our knowledge, or with some *department* of that system . . .
>
> A *mere* fact [is] neither true nor false, but unmeaning; so soon as it has a meaning, or is interpreted, the interpretation is either true or false as it will or will not square with [the] system of knowledge.[87]

In this exposition of his theory of thinking Green draws a parallel between the progressive nature of knowledge as evidenced in everyday life experience and the manner in which

---

[85]   *Ibid.*
[86]   *Ibid.*, p. 3.
[87]   *Ibid.*

scientific conceptions develop. Both of these cases are instances of one and the same process of thinking activity, but as the progressive nature of scientific understanding is more readily documented, Green turns to the corpus of knowledge represented by the various sciences to illuminate the development of knowledge as factually as possible.

Progress in scientific knowledge is, of course, primarily dependent on new facts necessitating a revision of earlier conceptions. But this synthetic character of scientific conceptions is rendered possible by the activity of a mechanism analogous to the self-assertion of reason.

> Thus, on [the] one hand, science is progressive: it meets with new facts by which old theories are modified.
>
> On [the] other, it in a way creates itself: i.e. no stage of it is so primary as that in it the materials of the science are absolutely 'raw', wholly unformed by thought. The new facts dealt with by actual sciences are, of course even in their first discovery conditioned by previous knowledge, which they afterwards modify.[88]

It may be concluded from this manuscript that Green's earlier theory of knowledge proceeded on a coherence theory of truth. This conclusion makes it all the more remarkable to find that coherence was replaced by the seemingly much less sophisticated unalterability criterion which we found in the argument of *Prolegomena*. It seems to me that coherence forms a far more powerful basis for an epistemology than the evidently disappointing notion of unalterability which Green employed in his later work. For, by its very nature, the notion of unalterability is dependent on the period of time on which one focuses. The mere fact that something has the same outlook over a certain period of time does not guarantee that it will remain that way forever.

The only possible hypothesis that could help to explain this rather implausible development in Green's position links up with the perspective of Green's intellectual development. It was already suggested that Green's initial rationalism gradually gave way to a more ambivalent position according as Green grew more and more convinced of the difficulties of a consistently rationalist ethical theory. Now, the only conceivable explanation of Green's move from the coherence criterion in his earlier work to the unalterability criterion in his *Prolegomena* is that the eventual stage of a development, i.e. as it is

---

[88]   *Ibid.*

completed, is construed as eternally complete and, in that sense, unalterable. But it seems to me that Green's change in position only constitutes a change for the worse. For, it turns a potentially open system of knowledge into an essentially closed and therefore *a priori* conception of human knowledge. A second question which rises in connection with Green's move from the coherence to the unalterability criterion is why Green considered the former criterion to be inadequate for the task it had to perform in the context of *Prolegomena*.

H. Conclusion

In this chapter we have set out Green's system of idealist first principles and sought to make clear the function Green wants his metaphysics to perform. To the extent the doctrine of self-assertion of reason was less evident from his published metaphysics, we have sought to enlarge upon this doctrine by drawing from Green's earlier manuscripts. Through this fuller account of the metaphysical basis of Green's system of philosophy it became possible to place the notion of an eternal consciousness in the context in which Green construed it. Green in fact saw the eternal consciousness both as the presupposition and as the outcome of a process, to which he referred as the self-assertion of reason. This doctrine features in a number of manuscripts, in particular those from his earlier years. An account of Green's thinking on this point leaves us in a better position to consider the relationship between this eternal and the finite consciousness, another point in respect of which the argument of *Prolegomena* was shown to be insufficient. Green's views on the relationship between eternal and finite consciousness will help to bring to the fore the practical relevance of Green's metaphysical principles, which will be considered in the following two chapters.

Chapter III

Positive Freedom

Green's reputation as a philosopher was primarily in the field of ethics and political theory. However, if my reading of his unpublished manuscripts is correct, metaphysics played a far more central part in Green's thinking than was traditionally known. The system of first principles, as outlined in the previous chapter, forms the key to each of the separate realms in which Green was philosophically active. Green himself construed these separate realms as forming part of a comprehensive theoretical system. This is, in my view, the main point at which the standard interpretation of Green needs to be corrected. Proceeding from this conclusion I propose to explore in this chapter the implications for his political theory which may be drawn from this new assessment of the central place of metaphysics in Green's thinking.

As a political thinker, Green was chiefly known for his *Lectures on the Principles of Political Obligation*, based on his notes for a series of professorial lectures. But if we do not restrict ourselves to his academic writings, there can be no room for doubt about the concept which was to be more influential than any other single concept of his political theory. This was the notion of positive freedom, the origin of which we traced to Hegel's *Propädeutik* in Chapter One. But, in point of fact, this term acquired in Green's hands a far greater practical significance than it ever had in Hegel's political doctrine.

One of the more remarkable features to be observed with respect to Green's use of the term is that he does not employ it in his academic lectures. The only definition which he ever provided of the concept of positive freedom was given in the course of a party political speech. Green's concept marks a crucial stage in the transition to the modern welfare state in Britain. Given the actual impact of his doctrine, Green may be regarded as the first theorist of the welfare state. In the fourth chapter it will be argued that Green in fact has a better title to this claim than theorists like John Stuart Mill, even though this predicate would not at all be inappropriate if applied to the latter thinker.

The concept of positive freedom therefore became known as a separate idea and not — as Green must have understood it — as part of a comprehensive theoretical system. Owing to this misapprehension, Green's theory of positive freedom was open to the criticism of conceptual confusion, as was indeed levelled against Green at a later stage.[1] In fact, this line of criticism may be rejoined with a far more powerful defence than was actually made on behalf of Green's doctrine.

In this chapter I will set out the way in which Green's positive notion of freedom forms part of a general theoretical system. I will begin by giving an account of what, for present purposes, may be termed the popularised version of Green's notion of positive freedom. I will then go on to reconstruct a more genuine statement of this doctrine which may be seen to 'follow' from the first principles as set out in the previous chapter. The chapter concludes with a sketch of the immediate systematic context in which Green situated his doctrine of positive freedom, i.e. his moral and political theory. Special attention will be given to the mutual and close connection of these two realms in Green's thinking.

A. Green's Theory of Positive Freedom in his Political Speech

Green delivered his speech before the Leicester Liberal Association early in 1881. It was initially published privately by Slatter and Rose in Oxford and later included in the volume of miscellaneous writings when his collected *Works* were issued. Green began his lecture by pointing out the significance and timely nature of his argument. For this purpose he referred to the actual arguments levelled against two bills which had been proposed in the last parliamentary session. These two proposals by Gladstone's second cabinet were opposed on the ground that they interfered with the freedom of the individual parties to contracts. First was the Ground Game Act, prohibiting all clauses in tenancy agreements granting the exclusive

---

[1]   W.L. Weinstein, 'The Concept of Liberty in Nineteenth Century English Political Thought,' *Political Studies*, 13 (1965), pp. 145-62.

hunting rights to the landlords. In a similar manner, the Employers Liability Act was said to interfere with parties' freedom of contract in that it sought to reverse the burden of proof with respect to measuring out the responsibility in cases of industrial injuries. In the absence of a clause to the contrary the act held the employer to be responsible for any injuries sustained in the course of labour carried out under the terms of the labour contract.

This new kind of proposed legislation constituted a special problem for Liberals: for, while most supporters of the Liberal party were in favour of the bills proposed, it was clear that they ran counter to the classical liberal ideal of a maximum possible amount of individual freedom. These considerations may help us to come to a better understanding of the object of the theoretical intervention Green sought to make with his public speech. In fact, on the basis of Green's text, two ways suggest themselves in which a 'problem statement' of his lecture may be pointed out.

In the first place Green drew attention to a qualitative change in the kind of legislation which was being sought and, to an increasing extent, being carried into practice. While earlier reform legislation could always be classified and defended as an increase of the liberty of the individual, it would be difficult to make this claim for the protective measures that were recently proposed.

A further derivative point to be discerned in Green's text is the observation that the new kind of liberal legislation shows a clear break with the efforts and ends of earlier generations of liberal reformers. As a liberal, Green rejoiced in the thought that it was his fellow liberals in earlier periods of English political history who had propelled the great social and political reforms. But whereas liberalism had so far been adequately characterised by its struggle to increase the liberty of the individual, it would be difficult to make the same claim for the recent Liberal proposals for reform. Of course, these two 'problem statements' are intrinsically linked: the first centres on the conception of freedom itself, whereas the second looks at the nature of liberal policy through the years. Either way a problem can be identified which the positive conception of freedom intended to resolve; however, prior to investigating Green's actual definition of positive freedom, it will be helpful to consider the way in which Green sought to make his case.

Green's Method of Argument

In order to point out Green's method of argument, I need to draw attention to something concerning the specific character-istics of all normative judgments. This relates to their inter-subjective nature: on the one hand, all value judgments are in principle problematic in that it will always prove to be possible to disagree about certain values, even among reasonable agents; on the other hand, norms, whether political or ethical, are not altogether subjective; all norms are open to argumenta-tion and it is always possible to convince others of their valid-ity by giving reasons to support these norms. This feature of norms and values may be brought to bear on the manner in which norms can be conveyed and the way in which others may be persuaded of their intrinsic merit.

In view of this intersubjective nature of norms and values and the consequent potentially problematic nature of the con-veyance of norms and the criteria for their validity, Green was searching for a standard or reference point and he thought this was to be found in all the instances of legislative interference with individual freedom with which people were already acquainted and which they already accepted as legitimate forms of state interference. His argument therefore proceeded on an analysis of a number of concrete cases of protective legis-lation which were — on the whole — subscribed to. For this purpose he reviewed all prescriptions in the realm of labour legislation and education which were no longer regarded as controversial instances of state interference.

Green's second step was then to formulate some principle in terms of which these various separate legislative measures could be summed up. Such a principle would furthermore constitute a useful indication for assessing new and more advanced forms of restrictive legislation. By deriving a com-mon principle from forms of legislative interference in society which were already seen as legitimate, Green sought to sup-port a number of prescriptive measures in the field of temper-ance legislation and land reform which he would like to see carried through but which remained, as yet, controversial issues. Once he succeeded in demonstrating that there is a sin-gle principle underlying the various instances of legislative interference, he would have produced an argument why restrictive measures in the field of liquor traffic and land reform must equally be taken as desirable.

By identifying a certain common principle, a definite unity is imposed upon what otherwise would remain an aggregate of separate legislative measures. The reference to a principle summing up the reasons why each of the individual instances need to be seen as legitimate or desirable provides this unity. In the absence of such a common principle each case would remain separate; and in view of the special nature of norms and values each individual case would necessarily have to be judged on its own, individual merits.

Definitions of Positive Freedom

Having explored Green's working method in his public speech we may now go on to consider the actual definition he gave of positive freedom. In the course of his speech Green set out a number of alternative descriptions of the positive concept of freedom. In order to be able to contrast the 'genuine statement' of Green's doctrine, as is to be worked up in this chapter, with the more familiar popular version of his doctrine, I shall begin by discussing the various forms in which he phrased his conception of positive freedom.

In fact, there are three descriptions of positive freedom to be found in Green's lecture. While all three descriptions are of course closely linked, each separate rendering brings out a different aspect of the concept. On one occasion 'the idea of true freedom' is described as 'the maximum of power for all members of human society alike to make the best of themselves'.[2] In this description Green puts special emphasis on the self-realization of the individual. A second rendering defines freedom in the positive sense as 'the liberation of the powers of all men equally for contributions to a common good'.[3] This seems primarily to point to equal opportunity for all individual citizens. For the purpose of our present inquiry, however, we will chiefly base ourselves on what could be viewed as the classical definition of positive freedom. This concept is contrasted to the then current notion, which, in order to distinguish it from Green's redefinition of the term, is referred to as 'negative' freedom.

> We shall probably all agree that freedom, rightly understood, is the greatest of blessings; that its attainment is the true end of all our efforts as citizens. But when we thus speak of freedom, we

[2] *Works*, iii, p. 372.
[3] *Ibid.*

should consider carefully what we mean by it. We do not mean merely freedom from restraint or compulsion. We do not mean merely freedom to do as we like irrespectively of what it is that we like. We do not mean a freedom that can be enjoyed by one man or one set of men at the cost of a loss of freedom to others. When we speak of freedom as something to be so highly prized, we mean a positive power or capacity of doing or enjoying something worth doing or enjoying, and that, too, something that we enjoy in common with others. We mean by it a power which each man exercises through the help or security given him by his fellow-men, and which he in turn helps to secure for them.[4]

This rendering of freedom soon established itself as the classical definition of positive freedom. Two remarks suggest themselves in connection with this definition. In the first place it is important to draw attention to the fact that Green explicitly links his redefinition of 'freedom' to its function as a political ideal. Its nature as a political ideal carries a number of qualifications which he specifies in the rest of his lecture. A second observation relates to the form in which Green phrases this classical definition of freedom. He explains the intrinsic qualifications carried by the negative notion of freedom as following from its nature as a political ideal. This is set out by specifying three elements in which the difference with negative freedom consists. Again, these three elements are presented as building on one another.

He begins with a series of three negative characteristics, which are subsequently contrasted to the more appropriate conception of freedom by means of a parallel series of three determinations, culminating in a final point about the essentially social nature of freedom. When juxtaposing both series, four points result which enable us to clarify the difference between positive and negative freedom. First, the condition of absence of coercion is compared with 'a positive power or capacity of doing something'. The second distinguishing feature points to the formal, unspecified nature of the condition of absence of coercion: 'merely freedom to do as we like irrespectively of what it is that we like' is contrasted with 'doing or enjoying something worth doing or enjoying.' The third element centres on the compatibility of the exercise of various specific forms of freedom by different people: 'freedom that can be enjoyed by one man or one set of men at the cost of a loss of freedom to others' is opposed to those forms of freedom which do not interfere with the exercise of similar forms of freedom by others. These three elements prepare the way for the conclusion about the social nature of freedom. Genuine freedom can only be exercised 'through the help or security given to him by his fellow-men, and which he in turn helps to secure for them.'

Freedom and Coercion

A crucial point in Green's discourse consists in his position on the obligatory nature of the kind of legal measures he sought to introduce. His opinions on the relationship of freedom and coercion clearly emerge when he discusses the relationship of positive freedom and the negative conception of freedom which so far had been current. Green discusses this latter concept of freedom as a means to an ulterior end:

> If I have given a true account of that freedom which forms the goal of social effort, we shall see that freedom . . . in all the forms of doing what one will with one's own, is valuable only as a means to an end. That end is what I call freedom in the positive sense . . . [5]

It is significant to observe that Green does not so much refer to the obligatory character of the legal measures intended, as to the formal, unspecified nature of the negative conception of freedom. But it is obvious that there may be cases in which the project of 'the liberation of all men equally for contributions to the common good' needs to be enforced by the law. In the context of his political speech it is easy to avoid this impingement on negative freedom; in this manner Green states in the same breath that

> though of course there can be no freedom among men who act not willingly but under compulsion, yet on the other hand the mere removal of compulsion, the mere enabling a man to do as he likes, is in itself no contribution to true freedom. [6]

No doubt, in this respect the repeated use of the qualifying 'mere' is significant for Green's intention. If taken at face value, this passage would seem to imply that absence of coercion, as well as the further qualification following from the ulterior end of this 'negative' conception of freedom, are to be seen as two cumulative criteria. However, as will be pointed out in the next section, such a reading of Green would not be in

[5] *Ibid.*, p. 372.
[6] *Ibid.*, p. 371.

line with the structure of his argumentation. In all cases in which the law prescribes a certain conduct which a conscientious man would have done voluntarily, the true moral agent will look upon the law as a 'powerful friend'. In a similar manner, Green argues that social legislation makes room for new efforts in realms which the individual would not be able to consider when the arrangements thus enforced by the law would have been left to the moral initiative of individual agents. Green apparently assumes that moral effort must be seen as a scarce good: when spending one's moral effort or 'energy' in one field, this will be at the cost of care and attention in other fields.

By way of provisional summary of this point it may be concluded that while Green, as much as any genuine liberal, is opposed to the enforcement of a certain desirable state of affairs by means of the law, his position on state interference yet differs in a crucial sense from theirs. Green is prepared to leave things to their own course, it would seem, as long as this produces the right result; if not, he seems to be saying, the use of force is appropriate in all those cases in which this result is nevertheless needed. In this respect his liberal position seems altogether invalidated. As long as it produces the right result, voluntary activity of individuals is to be preferred; but once this is no longer the case, force seems to be appropriate. In contrast with a thinker like Mill (at least in his *On Liberty*) Green apparently does not dare to rely on the outcome of individual initiative. In spite of his genuinely liberal attitude, and however much he values the principle of voluntariness, Green stands for a new kind of liberalism which no longer accepted the condition of absence of restraint as an end in itself.[7]

Legal Obligations and Moral Autonomy

In the course of his discussion of the various legal measures in the field of public health and labour legislation Green also addresses the question as to whether independence and self-reliance do not, in the long run, constitute a better guarantee against the evils social legislation sought to remedy. 'Might not our people,' he puts this imaginary counter argument,

> have been trusted to learn in time for themselves to eschew unhealthy dwellings, to refuse dangerous and degrading

---

[7]   Compare also Chapter IV, Section F on Green and Mill.

employment, to get their children the schooling necessary for making their way in the world? Would they not for their own comfort, if not from more chivalrous feeling, keep their wives and daughters from overwork? Or, failing this, ought not women, like men, to learn to protect themselves? Might not all the rules, in short, which legislation of the kind we have been discussing is intended to attain, have been attained without it; not so quickly, perhaps, but without tampering so dangerously with the independence and self-reliance of the people?[8]

Of course, a situation in which all these desiderata are provided for by the spontaneous activity of the individuals concerned, would be preferred to legal sanctions, Green is eager to point out. 'But,' as he goes on to say, 'we must take men as we find them.' As long as individuals do not voluntarily take care of a number of essential matters, the law will need to provide for this by means of legal regulations. It would be premature, however, to conclude that this would be necessarily at the cost of the moral autonomy and self-reliance of the individual. An agent who would have done voluntarily what is prescribed by law, will not look upon such enactment as an unwelcome interference with his affairs:

> Such a man does not feel the law as constraint at all. To him it is simply a powerful friend. It gives him security for that being done efficiently which, with the best wishes, he might have much trouble in getting done efficiently if left to himself. No doubt it relieves him from some of the responsibility which would otherwise fall to him as a head of a family, but, if he is what we are supposing him to be, in proportion as he is relieved of responsibilities in one direction he will assume them in another. The security which the state gives him for safe housing and sufficient schooling of his family will only make him more careful for their well-being in other respects, which he is left to look after for himself.[9]

It follows that there is no reason to fear that legal regulations would leave no room for the moral responsibility of the individual. Green finds his way out of this potential difficulty by stipulating the clause of a certain minimum 'standard of moral and material well-being'. Proceeding on this stipulation, Green's argument is that, as far as the social evils he drew attention to were concerned, this precondition simply had not yet been met.

---

[8] *Works*, iii, p. 375.
[9] *Ibid.*, pp. 375–6.

> Given a certain standard of moral and material well-being, people
> may be trusted not to sell their labour, or the labour of their chil-
> dren, on terms which would not allow that standard to be main-
> tained. But with large masses of our population, until the laws we
> have been considering took effect, there was no such standard.
> There was nothing on their part, in the way either of self-respect
> or established demand for comforts, to prevent them from work-
> ing and living . . . in a way in which no one who is to be a healthy
> and free citizen can work and live.[10]

A further argument Green develops to support his account
of principles of state-interference is reminiscent of the free-
rider argument in theories of collective action. Not only is the
wise exercise of state interference perfectly compatible with
the exercise of virtue; conscientious employers, for example,
'could not prevent less scrupulous hirers of labour from hiring
it on the cheapest terms'.[11] And the plea for legislative interference to relieve the sufferings of underprivileged classes culminates in the following statement:

> The danger of legislation, either in the interests of a privileged
> class or for the promotion of particular religious opinions, we
> may fairly assume to be over. The popular jealousy of law, once
> justifiable enough, is therefore out of date. The citizens of England
> now make its law.[12]

The preceding account of Green's political speech already
pointed to an important difference between Green and Mill
with respect to their ideas as to the use of legal prescriptions as
an instrument to bring about a certain desired state of affairs.
The statement just quoted constitutes a second point on which
Green clearly distinguishes himself from the more classical
liberal political thinkers. It adds an even more clearly
Rousseauesque feature to his position than was already suggested.

B. Metaphysical Foundations of Green's Positive Concept of Freedom

In order to appreciate Green's doctrine of positive freedom in
its proper context, it should be considered in connection with
the idealist philosophy of consciousness. As was explained in
the foregoing chapter, Green interpreted the development of

---

[10] *Ibid.*, p. 376.
[11] *Ibid.*
[12] *Ibid.*, p. 386.

both individual and collective human consciousness in terms of a doctrine of self-assertion of reason. In the same way as negative freedom is defined as a condition of absence of restraint, positive freedom should be seen as a condition in which man determines himself according to what Green refers to in his professorial lectures as 'the law of his being'.[13]

According to the idealist philosophy of consciousness it is inherent in the developmental logic of individual consciousness that individual man will recognise his fellow men as equally gifted with rational faculties and for that reason essentially equal to himself. It is on this mutual recognition by the members of a community that the entire fabric of society rests. As a first step in reconstructing the metaphysical basis of Green's positive conception of freedom, I will explore Green's claim that such a recognition is indeed inherent in the development of human consciousness. In order to explain this point I need to elaborate a part of his philosophy of consciousness, notably the part dealing with human willing, or practical reason.

According to idealist moral psychology, individual man presents to himself images of states of affairs which he holds to be desirable. This continually presenting himself ends or ideals is intrinsic to the way in which he relates to the external world. It constitutes a distinguishing feature of human nature. Each agent conjectures a certain image of what, at a given point in time, his personal good consists in. This conception of personal good, or representation of a certain desirable state of things governs his activity; it is by means of his activity that he will try to bring such an ideal state into existence. As consciousness grows, such a practical conception develops accordingly. A given practical conception directs human conduct and structures the activity of each individual agent.

The central thesis of Green's moral psychology, then, is that this development actually shows an ever increasing rationalization. As was explained in Chapter Two, Green develops two complementary lines of argument to substantiate this thesis. On the one hand he makes a purely empirical claim: the actual course of human history indeed reveals such a process

---

[13] 'On the Different Senses of 'Freedom' as Applied to Will and to the Moral Progress of Man,' p. 228; cf. 242–9. This text will hereafter be cited as *Different Senses*. References are to the critical edition by Harris and Morrow (CUP 1986).

of rationalization, both in terms of the moral norms held in society and at the level of individual human agents. On the other hand, Green argues that such a development can only be explained teleologically, in terms of the self-realization of reason. In his view, this assumption must be made in order to explain why at each stage in the process of social development individual agents are aware of a certain moral ideal with which they identify their practical conception of well-being. Moral conduct can be adequately understood only by rendering human activity in terms of some 'consciously self-realising principle,' i.e.

> a principle that is determined to action by the conception of its own perfection, or by the idea of giving reality to possibilities which are involved in it and of which it is conscious as so involved; or, more precisely, a principle which at each stage of its existence is conscious of a more perfect form of existence as possible for itself, and is moved to action by that consciousness. [14]

A further argument which Green adduces in support of the central thesis of his moral psychology, we saw, may be derived from the parallel pattern to be discerned in the development of theoretical reason, or human understanding. And, as was explained in the previous chapter, this development may be seen equally at the collective and the individual level. What can be said about the development of individual consciousness, also applies to the progress of the entire corpus of human knowledge.

Dominion and Servitude

This philosophy of consciousness underlies Green's entire social philosophy. In fact, the essentials of his political and ethical theory may be derived from an analysis of the structure of human consciousness. The manner in which rights and political obligations logically follow from the development of human consciousness is explained in the allegory of 'Dominion and Servitude' in *Phenomenology of Mind*. In all likelihood, Green's version of this doctrine was taken from the Nürnberg *Phenomenology*. [15] By its very nature, each individual self-conscious agent aims at changing and interfering in the natural order of things so as to make it fit his own practical concep-

---

[14]   *Different Senses*, pp. 243–4.
[15]   See the account of the Nürnberg *Phenomenology* in Chapter I, Section C.

tions. This aim necessarily brings him into conflict with other agents whose activity is equally governed by the intention to create an order according to their preconceived ideas about the ends of life. This inevitable conflict is first settled by means of a life-and-death struggle between parties in which the one who prefers life to liberty will be subjected by the party which prefers to die rather than to live in slavery.

This conflict is inherent in the way human consciousness operates and is in that sense inevitable. It follows that the first form of contact among human beings must have been a relationship of master and slave, characterised by fundamental inequality. However, the developmental logic of the self-same process which brought this state into being, already points to the manner in which this first form of human interaction will disappear again and inevitably pass into a subsequent stage: the slave, who owes his life to the master, is obliged to work for the master and must satisfy the latter's needs; owing to this course of events the master will eventually become as dependent on the labour of the slave as, vice versa, the slave was dependent on the master for his security. In this manner, the initial state of one-sided dependency will gradually be substituted by a relationship of mutual dependence, in which both parties will have to recognise one another as persons, equally gifted with rational capacities. It is this mutual recognition which underlies all rights and obligations operating in a given society. This also constitutes the basis of the right, or the political ideal, of 'negative' freedom. In other words: the identification of the condition of absence of restraint as an intrinsic good, something which is in itself desirable, equally rests on this mutual recognition of individual members of a community as persons. This recognition requires — and is manifested in — the respect for another man's acts of will.

People must eventually recognise each other as equal to themselves. This matter of fact may both be discerned in the actual social development of man and concluded from the structure of human consciousness. In this sense, man's social nature forms part of the '*a priori* furniture' of the mind, as Green phrased it on one occasion. In the same way as mutual recognition by the members of a political community is inherent in the developmental logic of human consciousness, this process will eventually produce an identity of interests on the part of different individual agents.

On this point, we discern once again the characteristic two-fold mode of reasoning by which Green argues practically all his positions adopted in the field of ethical theory. On the one hand, the recognition of some identity of interests, or common good, on the part of the members of a political community is presented as an empirical fact, which may be verified in existing societies. On the other hand, Green seems to be saying that this must be regarded as a necessary element in the social development of mankind and argues that, properly speaking, there can be no society unless such a common interest is actually recognised. The common good thus must be seen as a necessary condition for a political community.

Negative Freedom Superceded

In view of this theory of human consciousness 'negative' freedom can no longer be understood as a 'stand-alone' value: it is rather to be seen as a natural outcome of the development of human consciousness. The political ideal of negative freedom corresponds to a certain stage in the social development of mankind, a process which, in turn, may be seen as a result analogous to the development of individual consciousness.

As was the case with earlier transitions to higher stages in the development of human consciousness, the process making negative freedom into a political ideal already carries the elements which will eventually supersede it. The product of a certain stage in the social development, this political ideal will be rendered out of date by further developments, or, at any rate, it will be viewed in a wider perspective. Respect for the individual person and his acts of will constitutes the basis of society. But the very fact that man is dependent on his fellow men (which was the significance of the allegory of 'Dominion and Servitude') already points to the conclusion that individual agents cannot do everything they might conceivably want to do, without any restrictions. If the integrity of individual personality was to be erected into an absolute value among all political ends, this would sooner or later result in an interference with the integrity of other persons. It follows that, while respect for other people's acts of will thus must be seen as a primary political value, a principle structuring the political order, its actual operation in society already shows a number of inherent restrictions. Respect for someone else's person (which, for present purposes, may be identified with freedom in the negative sense) cannot be turned into an absolute political value; as a principle, it can never be carried through unqualifiedly since human activity, as long as it is not organised or directed, may very well come into conflict with other people's acts.

Apart from this inherent limitation to the principle, there is yet another restriction which is of an altogether different nature. This qualification follows from the further development of human consciousness. The condition of absence of restraint cannot be a political ideal of absolute validity, invariable, fixed and determined once and for all. The value attached to unqualified absence of restraint rather becomes a product of a certain stage in social development, which will be rendered out of date in the course of further progress. When conceiving of the progress of human consciousness as a process of development, negative freedom can no longer count as an absolute and universal political ideal.

The rationale of society consists in its being contributory to the further self-realization of individual agents. In *Political Obligation* Green pointed out that rights adhere to individual people as members of a community, a consideration which rendered impossible the idea of a right which individuals could claim against society.[16] In a similar fashion, it could be concluded that negative freedom cannot be exercised when it runs counter to the ulterior end with reference to which it derives its justification.

Green's Professorial Lectures on the Concept of Freedom[17]

Green never gave a full statement of the metaphysical foundations of his concept of positive freedom. In this respect the

[16] The central argument he set out against natural right theories in his academic lectures on political theory was that rights essentially follow from the mutual recognition of their fellow men as equals on the part of all members of a political community. Therefore individuals can only have rights as members of that community. A relatively extreme conclusion Green draws from this is the consideration that 'a right against society, as such, is an impossibility.' Sect. 143. Cf. 31, 113, 139, 143.

[17] This lecture also forms a central part in a number of recent analyses of Green's theory of freedom. See Peter Nicholson, *The Political Philosophy of the British Idealists*, Cambridge, 1990, pp. 116–22; Tyler, *Thomas Hill Green and the Philosophical Foundations of Politics*, pp. 34–72; and Dimova-Cookson, *T.H. Green's Moral and Political Philosophy*, pp. 108–15. Her interpretation of Green's theory of freedom is taken beyond Green in 'A New Scheme of Positive and Negative Freedom: Reconstructing T.H. Green on Freedom.'

foregoing reconstruction of this argumentation supplements Green's own lectures. In this sense we are 'saying here for Green what he did not say for himself,' in the same way as Green once commented in his essay on Aristotle.[18] But, where a complete account of the argumentation underlying his views on the subject of political freedom is lacking in the published Green, his surviving academic writings do provide a number of important arguments which may be adduced to support the above reconstruction of his theory. Green explicitly commented on the problem of the meaning of freedom in the course of his 1879 professorial lectures.[19] While these lectures were on moral philosophy and may be regarded as an earlier version of *Prolegomena*, these arguments nevertheless have a direct bearing on the discussion about the political implications of the positive concept of freedom. The remainder of this section presents the chief arguments which may be cited to support the earlier reconstruction of Green's argumentation.

Green's professorial lectures on freedom are particularly interesting since it would seem that, on this occasion, he seeks to meet a number of criticisms which, in their full force, would be voiced only long after Green's death. In particular he seems concerned with the likely reproach of conceptual confusion inherent in appropriating a term which already had a clear and definite meaning attached to it.[20] Green's defence proceeds as follows. He begins by conceding to his opponents that freedom in its negative sense must be taken to be the 'primary' meaning.

> As to the sense given to 'freedom', it must of course be admitted that every usage of the term to express anything but a social and political relation of one man to others involves a metaphor.[21]

He then goes on to point out the actual development of the meaning given to the term. Drawing attention to the fact that it is not up to any individual to decide upon the meaning of words, he points out that people actually also attribute different meanings to this term. In this respect language is as inde-

---

[18] *Works*, iii, p. 83.
[19] Ms 24. Nettleship published selections from this Ms as 'On the Different Senses of "Freedom" as Applied to Will and to the Moral Progress of Man.'
[20] Berlin, *Four Essays on Liberty*; Weinstein, 'The Concept of Liberty in Nineteenth Century English Political Thought.'
[21] *Different Senses*, p. 229.

pendent of an individual man's intention as are biological processes in the world of nature.

Having pointed out the factual use made of the term, Green wants to make crystal clear that he considers this to be in many ways a regrettable development which would better have been prevented since it gave rise to much confusion and disputes.

> If it were ever reasonable to wish that the usage of words had been other than it has been . . . one might be inclined to wish that the term 'freedom' had been confined to the juristic sense of the power to 'do what one wills': for the extension of its meaning seems to have caused much controversy and confusion.[22]

Having thus attempted to parry the first blow of what he must have taken to be a most likely criticism of his re-definition of freedom, Green went on to sum up the reasons why he thought he was nevertheless entitled to use the term 'freedom'. To substantiate his position he appealed both to the metaphysical theory of self-assertion of reason and to intuitive experience. The argument on intuitions about freedom is remarkable for two reasons. First, it is exactly analogous to the assertion concerning the eventual coincidence of faith and religious intuitions, on the one hand, and reason, on the other. This argument, it will be recalled, played a central role in his philosophy of religion and, at a more general level, in his efforts to find a solution to the apparently contradictory claims of religious faith and scientific knowledge.[23] Secondly, Green's appeal to intuitions about freedom to justify his terminology is unexpected since, interestingly enough, it anticipates an argument which was to be voiced only seventy years after his death. In fact, this argument was made in a study intended to show that there is no room for more than one meaning of freedom in English, and which, consequently, aimed at undoing the conceptual innovation Green sought to introduce.[24]

Green's argument on intuitions about freedom is of a purely empirical nature. Once people have grown familiar with the metaphorical use of the word, he claims, and the negative notion of freedom has thus been departed from

---

[22] *Ibid.*, p. 234.
[23] See the section on 'Idealism and Religion' in the Introduction, also the account in Chapter I, Section D.
[24] Cranston, *Freedom: A New Analysis*, Part I, Chapter 2.

> . . . certainly the unsophisticated man . . . can much more readily assimilate the notion of states of the inner man described as . . . freedom from sin and law, freedom in the consciousness of union with God or of the harmony with the true law of one's being, freedom of true loyalty, freedom in devotion to self-imposed duties, than he can assimilate the notion of freedom as freedom to will anything and everything, or as exemption from determination by motives, or the constitution by himself of the motives which determine his will.[25]

In view of the actual sense of freedom people may experience there is more to justify the positive than the negative notion of freedom. There are just too many cases in which the positive notion links up with the norms and beliefs of ordinary people, at the individual as well as the collective level.

> To any popular audience interested in any work of self-improvement . . . it is as an effort to attain *freedom* that such work can be most effectively presented. It is easy to tell such people that the term is misapplied; that they are quite 'free' as it is, because every one can do as he likes so long as he does not prevent another from doing so; that . . . to get drunk is as much an act of free will as anything else. Still the feeling of oppression, which always goes along with the consciousness of unfulfilled possibilities, will always give meaning to the representation of the effort after any kind of self-improvement as a demand for 'freedom'.[26]

A further claim made in this context, which may be regarded as a separate step in Green's argumentation, is his statement that the mere possibility of doing something cannot produce a lasting satisfaction. For that reason, mere capacities or possibilities are unfit to serve as a genuine end of human activity. Only in an initial stage it is conceivable that newly created possibilities are by themselves capable of producing satisfaction. But, by its very nature, a mere possibility cannot give durable satisfaction or serve as an end of man's activity. The point Green is trying to prove is that, in the same way as other matters which can only be described in negative terms, the condition of absence of restraint can perform the function of a valid political ideal only in an initial stage. It is as it were inherent in its negative nature that it cannot serve as a lasting end of life. Green illustrates his claim with the example of prisoners and children:

---

[25] *Different Senses*, p. 240.
[26] *Ibid.*, p. 242.

To a captive[27] on first winning his liberty, as to a child in the early experience of power over his limbs and through them over material things, this feeling of a boundless possibility of becoming may give real joy; but gradually the sense of what is not — of the very little that it amounts to — must predominate over the sense of actual good as attained in it. Thus to the grown man, bred to civil liberty in a society which has learnt to make nature its instrument, there is no self-enjoyment in the mere consciousness of freedom as exemption from external control, no sense of an object in which he can satisfy himself having been obtained.[28]

Logical Continuity

A further argument to be found in Green's 1879 professorial lectures relates to the logical and historical connection which can be construed between both political ideals. It will be recalled that the theory of self-assertion of reason looks upon both conceptions of freedom as various stages of reflection upon the same self-asserting principle. On that point of view, positive freedom is presented as a higher expression of this principle than the current ideal of negative freedom. Once this point of view is adopted, the opposition between the condition of absence of restraint and the state in which all men are equally capable of pursuing their self-realization becomes as significant as construing a contradiction between two phases in the same process of development. In terms of the logic of this process of self-assertion of reason, the continuity between the two conditions respectively denoted by negative and positive freedom, is brought out as follows:

> The reflecting man is not content with the first announcement which analysis makes as to the inward condition of the free man — viz. that he can do what he likes, that he has the power of acting according to his will or preference. In virtue of the same principle which has led him to assert himself against others, and thus to cause there to be such a thing as (outward) freedom, he distinguishes himself from his preference, and asks how he is related to it — whether he determines it or how it is determined. Is he free to will, as he is free to act; or, as the act is determined by the preference, is the preference determined by something else?[29]

After a detailed, but condensed consideration of the relationship between man, his will and preferences, which has since received extensive treatment in the second book of *Prolegom-*

[27] The MS gives 'slave' as an alternative for 'captive'. Harris and Morrow, p. 371.
[28] *Different Senses.*, p. 241.
[29] *Ibid.*, pp. 234-5.

ena, Green characteristically advances the view that the question whether man is free is asked in inappropriate terms and is for that reason unanswerable. And the terms of the question are inappropriate, because they can only be answered on the self-denying hypothesis that there is 'some agency beyond the will which determines what the will shall be'.[30] But, as he goes on to point out, in a political sense ' . . . there is a real community of meaning between "freedom" as expressing the condition of a citizen of a civilised state, and "freedom" as expressing the condition of a man who is inwardly "master of himself".'[31] For,

> . . . the practical conception by a man . . . of a self-satisfaction to be attained in his becoming what he should be . . . is the outcome of the same self-seeking principle which appears in a man's assertion of himself against other men and against nature.[32]

A man's 'assertion of himself against nature' consists primarily in his ability to make use of nature so as to bring about his own ends; whereas his 'asserting himself against other men' is substantiated as 'claiming their recognition of him as being what they are'. It is in view of this common origin of both practical ideals that Green finds a justification for presenting self-realization as a form of freedom.

> . . . just as the demand for and attainment of freedom from external control is the expression of that same self-seeking principle from which the quest for such an object proceeds, so 'freedom' is the natural term by which the man describes such an object to himself — describes to himself the state in which he shall have realised his ideal of himself, shall be at one with the law which he recognises as that which he ought to obey, shall have become all that he has it in him to be, and so fulfil the law of his being . . .[33]

These are the chief arguments with which the earlier reconstruction of the metaphysical foundation of Green's doctrine of positive freedom may be supported. To an extent they state explicitly separate elements in the argumentation underlying Green's position on positive freedom as it was worked up earlier in the present chapter. Having presented the various arguments which can be related to the metaphysical basis of his doctrine, we may now go on to consider the political implica-

[30]   *Ibid.*, p. 238.
[31]   *Ibid.*, p. 240.
[32]   *Ibid.*, pp. 240–1.
[33]   *Ibid.*, p. 241.

tions of the preceding 'genuine statement' of Green's positive conception of freedom.

Some Implications of the Present Re-Statement of Green's Doctrine

One of the principal objections against the notion of positive freedom is that it does not allow for a precise determination of what is involved in it. This evasive nature of 'positive freedom' follows directly from its identification with self-realization. It is perhaps one of the less satisfactory aspects of his public lecture that the intrinsic link with his general philosophy is not made more evident.

But, in spite of this defect, there is a genuine philosophical argument to be made on the basis of Green's metaphysical principles. This has to do with the attention he draws to the interrelation of all the various conditions which may be discerned in the process of each individual's self-realization. Admittedly, as it is hard to make out whether any such inventory of conditions is exhaustive, this argument is to a lesser extent liable to the reproach that it would be impossible to establish beforehand what exactly is involved in the definition. This is all very well, we may conclude, for an ethical doctrine, but it is certainly less than satisfactory in a discourse on actual political questions. Whereas it may be difficult or even impossible to draw up an exhaustive inventory of conditions involved in self-realization, the force of Green's argument remains intact as a criticism of the undue emphasis on what can be shown to be but one condition among the many relating to an individual's self-realization.

This argument is directly derived from Green's more general metaphysical principles. It has a definite bearing on matters of practical politics since it questions the uncritical reliance on the political ideal of absence of restraint at the cost of a more balanced, wider view of conditions of self-realization. Negative freedom in the sense of conditions of self-realization is thus not so much invalidated, but placed in a wider perspective.[34] As such, it remains of intrinsic value. It becomes a subordinate standard which must be balanced

---

[34] Compare Milne, *The Social Philosophy of English Idealism*, pp. 22–55, on the theory of rational activity.

against other conditions of self-realization which may be newly discerned.

A further observation regards the relationship between the two rival definitions of freedom and their corresponding principles of state-interference. Since champions of negative freedom render absolute the condition of absence of restraint there must be an inherent presumption against state interference in their political theory. In most cases this is remedied by the common sense consideration, that while it must be seen as an evil, it may be necessary to prevent something worse. However, while the two schools of political theory may thus be not too far apart in terms of the practical inferences which may judiciously be drawn from either of them, there remains an important difference of emphasis between the two.

Needless to say Green, whose only definition of positive freedom claiming a certain completeness was given in the context of a political speech, was less than consistent with his own principles in working out the implications of his theoretical position. It will be clear that, where he does not find himself in circumstances in which he was likely to be held to his metaphysical principles, he is apt to make statements which may turn out to contradict his metaphysics, as long as they do not appear to be in conflict with premises of a less abstract nature.

It would seem that the chief inconsistency Green is guilty of in his speech on *Liberal Legislation* regards the relationship between positive and negative freedom. He simply stipulates that there is no contradiction between the two conceptions of freedom.

Optimal conditions for the realization of self will coincide with absence of restraint only in special circumstances, and it is only in these instances that positive freedom may be presented as a further determination of the condition of absence of restraint. It certainly will not do to suggest that the two always go together. This in fact comes down to assuming some mysterious pre-established harmony in the actual political ends pursued by individual agents.[35] Perhaps Green would have been better off admitting that maintenance of the optimal conditions for self-realization generally will not go together with the condition of absence of restraint. In ordinary cases, optimizing the conditions for the self-realization of A will require a restriction of the exercise of freedoms by B.

---

[35] Berlin, *Four Essays on Liberty*.

C. Positive Freedom and Political Obligation

In the second chapter I have sought to enlarge upon Green's metaphysical doctrine by drawing from his unpublished manuscripts. On the basis of this fuller statement of its metaphysical foundation, it was attempted to bring out the unity which pervades the separate provinces of Green's system of philosophy. This was demonstrated by the identification of certain basic principles, operative in his metaphysics, which can be shown to recur in a number of other realms of his system. In this manner a comprehensive system of philosophy emerges. However, if we have been arguing the interrelationship between separate realms of his philosophy and his metaphysics, this applies *a fortiori* to the connection between moral and political philosophy. In order to set Green's doctrine of positive freedom, as it was derived from his metaphysical principles in the preceding section of the present chapter, in the context of his theory of political obligation, we shall now turn to his major publication in the field of political theory.

Green's *Lectures on the Principles of Political Obligation* were published posthumously. The text which was issued under this title was initially included in the *Works*, but due to its wide popularity with students of political theory it was later issued under separate cover. The manuscript lecture notes stem from lectures which Green delivered on the subject in the Michaelmas and Lent Terms of 1879-1880.

Green's professorial lectures on political obligation represent by far the best example of his method of philosophical criticism. At any rate it is more representative of his working method than his treatise on moral philosophy, which entirely lacks the precise criticism of the work of predecessors. Rather than criticism on which to build his own doctrine, Green's *Prolegomena* gives an independent statement of his own positive doctrine, which more or less results in an open polemic against a contemporary publication, Sidgwick's *Methods of Ethics*. The earlier publication of the *Introductions* to Hume may count as an example of the other extreme. As may be expected from the nature of such a work, Green's approach in it is entirely critical and, while his positive views are implied throughout and occasionally come to the surface, he does not come anywhere near to a full statement. According to his own method of philosophical criticism he would have had to develop his critical investigation beyond Kant and Hegel before he could have stated his own doctrine. The philosophical method to which he committed himself requires that his own arguments should not simply be posited. In terms of Green's methodology his own views need to be presented as following from the views of his predecessor by intellectual necessity. A statement of his own positive doctrine must therefore be preceded by a critical review of all relevant theories which have been produced on the subject. By considering the arguments of his predecessors and disentangling what is of permanent worth from the points on which they can be shown to be defective, Green, as it were, constructs a basis from which he can advance his own point of view. To some extent this method of philosophical criticism features in all his writings, published as well as unpublished.

Political Obligation is organised entirely in accordance with this methodological ideal. The lectures fall into three parts, the first being an introductory discussion on what Green calls 'the true function of the law,' in which he sets out the intrinsic relation between moral and political theory.[36] It is in the function which legal enactments fulfill in making moral activity possible that the 'Grounds of Political Obligation' are to be found, in the terms which Nettleship assigned to this first part of Green's lectures.[37]

The second part is entirely critical and discusses the political doctrines of Spinoza, Hobbes, Locke, Rousseau and finally Austin, whose doctrine may be taken as representative of the English learned opinions chiefly used to oppose Rousseau's concept of sovereignty. On the basis of the first three authors, Green works out his case against the notion of any system of natural rights, prior to society, from which the existing legal order derives its justification. With Hobbes and Locke this takes the form of a social pact by which people assign sovereign power to the prince. In Green's opinion, it begs the question as to the origin of the sovereignty of civil government in a fundamental sense. For, in order to be able to sign away their rights to self-determination to a civil government, individual citizens must possess them first. Hence arises the question as to the origin of these natural rights. While all theories of natural law proceed on the notion of certain rights which belong to

---

[36] *Political Obligation*, sect. 1.
[37] *Ibid.*, sects 1–31.

individuals as such, they invariably fail to account for the origin of these rights.[38]

Having gathered material for a strong case against natural law theory, Green goes on to consider a more peculiar instance of social contract theory in the work of Rousseau, and it is here that he finds a more workable argument in the reference to the concept of a general will. In fact, according to Green, the perceptive reader will find much of permanent value in Rousseau. It is merely owing to the burden of the predominant 'nominalistic logic and psychology of individual introspection,' as he describes it on another occasion,[39] that Rousseau was unable to escape the notion of a social contract, thereby condemning him to the same metaphysical mistake of assuming an individual vested with a number of natural rights prior to the establishment of the political order as enforced by civil government. On the basis of the important concept of a general will, Green seeks to work out his own theory of sovereignty by, as it were, playing off Rousseau against Austin. It is not until he has thus investigated the whole range of theories of sovereignty that he comes to his own positive statement.

Green's main contention is that the system of law as we find it enforced in civilized nations does not depend on force, but on mutual recognition on the part of the members of a community as all equally vested with rational will and the capacity of being determined by a conception of the common good of that community.

After this first principle of political obligation is stated in detail, Green proceeds to the third part of his lectures and goes on to consider some of its main applications as they are to be found in modern European legal systems: first and foremost the right to life and liberty which cannot be conceived of separately and which are for that reason better joined into a right to free life; property rights; rights concerning the promotion of morality; and finally the section on 'rights and virtues,' which is the only remaining fragment of an inventory of social virtues Green had in mind.[40] In the section 'Has the citizen rights

---

[38] Cf. the account of the origins of Green's concept of rights by Rex Martin, in Andrew Vincent, ed., *The Philosophy of T.H.Green*, Aldershot, 1986.

[39] *Works*, iii, p. 124.

[40] Compare the official announcement of Green's lectures on *Political Obligation*, which also refers to 'Social virtues,' *Memoir*, p. cxxv. Cf. the account of the *Propädeutik* in Chapter I, Section C.

against the state?' he discusses the possibility of civil disobedience.

Political Obligation and Moral Duty

Having outlined the structure of his main treatise in political theory we may now concentrate on the close relationship Green construes between political obligation and moral duty. In *Political Obligation* Green emphasizes the intrinsic relation between the system of law enforced by a political superior and the exercise of moral duties. Moral goodness is then described as an 'attribute of character so far as it issued in acts done for the sake of their goodness, not for the sake of any pleasure or any satisfaction of desire which they bring to the agent.'[41] This definition makes it clear that goodness can only be characterized in formal terms.

In his moral treatise, Green had definitely adopted the view that goodness can only be defined in its own terms.[42] Moreover, he stated explicitly that this is inherent in the nature of the good. This argument is worked out in great detail in his controversy with Sidgwick as to which of the two systems of ethics provided the best guide to moral conduct.[43]

The remarkable feature of the opening paragraphs of *Political Obligation*, however, is that it does attempt to find ways to describe goodness otherwise than in its own terms. Green develops here an altogether different argument on the circular nature of any definition of the moral ideal. What he drives at is nothing short of an attempt to evade the circular reasoning. He even goes so far as to postulate a sort of 'prior morality,' i.e. a system of norms which as yet fall short of 'pure' morality from which eventual morality is derived. Without such a system of prior morality, Green maintains, moral duty would remain an empty conception.[44]

Now, it is easier to see *what* problem Green is trying to resolve with his postulate of prior morality than it is to comprehend *how* he is thinking of solving it. The problem he envisaged goes back to what is known as Kant's formalism in his ethical theory. The notorious problem of Kantian ethics is that it concentrated all attention on the disposition from which a

[41]   *Political Obligation*, sect. 2.
[42]   *Prolegomena*, sects. 171–3, 367.
[43]   *Ibid.*, Book IV, Chapter 4.
[44]   *Political Obligation*, sect. 2.

moral act should be accomplished in order to qualify as properly moral, so that its contents are completely resolved in the definition. It is this aspect of Kant which Green finds most unsatisfactory and consequently he tries to work his way around a formal definition of the moral good. However, in suggesting the curious argument of a 'prior morality,' Green does not seem to be aware that he is not solving the problem as to the 'contents' of moral duties. In fact, as long as he does not make clear the source of this 'prior morality,' he merely carries the argument to another level. He goes on to say that once the 'contents' of 'pure' morality is established in this manner, it must serve to criticise the self-same 'prior morality'. Green's argument in the opening lecture of *Political Obligation* can thus be shown to involve a circular argument and the reader is left with the question why Green wanted so clearly to create the impression he was in a position to solve the problem of Kantian ethics by emphasizing that without certain preliminary norms 'it would be impossible to say what the good actions were, that were to be done for the sake of their goodness.'[45]

Green's construction of two categories of moral norms may become more intelligible when we take into account the objectives of his reconstruction of the history of moral philosophy. No doubt, these are best established in the perspective of the various approximations which can be gathered from his lecturing on the subject of moral philosophy over the years.

Green clearly wanted to go beyond Kantian ethics. Kant, too, had confined himself to a formal description of the categorical imperative, but he was less cryptic about this than Green in his *Prolegomena*. In his work Green even explicitly criticizes Kant on this point, in which he was of course strongly inspired by Hegel's criticism of Kant; but eventually Green too must admit that the moral ideal does not admit of a positive statement. His advance on Kant's position is that he describes the 'content' of moral conduct more precisely, although, in the end, he is forced to admit that a complete determination would be self-defeating. That this was nevertheless what Green had in mind concerning the relationship of moral duty and political obligation can be gathered from his earlier courses on moral philosophy which are to be presented in the following section of this chapter. From these earlier lectures it

[45] *Ibid.*

emerges that Green intended to 'fill in' the empty form provided by a rationalistic ethics, such as defended by Kant, with
the historical events actually manifesting this gradual substantiation of the moral ideal. Green, in other words, suggested a kind of synthesis of Kantian ethics and the theory of
moral sentiments as was defended, characteristically, by eigh-
teenth century British moralists.[46]

We have already seen that, in *Political Obligation*, Green
chose to term the existing system of norms 'moral sentiments'.
The criticism of these norms in terms of higher moral norms
became 'a theory of moral sentiments,' in this terminology.
Green elaborates his thesis by distinguishing two kinds of
non-moral rules which are recognised in society, depending
on whether or not they are codified in positive law. Non-moral
rules of the latter type may be termed 'laws of opinion'. These
two systems of non-moral norms relate as a species to a genus;
but as generally accepted 'laws of opinion' cannot be considered separately from the entire social fabric, Green proposes to
begin his inquiry by an investigation of

> what is of permanent moral value in the institutions of civil life, as
> established in Europe; in what way have they contributed and
> contribute to the possibility of morality in the higher sense of the
> term, and are justified, or have a moral claim upon our loyal con-
> formity, in consequence.[47]

From the discussion of Green's moral psychology it will be
recalled that the human self realizes itself essentially in universal acts of will, by which Green was referring to acts which
are capable of generalisation.[48] Proceeding from a conception
of self to be realized, the self-conscious agent conceives of society's well-being as identical with his own well-being. This is
necessarily so since, as a rational agent, he cannot conceive of
his well-being otherwise than in terms which could be erected
into a general norm for the community as a whole. In line with
this position in moral psychology Green concludes his preliminary investigation into the nature of political obligation with
the assertion that the rationale of 'institutions of civil life' consists in their being contributive to the realization of the moral
ideal and in the same way institutions of civil life can also be
judged by this ulterior standard.

[46] Ms 12.
[47] *Political Obligation*, sect. 5.
[48] See also the doctrine in the *Propädeutik*, set out in Chapter I, Section C.

We already drew attention to Green's special liking for stipulative definitions when discussing his use of the term 'moral sentiments'. In the course of establishing the precise relation of moral duty and political obligation Green postulates 'jus naturae' in a similar fashion. And, while he warns his audience that the discussion of this issue is rendered more difficult by the absence of any English equivalent to represent the full meaning of *jus* or *Recht* as 'a system of correlative rights and obligations, actually enforced or that should be enforced by law', he somewhat remarkably altogether neglects the conceptual confusion stemming from his own stipulative definition in terms of 'law as it ought to be,' while omitting to provide any further criteria. However, the questions which he contemplates for this part of his investigation readily show what he had in mind:

> The essential questions are: (1) whether we are entitled to distinguish the rights and obligations which are anywhere actually enforced by law from rights and obligations which really exist though not enforced; and (2), if we are entitled to do so, what is to be our criterion of rights and obligations which are actually valid, in distinction from those that are actually enforced.[49]

It will be clear that if the system of legal enactments as it is actually enforced serves as an ultimate standard for their legitimacy, citizens would be bound to conformity with existing laws, and there would be no need for a further theory of political obligation. But Green does not leave his audience in uncertainty for long:

> No one would seriously maintain that the system of rights and obligations, as it is anywhere enforced by law — the *ius* or *Recht* of any nation — is all that ought to be.[50]

The question following logically from this admission cannot satisfactorily be answered with an appeal to 'natural rights'. For, it is by no means clear what exactly this term is taken to denote. Green draws up three possible theoretical arguments fitting this context which could be implied by a reference to 'natural rights': first, a 'state of nature' in which everyone is free to do as he likes; second, rights and obligations as authorized by means of a contract; or third, reference to 'natural rights' taken to imply that after the political community has

---

[49] *Political Obligation*, sect. 8.
[50] *Ibid.*, sect. 9.

been established by means of such a contract, the individual retains certain rights which belong to him as a person and with which legal obligations developing out of the social contract should not interfere.[51]

Any theory proceeding from the postulate of a system of rights prior to the constitution is insufficient in the sense that it merely carries the question further back to an earlier level. To explain civil rights by a presupposed system of natural rights begs the question as to where these natural rights may be derived from. It was this very point which Green levelled against earlier theorists of social contract. It follows that the only valid use of the term 'natural' rights and obligations is in the sense Green attributes to it, by which 'natural' rights acquire a logical status comparable to 'unfulfilled duties':

> There is a system of rights and obligations which *should be* maintained by law, whether it is so or not, and which may properly be called '*natural*' . . . because necessary to the end which it is in the vocation of human society to realise.[52]

The next stage in Green's inquiry into the nature of political obligation is further to distinguish it from moral duty by a feature which is logically incompatible with the latter concept. Since all political obligations are enforced by law, moral duties are by definition excluded from this category. But it does not follow that political obligations 'do not have anything to do with moral activity.'[53] The system of legal and political obligations enforced in society forms, as Green puts it, 'the negative realisation' of man's capacity for morality.[54] On Green's principles, moral activity would not be possible without a framework of positive law. In the first series of lectures of *Political Obligation* there is not much to substantiate this thesis. Green merely postulates positive law as a condition *sine qua non* for the exercise of moral activity and then goes on to explain the rationale of political obligation in these terms. For a proper derivation of this argument we shall have to turn to the general structure of Green's theoretical system, as was expounded in Chapter Two of the present book.

In his lectures on political obligation Green seems primarily engaged by the question of the practical implication of the

---

[51]   *Ibid.*, sect. 113. Cf. Lecture 'H': 'Has the citizen rights against the state?'
[52]   *Ibid.*, sect. 9.
[53]   Ms 10a, general essay, p. 28.
[54]   *Political Obligation*, sect. 25.

relationship between morals and politics. One of the criteria which he develops to restrict political obligation to its proper province is that it should not limit the range of possibilities for moral agents to exercise moral duties. The dilemma is obvious. On the one hand, if the system of positive law exceeds its province, it diminishes the possibility of moral acts. On the other hand, as this constitutes an argument against any form of legal interference, it would seem to point in the direction of complete absence of any legislation whatsoever. It follows that there must always be a presumption against legal enactments: only those matters which are necessary to maintain the conditions rendering moral activity possible should be the object of legal obligations.[55]

As to this point there is a noticeable difference between *Political Obligation* and Green's public lecture on the principles of state interference. We already saw that, in the latter lecture, Green goes substantially out of his way to make clear that positive law does not necessarily frustrate virtuous conduct. In case a positive legal enactment coincides with what the virtuous man would do irrespective of whether there is any obligation or not, such a moral agent will look upon the law as 'a powerful friend'.[56] It is true that in this manner certain responsibilities are taken away from the virtuous citizens, but these will be reinvested in new responsibilities which otherwise would not have been contemplated.

In order to account for this remarkable difference between Green's public lecture for the Liberal Association in 1881 and his academic lectures on the same subject delivered only two years earlier, it may be suggested that, in setting out formal principles of state interference in his *Political Obligation*, Green was more cautious than he was when it came to recommending actual political questions. To supply a theoretical defence to support a limited number of instances is always safer than establishing general rules as was required for the type of pure theory which he gave in *Political Obligation*.

It is on the topic of temperance legislation that Green adopts his most extreme position on state interference.[57] With regard to the subject of liquor traffic he does not seem at all afraid of

---

[55] *Ibid.*, sect. 15.
[56] 'Liberal Legislation,' *Works*, iii, p. 375.
[57] An analysis of Green's radical position on temperance legislation is given by Nicholson, *The Political Philosophy of the British Idealists*, pp. 177–80.

the danger of excessively confining the possibilities of moral activity, a fear which is characteristic of his more theoretically oriented *Political Obligation*. It was already pointed out that, in his political speech, Green even refutes a counter argument which to the unprejudiced reader may seem very much in the spirit of his *Political Obligation*. Restrictive legislation, according to that argument, is but a self-defeating 'shortcut to a good end.'[58] To rely on the moral autonomy of the individual in these matters may not be so rapid a solution, but it will prove more lasting. Green replies to this, somewhat unexpectedly, that 'every year the evil left to itself, it becomes greater.'[59] Restrictive laws on liquor traffic are thus legitimate and there is no danger of interfering with the possibilities of the individual agent for moral activity. On the contrary, when liquor traffic was subjected to a rigid system of licences, 'the spirit of self-reliance and independence was not weakened by those acts.'[60] Rather it formed a stimulus for the pursuit of higher objects. And he concluded his discussion of this topic with the following statement: 'When all temptations are removed which the law can remove, there will be still enough, nay, much more room, for the play of our moral energies.'[61]

It would seem, therefore, that Green's pre-occupation with possible negative effects of excessive legislation on the moral initiative of the individual agent has largely disappeared when it comes to the question of liquor traffic. In working out his general principles in this particular instance Green seems to have drifted a considerable distance from the prudent tone in which he set out his academic political philosophy. One is entitled to ask why legislative interference with excessive drinking should be less of an interference with the moral autonomy of the individual than in other instances of legal obligations. The difference remains unaccounted for by Green's principles and in this sense his unqualified support for restrictive measures in the field of temperance legislation forms a weak element in his theoretical position.

---

[58] *Works*, iii, p. 384.
[59] *Ibid.*, p. 385.
[60] *Ibid.*, p. 386.
[61] *Ibid.*

A Different Interpretation of Green on State Interference

To sum up: the intrinsic link of political obligation and moral duty in Green's philosophy receives somewhat more conservative treatment in his general theoretical work as compared to the application of these principles in concrete cases, as evidenced by his public speech. In this light it is remarkable that Melvin Richter in his biography of Green comes exactly to the opposite conclusion, when he discusses Green's theory of property rights. Richter's thesis is that as far as the exposition of property rights in *Political Obligation* is concerned, Green was most uncritical of the capitalist system.[62]

He then goes on to play down the socialist implications of Green's political speech, pointing out that Green's pamphlet was incorrectly taken as a general defence of state interference. '[T]his whole essay has often been misinterpreted as a general sanction for state-interference,' Richter contends in his biography.

> This was not Green's meaning. The lecture was delivered to a Liberal party organisation; it naturally stated Green's positive opinions summarily and without the qualification that appears in *Political Obligation*.[63]

Richter's thesis thus seeks to establish that the difference in tone between Green's political speech and his academic lectures must be seen as deriving from the fact that his exposition on the former occasion was less complete than the more detailed account of the same matter in his academic lectures. And he further suggests that, in his speech on *Liberal Legislation*, Green was addressing an audience which did not need to be convinced as to the desirability of the new style of liberal legislation so that he could afford to discuss these matters more briefly.

However, in whatever way one looks upon the circumstances of the public lecture, it is difficult to conceive anything self-evident or 'natural' in Richter's explanation. Had Green really been concerned about possible excesses of regulative activity by the state and the danger of impingements upon individual liberties, as much as Richter wants us to believe, it would seem to become all the more relevant as a topic to be discussed in front of an audience favourably disposed

---

[62] *The Politics of Conscience: T.H.Green and his Age*, p. 274.
[63] *Ibid.*, p. 283.

towards strong governmental activity to relieve the sufferings of the poor.

D. The Relationship of Morality and Politics in Green's Earlier Lectures

Before presenting Green's earlier lectures on moral and political philosophy it will be helpful to point out a number of biographical details about his academic career, in addition to what was already mentioned on this point in the first chapter, so as to situate the intensive study he made of Hegel in the course of the 1860s. In fact, Green did not get a place on the permanent staff of Balliol until the death of one of his tutors from his undergraduate years, J. Riddell, in 1866. Until that year he had been employed as a supernumerary lecturer at the instance of Benjamin Jowett immediately after he had finished at the school of law and history. In the years preceding his permanent appointment he had been undecided as to whether he should sign the thirty-nine articles of the Established Church, a circumstance which for some time prevented him from taking his MA; but he eventually decided that 'one kiss does not make marriage'.[64] Thus, the last obstacle in the way of his academic career was removed.

We learn from a letter of 20 June, 1866, that Benjamin Jowett was trying to get him a regular lecture on moral philosophy in the College, and the Deansbook of Balliol records that on 12 October of the same year an 'Ethical lectureship' was created for one year with a stipend of £100.[65]

Manuscript 15: The State as the Realization of Freedom

It would seem legitimate to conjecture that the lecture notes for this first independent series of lectures on moral philosophy are to be found among the documents which make up manuscript 15.[66] In any event, these notes were written on official stationary of the Schools Inquiry Commission, for which Green served as an assistant commissioner in 1865, and from April to September 1866. Also, they would seem to represent

---

[64] P. Grosskurth, *John Addington Symonds: a Biography*, London, 1964, p. 104; cf. A. and E.M. Sidgwick, *Henry Sidgwick: A Memoir*, London, 1906, p. 105.

[65] Ms extracts from Balliol's Deansbook made by Nettleship.

[66] This manuscript has now been published in vol. v of Nicholson, ed., *Collected Works of T.H. Green*, pp. 188–92.

the earlier stages of Green's thinking on moral and political philosophy and allow us an interesting insight into the character of Green's lecturing when he was able for the first time to organize a course by himself, as opposed to delivering the obligatory commentary on the *Nichomachean Ethics*, on which he had lectured before he was appointed on a permanent basis.

The manuscript makes clear that by 1866 Green had already adopted in his theoretical system the relationship between moral duty and political obligation essentially in the terms which he continued to endorse in his professorial period. It will be recalled that the origin of the peculiar correlation between obligations and duties was traced to Hegel's *Propädeutik*. In manuscript 15 Green develops a doctrine along the lines of these two correlative concepts in answer to the question 'In wt sense is [the] "state [the] realization of freedom" & with it [the realization] of the idea of duty?'[67]

As to the relationship of positive legislation and the realization of freedom, Green draws the following conclusion:

> Thus the systematic custom & law of society [is] really [a] projection or expression of the universality of [the] self though never fully adequate.
>
> In being determined by it, man is determined by [the] self. Thus [he] realizes [the] idea of duty. But this implies conformity to custom &c, be loyal i.e. for its own sake, & according to [the] spirit not to [the] letter.[68]

Green thus already renders here the idea that the legal rules which are enforced in a society somehow 'follow' from the development of the human self. In abiding by the law one ultimately obeys oneself. At the same time he makes clear that these social institutions and norms held are just partial reflections of the 'universality of the self,' in which conception the reader of *Prolegomena* will recognise an earlier version of the 'eternal consciousness'.

A further point which emerges from his first course of lectures on moral philosophy is his emphasis on the parallel between his metaphysic of ethics and his epistemology. Owing to the analogous structure of these two forms of human activity, Green saw fit to explain the role of formal ideas in the constitution of moral activity by drawing from an analysis of the conditions of knowledge:

---

[67] Ms 15, p. 3.
[68] *Ibid.*, p. 4.

> An idea is *formal* when there is no existence corresponding it. So [the] idea of [the] absolute [is] formal. [There is] no phenomenon corresponding to it. But without [the action] of this idea [there could be] no account for [the] effort to reduce experience to a unity, without which [there would be] no knowledge.[69]

An analogous application of this doctrine to moral activity forms the basis of Green's metaphysic of ethics. In the same sense as the activity of a self-distinguishing agency must be presupposed to account for human knowledge, a self-distinguishing agent forms the primary condition of all moral activity. This is, however, a completely formal analysis of human activity. It does not follow from the mere supposition of a self-conscious agency that all its activity will for that reason satisfy the standard of morality, but it must nevertheless be taken as a pre-condition of moral activity, indeed of human activity in general. Self-consciousness is the condition of virtue and vice alike. By virtue of a man's self-consciousness human activity may be distinguished from animal appetite:

> This relation to self — active self-consciousness — gives man [the] conception of his good as a whole. As it is [the] condition of conflict of desires so [it is the condition] of adjustment of this conflict of [the] subjection of [the] immediate desire to [the] general good of the man.[70]

It follows that the first distinguishing feature of human character must be found in its capacity to distinguish itself from any desires, whether capricious or not, originating from his animal nature. By the act of distancing himself from his desires, man is the only creature capable of forming a conception of permanent good. It is by virtue of his reason that an individual agent possesses this capacity.

> It rules the man because it constitutes him [as a] man, because it is that which ... makes his appetitive & sensitive experience to a system.[71]

Green, in other words, eventually identifies such a 'relation to self' with 'reason'. Man's capacity for a conception of permanent good will in the end causes him to conceive his own, individual well-being as identical with that of his fellow men. This point anticipates Green's position in manuscripts which will be presented in the remainder of this section.

---

[69] *Ibid.*, p. 1.
[70] *Ibid.*
[71] *Ibid.*

To summarize the essentials of this important early manuscript on moral and political philosophy: as early as 1866 Green already exhibits a number of elements, which were traced to his study of the *Propädeutik* in the first chapter of this monograph. One such element is the parallel structure of his theory of human experience and his theory of human activity. He uses the epistemological argument to explain the particular nature of moral activity along the lines of his later findings regarding epistemology. A second conclusion which this first moral lecture course of Green's allows is as to the continuity of the correlative concepts of political obligation and moral duty in Green's thinking. Finally, we saw that the beginnings of his theory of human activity and his philosophy of character were already existent in this early manuscript.

Manuscript 10a: Freedom and Accountability in Human Conduct

The following manuscript which may be used to reconstruct the actual philosophical enterprise Green contemplated is a course on moral and political philosophy which he delivered in 1868. Like the previous document considered, this manuscript is able to be dated rather more precisely than most of the other material of Green's philosophical legacy owing to a list with the names of his audience.[72] The manuscript notebook consists of a general essay on moral philosophy and an essay dealing specifically with Kant. The general essay on moral philosophy provides us with a general idea of how Green organised his lectures on the subject in this period. His starting point was to consider the question of the essential difference between moral philosophy and physical science on the understanding that the different positions which could be taken on this issue would provide a 'true point of view from which to regard [the] modern speculation about Ethics'.[73] He then set out '3 popular answers' to this question in order to consider these in detail. By bringing out the tacit assumptions from which they proceed he tried to point out their untenable suppositions.

The first supposition on the relation between moral philosophy and physical science which Green singles out for a part in

---

[72] Ms 10a, back cover.
[73] Ms 10a, general essay, p. 2; the following quotations without footnote references are taken from the same Ms page.

the theoretical discussion he envisages is apparently intended to stand for what he refers to elsewhere in his manuscript as 'sense philosophy'. This position is paraphrased as follows:

> physical science deals with [the] world revealed to us by our senses; these are its test, to these it appeals. Moral philosophy [deals] with some inner consciousness, the facts of which [if so at all] can only be ascertained by each man's individual experience. Hence [it is] cumbered with [a] diversity of views which can never be got rid of.

The second statement represents Green's assessment of the scientific view:

> Object of [physical science] consists of uniform coexistences & sequences which by experiment can be precisely ascertained. [The] object of [moral philosophy, on the other hand,] cannot be dealt with by experiment; it is thus impossible to ascertain precisely what does happen in any case of moral action. Further, in moral action there is an element of wilfulness, a possibility of unmotivated origination, which, if you could ascertain all conditions of a given act, would make it impossible to conclude that what results from those conditions in the given case would result in another.

The third 'popular answer' to the question as to the relation between the moral and the physical world Green puts as follows:

> There is no such element of wilfulness in [the] object-matter of moral philosophy. This matter consists of phenomena of social life, which only differ from the 'natural' in their greater complexity, & in [the] difficulty of applying [an] experiment to them, which however only differs in degree from the [difficulty] of applying it to phenomena & [a] living animal.

The assumption on which sense philosophy proceeds urges Green to criticise the idea that our senses 'reveal' a world to us. He then goes on to set out the part played by reason in the constitution of both nature and human activity. Some important parts of his exposition on this point were already quoted in the account of Green's theory of the self-assertion of reason, as was given in Chapter Two.[74] The chief conclusion regarding ethics is that there is a fundamental and unbridgeable difference between these two worlds. Hence the impossibility of a 'natural theory of ethics'. Green's rendering of this argument in this 1868 manuscript may be summarized as follows. Rea-

---

[74]   Cf. Ms 10a, inside cover.

son constitutes the order of nature and our knowledge concerning nature as much as moral activity; but, whereas the natural order remains unchanged, and does not, at any rate, depend on our cognitive activity, moral judgments, which are equally provided by man's reason, do form an integral part of morality itself.

In reply to the 'scientific view,' Green sets out to refute the idea that 'human events' are 'unaccountable'. The reason why Green opposes this view is evident: if human activity could not be accounted for it would be impossible to consider effects of human activity, which view would render it impossible to hold people responsible for their actions. But it is equally clear, on the other hand, that there can be no necessary connection between any actual motives and act of will in the same way as exists within the order of nature. For, such a natural necessity would not leave room for any autonomy of the will. In this sense, Green finds himself confronted with a familiar dilemma in this manuscript. It is to resolve this dilemma regarding man's free will that he introduces the notion that self-conscious thought is essentially 'originative'; what he means by this is that self-conscious thought invariably goes into the constitution of a man's object of will. Presenting to himself a range of actual desires, man by virtue of his reason comes to conceive of some permanent good. His reason directs his actual preferences and will eventually form a conception of his well-being. So, ultimately, reason 'forms its own ends'.

In passing, Green also discusses the related question whether the notion of a 'regular sequence' in the world of morality, which is required to be able to hold people responsible for their actions, can be upheld alongside the claim that it is impossible to predict the moral future. Again, Green finds himself confronted with a dilemma: if there is a regular sequence to be discerned in the world of morality, why is it that we cannot say what will happen next, whereas the moral future, if already determined, would clearly exclude moral autonomy. In a similar fashion, he considers the problem whether the notion of a regular sequence in morality does not contradict the empirical fact of people converting themselves after a sinful life.

On the basis of the foregoing characterization of moral philosophy and its fundamental distinction from the natural sciences, Green proceeds to outline a number of specific realms in the study of morality and related disciplines. First of all is metaphysic of ethics. In the rendering of the manuscript presently under consideration, this kind of inquiry deals with the 'nature of reason as self-related, thus as giving a law to itself as originating action in expressing itself.'[75] Proceeding from this perspective, it seeks to establish the thesis that reason operates at once

> ... as source of an objective moral world & of [the] recognition on [the] part of [the] ind[ividua]l subj[ec]t of that world as "alter ego".

The exposition of metaphysic of ethics in this manuscript comprises three separate elements. First, it regards all human activity as manifestations of some self-seeking principle: in human willing and human activity, Green says, reason is 'self-related'. Second, an inquiry into the metaphysical foundation of ethics serves to explain how 'the self-assertion of reason' gives rise to moral norms and institutions which are universally accepted by the members of a community. Third, this discipline professes to explain the possibility that individual agents recognize such norms and institutions as a self-imposed authority.

Metaphysic of ethics is an entirely formal discipline. It exclusively deals with the structure of moral judgments and moral activity. It is restricted to outlining this general and abstract relationship between actual preferences of the individual moral agent and the system of moral norms and institutions in society. Its sole object is to specify the presuppositions on which actual moral activity can be understood and explained. As an abstract metaphysical science it does not provide any practical guidance.

> Met[aphysic] of Ethics goes very little way, for so soon as [the] question arises, w[ha]t is the law wh[ich] reason gives to itself, w[ha]t [is] the action wh[ich] it originates, it can only be answered by passing from reason in its abstraction to reason as manifested in real motives and acts.

The only substantial clause which metaphysic of ethics stipulates is that all men are in principle equally gifted with the faculty of reason. The first and most fundamental principle on which proceed all moral considerations properly so called,

---

[75] Ms 10a, general essay, p. 10; the following quotations without footnotes appear on the same Ms page.

according to Green, is the notion of 'equality of reason as self-determining principle in all men.'

There are three more concrete disciplines which proceed from the formal basis provided by metaphysic of ethics. These are:

    — jurisprudence, or the science of right;
    — moral psychology; and
    — sociology, or science of *Sittlichkeit*.

Entirely separated from these three disciplines based on metaphysic of ethics is the science of political economy. Not proceeding from the metaphysical foundation of ethics, the status of the laws of political economy is comparable to that of laws in the world of nature. For an adequate insight in each of the three related fields of inquiry it is helpful first to explore their common difference from the discipline of political economy.

> Pol[itical] Economy is a science of facts & results. It assumes [the] impulse to appropriate, & [the] freedom of appropriation secured, wh[ich] in society means free interchange. Given this principle, it enquires w[ha]t results acc[ording] to various complicated conditions of production and interchange.

Political Economy describes essentially non-moral regularities in the interaction of human agents. It is as impossible to act against the laws of political economy as it is to disobey the laws of nature. It is true, however, just as is the case when one acquires a fuller understanding of the order of nature, that a better insight into the laws of political economy may carry new moral obligations.

Jurisprudence

The most direct application of the principle of 'equality of reason as self-determining principle' is found in the administration and interpretation of the law. Proceeding from the simple principle of mutual recognition on the part of all members of a community as equally gifted with rational faculties, jurisprudence merely takes into account people's outward conduct, i.e. apart from any motives prompting such conduct. Jurisprudence thus

> ... takes no acc[oun]t of [the] variety of motives as constituted by feelings, of qualifying circumstances, of degrees of virtue. It simply applies to the various occasions of life the abstract idea of

independence of each person, with everything he can appropriate, ag[ain]st every other.

Jurisprudence [proper] considers [the] various forms wh[ich the] obligation in each to abstain from interfering with [the] outw[ar]d freedom of another takes acc[ording] to [the] circumstances. It is a science of obligations.

The difference between jurisprudence and morality is further explained in this 1868 manuscript by referring to two senses of freedom. Freedom in its legal sense differs in at least two fundamental respects from moral freedom. First, 'jurisprudence regards freedom as merely negative. Its "obligations" are all ultimately obligations to *abstain*.' Second, freedom in this sense is conceived in purely formal terms: freedom is defined irrespective of whether it is employed in pursuit of a desirable cause. The system of legal obligations in society grants a 'state in wh[ich] no one is his brother's keeper — a state of universal abstention.' In a legal sense, freedom merely implies the obligation to respect one's fellow through 'abstinence fr[om] interference.' On the other hand, in its ethical sense freedom implies 'a law for the will . . . a law to respect oneself in the way of actualising one's possibilities'. Ethical freedom consists in 'an inner life of rationalized desires.' [76]

Moral Psychology

We saw that Green views man as a self-distinguishing agent. In the terms of his moral psychology man is seen as a self-consciousness which is able at once to present to itself certain concrete desires, originating from man's 'animal nature' and to distance itself from these presentations. For Green, the human ego cannot be defined in terms of the concrete desires which man thus internalises and yet personal identity is something more than the sum of all desires thus adopted and made one's own. It is this capacity of the human self to distinguish itself from its 'constituent' desires which fundamentally distinguishes man from the world of nature and human willing from animal desire. By virtue of his reason man is able to form some conception of his personal good out of the 'manifold of

[76] Compare this with the analysis of Green's theory of freedom in Nicholson, *The Political Philosophy of the British Idealists*, and Maria Dimova-Cookson, *T.H. Green's Moral and Political Philosophy*, Chapter 4; as well as the more crystalised view in her article 'A New Scheme of Positive and Negative Freedom: Reconstructing T.H. Green on Freedom.'

desires' which, originating from his animal nature, are presented to him. He is able to form some practical conception or, as it was put in his lecture of 1868, some 'system of desires' in which conflicting desires are weighed against one another, thereby constituting a consistent whole out of an unordered 'chaos' of 'accidental' animal desires.

Such a practical conception directs man's activity. By means of activity man seeks to change the existing order of nature in conformity with his preconceived idea. In the final analysis, therefore, it is man's reason which transforms the manifold of animal desires to a consistent 'system of desires,' or as Green also puts it, 'a conception of permanent good'.

As a rational being, man is able to 'perfect' himself, i.e. to conceive of some better state of himself which he will subsequently seek to realize through his activity. Individual perfection will eventually coincide with the conception of personal good of other agents of the community of which one forms part. Perfection of the individual self implies the identity of personal good and the common good of society.

In the account of Green's moral psychology, as was set out in Chapter Two, we already addressed the question as to whether Green's rationalist position in ethical theory is consistent with the notion of moral autonomy. In a similar manner it was questioned whether Green's rationalist account adequately explains actual human activity. A central thesis of Green's moral psychology, we saw, was that the development in the practical conception of an individual human agent will exhibit an ever progressing rationalisation; the logical outcome of this process would seem to be the state in which reason is setting its own motive. In the manuscript under consideration this doctrine is referred to as 'originativeness of reason'. Green's argumentation differs in a crucial sense from Kant's in that the notion of 'self-assertion of reason,' as exhibited in human character as well as in human history and social institutions, is not so much presented as an *a priori* necessity, but rather an assumption which needs to be made in order to explain the actual course of events. The notion of self-assertion of reason is as much needed to explain the events in the social world as the assumption of gravitation is necessary to account for the natural world.[77]

---

[77] Ms. 10a, p. 24.

A second major element in Green's moral psychology, as expounded in this 1868 manuscript, is that man will recognise the same force directing his own willing in the work of reason as exhibited in the objective social world. Green's position ultimately does not seem tenable in that he insufficiently specifies what is and what is not to be seen as 'self-assertions of reason'. Consequently he is forced to accept that everything existing is good and rational. He can only avoid this unacceptable conclusion at what really seems too high a price, i.e. to distinguish between more and less adequate 'manifestations of reason' in the objective world. Without a further criterion by which to distinguish adequate self-assertions from less adequate ones, moral criticism of the existing social order is reduced to mere guesswork. This is, in summary form, the very same dilemma which Green's published ethical doctrine leaves unresolved.[78]

Morality and Politics[79]

In Chapter III, Section C an account was offered of Green's mature social philosophy. This account made sufficiently clear that morals and politics are closely related: moral duties and legal obligations have a common basis in that they equally contribute to the realization of the moral ideal. In the manuscript presently under consideration Green expressed himself more explicitly on the role of the state with regard to morality than in his published academic lectures.

Green begins the relevant paragraphs by refuting two misconceptions of the relationship of morals and politics. Whereas law and morality indeed constitute two separate fields, the two are 'not to be opposed as if there were not a moral obligation to obey the law,' Green says.[80] Legal regulations are characterised by a certain sanction to enforce the law if need be. Nevertheless their enforceable nature is by definition redundant in the sense that each obligation thus enforced ought to be done spontaneously by the moral agent. Note however that for Green the notion of a 'moral obligation to obey the law' signifies above all a certain respect for the law as a necessary institution required to help bring about the realization of the moral ideal. To abide by political obligations is

---

[78]   Cf. Chapter II and Chapter V, Section C.
[79]   This issue is also addressed in Lecture 'A' of *Political Obligation*.
[80]   Ms 10a, p. 28; the following quotations without footnote references are taken from this same Ms page.

done primarily out of respect for the law and it is thus primarily in this derivative sense that good citizens obey any specific legislative measures.

A similar misconception with regard to the relationship of morals and politics is the suggestion that legal and moral obligation differ in that the former are 'external' obligations in the sense that they are imposed on the individual by society, whereas moral imperatives are prompted by one's own conscience and are thus 'internal'. Green sets out to refute this suggestion by pointing out that both forms of obligation originate in the mutual recognition of certain claims on the part of individual agents. The difference, then, between moral duty and political obligation simply consists in the fact that, owing to the enforceable nature of political obligation, certain categories of activity are beforehand unfit to be subject of this form of obligation.

> ... since [a] magistrate can neither ascertain [the] disposition from which [an] act proceeds, nor determine it ... he properly confines himself to [the] prohibition or injunction of acts the commission or omission of which would interfere outwardly with [the] freedom of others, i.e. would prevent [the] free development & expression of good disposition.

However, as emerges from the sequel of Green's lecture, the ulterior standard by reference to which political obligation derives its rationale consists in its contributing to the 'inward' freedom of the individual citizen. Inward freedom is described as the 'state in which reason, as principle of self-determination in [the] individual is determined by a rational motive.' Something of the political implications which Green draws from this 'inward' mode of freedom emerges when he specifies the said 'rational motive' as 'a motive upon which everyone might act consistently with [the] organic well-being of society'. This, he then goes on to say, only means that 'reason as self-consciousness of [the] will of [the] individual is at one with [the] reason which orders the moral world.'

Green's conclusions with respect to the limitations set by the nature of morality to any form of state interference do not essentially differ from the exposition in his later professorial lectures on *Political Obligation*.[81] No doubt the major supplement to the later exposition of his argument on this point con-

---

[81] *Political Obligation,*sect. 15.

sists in the four specific arguments why government is nevertheless involved in moral issues.

> This limitation does not at all imply that [the] law — or [the] State as [the] author of law — has 'nothing to do with morality'. On [the] contrary; (1) outward freedom which it secures is of value just as [a] necessary condition of inward freedom . . .
>
> (2) [The l]imitation of its office is prescribed just with [a] view to its moral end. Its end being the disposition of freedom as above defined, [there is all] the more reason why it should not present [an] inadequate motive, sc: [a] motive in which fear is [an] ingredient.
>
> (3) The removal of obstacles to free development & expression of good disposition means really much greater action on [the] part of [the] Government (supreme or municipal) than exists. [This] does not at all mean that it leaves every one to do as he pleases, so long as he does not pick pockets &c. [A g]reat obstacle to such free development is disease & as [the] conditions of disease — specially in connection with [the] mode of work & housing — come to be better understood, [the] office of the state, under [the] limitations aforesaid, seems almost indefinitely to extend.
>
> (4) How about [the] relation of [the] state to education & religion? [the former] ought to keep its hands off [the] promotion of opinion, so far as opinion affects or is affected by good disposition. [It m]ay provide for teaching natural science. [The] mode in which a man receives his views about the stars does not affect his disposition. [There is, consequently,] no danger of his doing [a] right act from [an] unworthy motive because the state teaches him this. But an opinion about God and the manner of his revelation does so relate to moral life that such an opinion adopted from any but the highest reason — as when there is any interested motive to its adoption — is a vitiated motive. This [is] the ultimate ground of [the] objection to all State religions.[82]

These arguments fall essentially into three categories. Green's first point establishes that outward freedom is a necessary condition for 'inward' freedom. On this issue he thus exactly anticipates the statement about the relationship of the two forms of freedom he was to work up in his lecture on *Liberal Legislation*. Earlier in this chapter, we saw fit to criticize this position as inconsistent with the structure of his system of philosophy and his overall mode of argumentation.

Secondly Green mentions two important reasons against excessive state interference: the point about the need for a minimum necessary level of enforcement quoted above as number (2) comes in this category. This restriction also has a clear bear-

[82]   Ms 10a, pp. 28–30.

ing on Green's opinion on the part the state has to play in education and its relation to religion, as emerges from number (4).

However, in spite of all these limitations set to governmental activity by the nature of morality, it is crystal clear that Green cannot but take an ambiguous view when discussing the danger of excessive legislation. Whatever may be thought of these inherent limitations, the third point quoted establishes beyond doubt that, for Green, the notion of 'removal of obstacles' may carry quite substantial forms of state interference in society. When it concerns the creation of the conditions required for the self-realisation of the individual, for Green, 'the office of the state . . . seems almost indefinitely to extend.'

E. Conclusion

This concludes my exposition of Green's earlier manuscripts on ethics and political philosophy, and with this account a first major part of the present study of Green is completed. This chapter started off from the problem that the best-known concept in Green's political philosophy, positive freedom, was known only in a limited and one-sided view. The concept does not appear in his published *Lectures on Political Obligation* and consequently it is not clear how it forms part of Green's system of philosophy. In the popular understanding of Green's political theory, positive and negative freedom are therefore likely to be set over against each other as two opposing and irreconcilable renditions of the idea of freedom. The exposition of such a system of philosophy, as we set out in Chapter One on the basis of the manuscript translation of the *Propädeutik*, makes clear how an idealistic philosophy of consciousness provides us with a comprehensive perspective which allows for a more congenial interpretation of the relationship between positive and negative freedom. The exposition of some of the themes in his earlier manuscripts on ethics and political philosophy can be taken to support the suggestion that Green was indeed thinking along these lines. In particular, the relationship between morality and politics comes out more crystallised than would appear from the published Green.

The importance of such an exercise by far exceeds the need for an adequate interpretation of Green thinking. For, on the basis of the preceding reconstruction of the metaphysical basis of this familiar doctrine, it is possible to come to a far more powerful defence of Green's idea than has so far been levelled against the extensive criticism which was made of Green, either implicit or explicit. This claim will be worked up in Chapter Five. But, prior to this rejoinder to Green's posthumous critics, I first want to place my entire study of Green in a broader perspective by situating his political theory in the historical context in which it was developed and in which it sought to intervene. This forms the subject of the next chapter.

Chapter IV

Theory and Practice

By its very nature political theory is developed to meet some major political questions of the age in which it operates. Any political doctrine therefore requires some account of the political and socio-economic environment in which it was originally developed and applied so as to come to a full understanding of it. Green's theory of positive freedom is no exception. Having elaborated in the previous chapters the intrinsic link Green construed between idealist metaphysics and political theory, thereby situating his political theory and his concept of positive freedom in the context of his general philosophical system, we may now turn to the actual environment in which this doctrine was employed and attempt to reconstruct the problem Green sought to resolve with his theoretical intervention in the course of mid-Victorian England.

Such a reconstruction falls into two parts. First, it involves some account of the fundamental change occurring in the actual political and socio-economic condition of England in the mid-Victorian age and the new ideological needs which it involved. Second, we need to explore Green's views on utilitarianism, which was the social theory in vogue in the 1870s. According to Green, utilitarianism could not meet these new ideological requirements. Together these two factors form the background against which we need to understand Green's theoretical intervention in nineteenth-century British politics.

In Green's opinion the social condition of his times was characterized by a discrepancy between theory and practice. The practice of social reform was ahead of the social theory by reference to which these reforms were defended. The sort of affairs Green saw as desirable could not well be defended on the basis of an argument proceeding from utility. And, to the extent that social reforms had already been carried through, in spite of the absence of any sound theory to support them,

Green held that these reforms were not likely to endure. For this reason he viewed it as his task further to support and thereby to sustain the trend towards ever increasing state interference by formulating a more compelling theoretical defence of it than had been possible on the basis of utilitarianism, the social philosophy current at the beginning of his academic career.

The present chapter is structured in line with this two-fold problem statement. It will give some account of the political condition of England in the mid-Victorian age (Section A). It will then provide a further analysis of Green's views on the relationship between theory and practice (Section B). It will be pointed out that Green, while he apparently allowed for theory to lag to a certain extent behind developments in practical politics, nevertheless firmly believed in a strong connection between theory and practice in the sense that the absence of adequate theory in his time constituted an obstacle to further social reforms. Third, the chapter will provide an account of Green's actual criticism of utilitarianism (Section C). It will appear that, in the same way as his own positive doctrine, Green's criticism of utilitarian social philosophy flows from certain metaphysical considerations. Green's criticism on this point again triggers an investigation into the validity of his claim as to the limited range of goals in public policy that could be defended by classical Benthamite utilitarianism. Such an investigation, in turn, calls for an inquiry into the 'logic' of utilitarianism. In order to come to a balanced view of the state of affairs of liberal political thinking in the earlier half of the nineteenth century, it is important to distinguish between the 'logic' of classical Benthamite utilitarianism and the doctrine of *laissez faire*, which in terms of its practical results coincided in the main with classical Benthamite utilitarianism, but which in some respects could nevertheless be said to be diametrically opposed to it. This will be undertaken in Section D.

In addition to reconstructing in this way the problem Green sought to resolve with his doctrine of positive freedom, it will be pointed out in Section E that Green drew from his criticism of utilitarianism a number of practical inferences which are rather more significant than might be expected on the basis of the version which was eventually published.[1]

Finally, in order to make intelligible the full significance of Green's metaphysics, Section F will draw attention to a number of features in which a later generation of utilitarian theorists, such as John Stuart Mill, can be said to have anticipated Green's position. Mill was inspired by a similar reforming zeal as Green and for that reason sought to revise classical Benthamite utilitarianism so as to avoid the unsatisfactory results which it produced. According to Green, however, what Mill lacked, preventing him from a more satisfactory revision of classical Benthamite utilitarianism, was an adequate metaphysical foundation such as Green had found in idealism.

A. Politics in Mid-Victorian England

Electoral Reform

In 1859, the satirical magazine *Punch* published a cartoon in which Britain, portrayed as a sleeping lion, was prodded by three men with red-hot iron bars.[2] On each bar was the word 'Reform'. One of the men was John Bright, the Radical politician, who for many years had been agitating for parliamentary reform and for whom Green had great admiration.[3] In the two other men readers recognized the Whig leader Lord John Russell and the Conservative Disraeli. The cartoon provides a telling image of one of the major political issues dominating the British political scene in the 1860s. It brings out the central place occupied by electoral reform in the middle years of the nineteenth century as well as the persistent attempts which were being made by all political parties to bring about some sort of reform of the current electoral system. It was, however, not until the year 1867 that the Reform Bill was proposed which eventually became law.

An account of the circumstances leading to the passing of the 1867 Reform Bill logically starts with some reference to the arrangements of the earlier Reform Act of 1832 and the electioneering to which it gave rise. The earlier Act was the product of a unique alliance of a number of progressive forces of

[1] 'Professorial lectures,' Trinity Term 1879, Ms 20 Balliol College Library. This consists broadly of an earlier version of *Prolegomena*, Books III and IV.

[2] *Punch, or the London Charivari*, March 12, 1859.

[3] On Green's admiration for John Bright, see *Memoir*, p. xxiv.

heterogeneous signature, whose combined efforts affected all other political affairs in the two decades after Waterloo. But the eventual result proved a disappointment to many of those who had been involved in the Reform agitation. As was pointed out by a twentieth century historian:

> The discrepancy between the exaggerated hopes and lofty aspirations of those who backed the Bill and the realities of the Act's achievements betokened future instalments of reform: and that is perhaps the chief importance of the Act. It offered a taste of reform and whetted the appetite for more . . . it set a precedent for changing even the most antiquated and traditionalist of institutions by legislative action.[4]

In fact, the actual electoral arrangements of 1832 left much to be desired. It was still a man's property, rather than his person that was represented in Parliament. The extension of the franchise amounted to less than a fifty percent increase and the redistribution of seats, although remedying the worst of the old anomalies, was soon outdated by the continued process of urbanization. In order to prevent the forms of corruption, to which the earlier electoral system was liable, the Act prescribed electoral registration as a technical qualification for voting. But this system of registration merely opened the door to new and more intricate methods of corruption.

The workings of the mid-Victorian electoral system were well satirized by Charles Dickens in his *Pickwick Papers*. His description of the corrupt political practices at Eatanswill were, of course, greatly exaggerated but, if not characteristic of all mid-Victorian electioneering, it was sufficiently vivid a satire to bring home the defects of the electoral system as it was left by the 1832 Reform Act. By the time the cartoon delineated above was published in *Punch*, few Englishmen considered the provisions of the current system as final. The central issue was no longer whether or not the older electoral system was to be reformed but to what extent the electorate should be increased. This question seemed to immobilize parliamentary proceedings in the 1860s. As late as 1866, when Russell and Gladstone proposed a very moderate extension of the vote, it brought down the Whig-Liberal government. Green's correspondence with his family provides us with an account of his

---

[4]   David Thomson, *England in the Nineteenth Century*, Harmondsworth, Middlesex, 1950, p. 75.

opinions on this administration, which held office from October 1865 to June 1866.

> It is the best ministry we have had, but I fear too good to last. A gov[ernmen]t with a conscience in the present state of lassitude is likely to have a hard time.[5]

While the issue of electoral reform is perhaps more naturally associated with the policies of Whigs and Radicals, it was left, paradoxically, to Disraeli to bring in the Bill which eventually became law. It was generally felt that the Conservative government had 'dished the Whigs' and that the Liberals had lost the most popular plank in their platform. However, together with some of his more enlightened fellow Liberals, Green could not help approving the Bill, as it was eventually passed, especially since a number of the safeguards were dropped with which Disraeli had sought to guarantee a moderate electoral arrangement.[6]

> On such a question it is idle to talk of who wins or who loses. The winner in no party, whig, conservative, or radical. The whole nation wins by a measure which makes us for the first time one people. We who were reformers from the beginning, always said the enfranchisement of the people was an end in itself. We said ... that citizenship only makes the moral man; that citizenship only gives that self-respect, which is the true basis of respect of others, and without which there is no lasting social order or real morality. If we were asked what result we looked for from the enfranchisement of the people, we said, that is not the present question. Untie the man's legs, and then it will be time to speculate how he will walk.[7]

Green correctly saw that a more democratic electoral procedure would produce further substantial reforms in the field of social welfare legislation. In fact, the two processes amplified one another. Throughout the nineteenth century there was a constant interplay of extensions of the franchise and the development of social legislation. In view of all governmental concern for the welfare of the working classes it was not logical to deny them a say in governmental matters and, conversely, once these classes were represented in parliament, questions of social improvement were better attended to. For Green, it

---

[5]   Nettleship's Ms notebook on the Green papers, Balliol College Library; cf. *Memoir*, p. xlv.
[6]   Cf. E.L. Woodward, *The Age of Reform, 1815–1870*, Oxford, 1938, pp. 178 ff.
[7]   Speech at a dinner of the Wellington Lodge of Odd Fellows, February 1863, quoted in *Memoir*, p. cxii.

was therefore no coincidence that most issues relating to welfare legislation, which had been on the Liberal agenda for many years, were not finally settled until after 1868, when the first genuinely democratic House of Commons was elected. In so far as factory legislation were concerned, the beginning of which dated back until long before the 1860s, these earlier measures did not yet lay down a universal system. The system of factory legislation was perfected only after 1868. As to other instances of social welfare legislation, such as statutes relating to public health and education, the correlation between their being effectively settled by legal arrangement and the inauguration of a democratic parliament is more obvious since none of these matters were satisfactorily dealt with by legal arrangement until after 1868.[8]

Factory Acts and Public Health Legislation

The political condition of Green's age can be characterized by the new trend towards collectivism in public affairs. Throughout Victoria's reign there was a slow, but steady development of legislation seeking to regulate affairs which, in earlier periods, had been left to the free play of market forces. This new kind of legislation was chiefly on conditions of labour, public health, education, and land reform, for which areas binding regulations were laid down. In an earlier stage these things were mostly left to private initiative. As a general rule this new kind of legislation was intended to intervene in agreements involving individuals, or parties in society, which, according to Liberals of Green's generation, were not in the position to look after their own interests. As a result, these new Liberals feared, these people stood to lose by the free play of market forces.

To the extent that it brought about a state of affairs which the Liberals held to be desirable, the new trend towards collectivism carried an obvious theoretical dilemma, to which attention was already drawn in our discussion of Green's political speech at Leicester: while an earlier generation of liberal reformers had been able to refer to a consistent set of liberal principles so as to support their proposals for reform, the policy options for Liberals of Green's generation directly contradicted these classical liberal principles. The first two chief

---

[8]   'Liberal Legislation and Freedom of Contract,' *Works*, iii, pp. 368–9.

governmental measures in the field of factory legislation were the so called 'children's charter' of 1833 and the Ten Hours Act of 1847. These first two factory acts had two common features: first, both measures provided for the appointment of factory inspectors to see to it that the new regulations were being observed; second, both laws sought to restrict the number of daily working hours which children were allowed to work.

In the long run the former point was perhaps the more fundamental achievement. The logic of the latter point may be explained as follows. In this early stage, all proposals to regulate the conditions of labour proceeded from an appeal to humanity and such an appeal found the best response when made about children. However, in most branches of industry the number of children employed by far outnumbered the adults so that a restriction of the daily hours of work compelled the stoppage of the entire process of production.[9]

What the Reform Bill of 1832 was to later extensions of the franchise, these two factory acts were to all further extensions and refinements of the legislation as to the conditions of labour. The working of the Ten Hours Act was restricted to textile factories but in subsequent years its principles were extended to other branches of industry. Similarly, progressive extensions in 1860, 1864 and 1867 of the legal definition of what constituted a 'factory' produced an increase of the number of workers protected under the factory acts.

Alongside the persistent call for compulsory regulation of the conditions of labour, there were similar attempts to improve the living conditions of the urban working classes. One of the indirect consequences of the industrial revolution was a rapid process of urbanization, brought about by the new mode of production. Owing to the large-scale character of these demographical changes, the living conditions in the new industrial slums were deplorably bad, a state of affairs which progressively deteriorated as years went by. Lack of proper sanitation caused various epidemics of cholera, the last of which was as late as 1865–6. Edwin Chadwick's Public Health Bill of 1848 was carried under the pressure of an outbreak of cholera, too. However, Chadwick's public health legislation proceeded from the principle of permission, not compulsion to act. It was not until 1871 that its regulations were effectively implemented when, in the aftermath of the latest cholera epi-

[9]   Cf. *ibid*. p. 370.

demic, the Local Government Board was set up, which had the necessary powers to compel local authorities to make certain sanitary provisions.

Educational Reform

Although Green was much concerned with all forms of social welfare legislation, there were two issues in which he was interested in particular, i.e. educational reform and the temperance question. Green was engaged in the first topic in various ways. He served as an assistant commissioner on the Schools Inquiry Commission and throughout his life he was active in the organization and improvement of local education at Oxford.[10] Green's findings were incorporated in the final report of the Commission and formed the basis of the Endowed Schools Act of 1869. This act was part of a series of legislative measures intended to change the educational system as a whole. Central to this entire process was the Education Act of 1870 which dealt with elementary education. The act finally settled a uniform system of education to the age of thirteen for the entire country. Until that time there was no national system of education. The main reason for this remarkable omission in the social organization of mid-Victorian society was religious. Until 1870 there was a network of voluntary schools paid for by private subscription and organized according to the religious denominations of the founders. These so called National Schools were supported by a small government grant. The chief obstacle to a further extension of this grant was that such a move would antagonize the Dissenting denominations which were less organized in the majority of the rural areas.

The Education Act of 1870 provided a workable religious compromise. It doubled the grants for existing schools and introduced publicly controlled schools in areas where no education was provided on a voluntary basis. These new schools were to be governed by popularly elected School Boards. As to religious instruction, the new Board Schools were to abstain from any denominational teaching. In this manner an obstacle

[10]   For an account of Green's activities in the field of educational reform, see *Memoir*, pp. xlv–lviii, cxiii ff.; cf. Green's public lectures on this subject: 'The Grading of Secondary Schools,' delivered to the Birmingham Teachers' Association, 1877; 'The Elementary School System of England,' 1878; and 'The work to be done by the new Oxford High School for Boys,' 1882. *Works*, iii, pp. 387–476.

was removed which for many years had prevented the introduction of compulsory elementary education. Until the dispute about subsidies was settled, it was not practicable to make attendance everywhere compulsory. But once the funds were raised to set up schools in those areas where no voluntary schools were as yet set up, one could finally move to a system of universal compulsory elementary education, as was implemented in 1880.

A product of Gladstone's first cabinet, the 1870 Elementary Education Act did not please too many dissenters in the Liberal party. In fact, this act marked the first weakening in the position of this Reform cabinet.[11] Green was not altogether satisfied with the Act either, but whereas the grievances of the nonconformists centred on the Act's provisions in regard to religious instruction, Green's objection was of a more general nature and regarded the degree to which it laid down compulsory regulation. In this respect Green thought the act to be 'wholly insufficient'. Green set out his position in two lectures on 'The Elementary School System of England,' delivered at the Liberal Hall, Oxford, in February 1878. 'The authors of the act,' he complained on that occasion,

> seem only to have looked at one of the faults of the system already in operation. They allowed their attention to be concentrated solely on the palpable fact of its insufficiency for providing schools in the less favoured districts, and in their hurry to remedy this evil, did not consider that the plan which should supply schools most quickly might not, in the long run, be the best for the education of the country.[12]

Temperance[13]

The other public question which interested Green deeply was the problem of liquor traffic and its regulation. He took an active part in the solution of this problem.[14] Green's stand on matters of temperance is remarkably extreme. The licence system relating to the sale of alcohol is one of the chief realms of legislation to which Green sought to apply the principle of positive freedom in his speech on *Liberal Legislation*. This constitutes a form of state interference in which he was prepared

---

[11] R.C.K. Ensor, *England 1870–1914*, Oxford, 1936, p. 33.
[12] *Memoir*, p. cxiv.
[13] See for this topic also Nicholson, *The Political Philosophy of the British Idealists*, pp. 177–80.
[14] For Green's activities in the temperance movement, see *Memoir*, p. cxv.

to go to a considerable length in restricting individual liberty for the well-being of the lower social classes.[15]

In order to situate this sort of Liberal policy in a party-political context it must be pointed out that the champions of this kind of restrictive measure and their adversaries largely coincided with the cleavages between the two main political parties. The Liberals under Gladstone were noted for their efforts to take away every temptation to excessive drinking,[16] whereas the Conservatives on the whole represented the interests of the brewing companies and their shareholders, and this division in British party politics grew more obvious as years went by.[17]

In view of the older Whig tradition in the Liberal party, this was a most remarkable development. For, in an earlier stage of industrialization, the Whigs drew a substantial part of their following from the ranks of the rising industrial classes. But under the Evangelical influence which came over Liberal politics in the Gladstone era, a clear antagonism developed with the commercial interest, which, as Green cynically remarked, 'is fattening upon the evil, and of course doing all it can to disguise it.'[18] In reaction to the Liberal support for the temperance lobby this matter developed into an issue which increasingly came to colour other political affairs in the final decades of the nineteenth century.

Having thus provided some account of the wider political and social context in which Green's doctrine of positive freedom was to operate, we may now go on to consider Green's criticism of utilitarianism, the social theory in vogue at the time. The best introduction to Green's views on this point is to give some account of his ideas on the relationship of theory and practice.

B. Theory and Practice in Green's Thinking

The preceding chapter has highlighted the importance Green attached to matters of practical politics. In fact, Green always looked to the practical impact of a theoretical stand. The fact

---

[15] 'Liberal legislation,' *Works*, iii, pp. 382–6.
[16] Although, of course, not all policians and adherents of this party were as strict as Green, as can be gathered from his controversy with Sir William Harcourt, a Liberal M.P. for Oxford. See *Memoir*, p. cxvii for details.
[17] Cf. Ensor, *England 1870–1914*, pp. 22 ff.
[18] *Memoir*, p. cxvii.

that a theory was likely to produce adverse practical results would be sufficient reason for him to seek to refute it. Green's criticism of utilitarianism distinguishes between utilitarian political theory and utilitarian ethics. This difference in his assessment of these two species of utilitarian theory can also largely be explained in terms of the difference in their practical effects. For Green, the argument based on utility could hardly produce adverse results as long as it is applied to matters of public policy. A utilitarian theory of morality, on the other hand, is likely to be abused in order to justify selfish conduct.

Green's assessment of the practical dangers inherent in a utilitarian theory of morals can also be seen from the concluding book of *Prolegomena*. A somewhat new element which this later publication added to the analysis of his political speech on *Liberal Legislation* is that this danger tends to increase as people grow more accustomed to the use of theories to defend their private conduct. Green observed that, according as this feature grew more obvious, theories of human conduct ran the risk of being applied and interpreted for the agent's own benefit. Green's point, then, was that a theoretical construction as easily applicable as the hedonist calculus was more open to abuse than the 'ethics of perfection' which he developed in *Prolegomena*.

> It is not to be expected, however, in an age of intellectual emancipation, when a scientific test of right action has been announced which is in itself easy intelligible . . . , that educated men will fail to employ it in their judgments of what they individually should do and should not do. Having got to the water, the ducklings will swim.[19]

This is not to play down the beneficial effects which, on the whole, utilitarianism has brought about. To the extent it was applied to problems of public policy the argument based on utility did produce sound results. As Green readily admitted,

> . . . no other theory has been available for the social or political reformer, combining so much truth with such ready applicability. No other has offered so commanding a point of view from which to criticise the precepts and institutions presented as authoritative.[20]

The positive result of utilitarian social theory consists predominantly in the 'wider and more impartial range to public spirit'

[19] *Prolegomena*, sect. 335.
[20] *Ibid.*, sect. 329.

it provoked.[21] By emphasizing the quest for 'the greatest happiness of the greatest number' utilitarian social theory was bound to have a positive impact on the norms and policies of the day.

The Status of Theories of Human Conduct

The remarkable feature of Green's point of view concerning the merits and practical value which utilitarian political theory has shown in the past is that it could produce beneficial results despite its falling short of an adequate analysis of the well-being of society, an analysis which must be in one way or another the ulterior standard from which any doctrine of politics proceeds.[22] Thus, it is in a sense *in spite of* its defective qualities as a theory that it produced sound reforms. And, if this is a correct rendering of Green's point of view, it would seem that in his opinion earlier social and political reforms were not carried through because of any special merits on the part of utilitarian theory. On that account its beneficial results would be a matter of mere coincidence.

For a better understanding of this point we must take account of Green's views on the status of theories of human conduct, their relation to practice, as well as their relation to earlier, authoritative doctrines on the same subject. All these issues were matters in which Green's position was to a great extent shaped by his early study of Hegel. Rather than a matter of positive results achieved in spite of an untenable theoretical position, the effective workings of utilitarianism were related to the specific characteristics of the historical period in which it operated.

If we recall the Hegelian influence on Green's philosophical development, it is no surprise to find that, for Green, any social theory is determined by the historical conditions of the community it addresses. In the case of a utilitarian social theory these conditions involved the substantial inequalities which characterized English society in the earlier decades of the nineteenth century. These inequalities mostly concerned a number of archaic privileges from earlier centuries, the rationale of

---

[21]   *Ibid.*, sect. 332. As to the possible adverse practical effects of utilitarian moral philosophy, see *Prolegomena*, sects 333 and 335; but see also the qualification made in 336. The merits of utilitarian theory are set out in Book IV, Chapter 3, especially sects. 329–335. Cf. *Political Obligation*, sect. 23.

[22]   *Prolegomena*, sects 332–3.

which had long since disappeared. Given this state of affairs it was possible for utilitarianism, with the strong egalitarian implications of its hedonist calculus, to produce real improvements in spite of its lack of an adequate analysis of the well-being of society.[23] Since inequalities had assumed such vast proportions in early nineteenth century England, even an insufficient qualification of the common good to be pursued sufficed to produce improvements to society as a whole. In other words, the existence of vast forms of inequality in England in the earlier decades of the nineteenth century constituted a precondition for the effective functioning of classical Benthamite utilitarianism as a social theory. It was for this reason, in Green's opinion, that Bentham's doctrine was to produce such remarkable results.

However, as utilitarianism was more successful in reforming various legal statutes and institutions sustaining the inequalities of the British political system, it was eliminating the conditions for its own effective working. On the basis of this analysis it readily appears why Green thought in the end even utilitarian political theory had to be replaced by a better theory providing a more adequate insight into the nature of the common good in society, such as did his own. In order for public policy to be further pursued utilitarian precepts had to be replaced by idealist political theory.

Green provides his theory to support a certain tendency which was in fact already in the process of materializing, partly brought about by utilitarian inspired reforms, partly by the autonomous working of the moral ideal, which he presupposes behind all moral activity. On the basis of this observation a conclusion may be drawn concerning the status of theories of conduct in Green's thinking.

According to Hegel's famous allegory, the Owl of Minerva does not begin its flight until the fall of dusk. To foretell the future course of events, human understanding will always be too late. The philosopher's task, then, is not to predict, but to reflect upon and understand what exists to facilitate further developments. Green largely endorses this view. Strictly speaking, it is already presupposed by the very attempt to formulate a more adequate theory of politics which was Green's professed object. And, in fact, this view is implied throughout his work. The most explicit statement to this effect is to be

[23] *Ibid.*

found in his essay on 'Popular Philosophy in its Relation to Life,' where Green concluded that

> ... man, above all the modern man, must theorise his practice, and the failure adequately to do so, must cripple the practice itself.[24]

An essentially similar line of argument emerges from the way in which he explains the intention of his political speech. On that occasion Green observed that the modern generation of Liberals in fact approved of an extensive system of legal restrictions. This paradox must be understood in the original meaning of that word, i.e. an apparent contradiction which disappears on closer analysis. Given that state of affairs, Green thinks it appropriate to spell out the principles on which the new generation of liberals actually supported these restrictive legal measures.

> Here, then, is a great system of restriction, which yet hardly any impartial person wishes to see reversed; which many of us wish to see made more complete. Perhaps, however, we have never thoroughly considered the principles on which we approve it. It may be well, therefore, to spend a short time in ascertaining those principles. We shall then be on surer ground in approaching the more difficult questions of legislation which must shortly be dealt with, and of which the settlement is sure to be resisted in the name of individual liberty.[25]

It follows that, for Green, to formulate theories and principles of conduct at once codifies existing practice and provides new practical guidance. This is, as it were, the other side of Green's position on the relationship of theory and practice. He apparently holds that developments in practical politics may anticipate the formation of theories to support them. This is, for example, the case with the modern trend towards 'equity,' a principle which would seem to have found general recognition in contemporary Europe. As Green pointed out:

> The fabric of European society stands apparently square and strong on a basis of decent actual equity, but no adequate rationale of this equity is generally recognised.[26]

Green pointed to three surrogate doctrines which, in his view, have so far performed the task which could only be well performed by a more adequate philosophy of life. These surro-

---

[24] *Works*, iii, p. 124.
[25] *Ibid.*, p. 370.
[26] *Ibid.*, p. 117.

gate practical philosophies he saw at work in the contemplative poetry of Wordsworth, and the recent revival of Evangelical religion, as well as the conception of freedom and rights as propagated by Rousseau. However, as the conclusion of Green's essay makes clear, these three sources of inspiration were not a substitute for the philosophy of life which British public life needed so badly.

We may thus conclude that Green saw an adequate theory of conduct as a necessary requirement for sound practice. At the same time he points out unequivocally that all practical philosophy is continuously and unavoidably rendered out of date by progress in actual conduct, moral as well as political. In his *Prolegomena* he makes this point in so far as the formation of moral philosophy is concerned:

> . . . the best practical philosophy of any age has never been more than an assertion of partial truths, which had some special present function to fulfil in the deliverance or defence of the human soul. When they have done their work, these truths become insufficient for the expression of the highest practical convictions operating in man, while the speculative intellect, if enlisted in the service of the pleasure-seeking nature, can easily extract excuses from them for evading the cogency of those convictions. But the remedy for this evil is still not to be found in the abandonment of philosophy, but in its further pursuit.[27]

The fact that, when lagging behind actual developments in practice, theory may have an adverse effect on further developments is pointed out in Green's first lecture on *Political Obligation*, where he makes this observation with respect to the doctrine of *laissez-faire*, a theory which initially helped to further genuine reforms, but which was rendered out of date in the mean time.

> The laws which it has helped to get rid of were really mischievous, but mischievous for further reasons than those conceived of by the supporters of this theory. Having done its work, the theory now tends to become obstructive, because in fact advancing civilisation brings with it more and more interference with the liberty of the individual *to do as he likes*, and this theory affords a reason for resisting all positive reforms — all reforms which involve an action of the state in the way of promoting conditions favourable to moral life.[28]

---

[27] *Prolegomena*, sect. 312.
[28] *Political Obligation*, sect. 18.

We may conclude that, like Hegel, Green holds that it is not for theory to lead the way for practice. Nevertheless, practice requires theoretical activity. The social theorist has an essential part to play with regard to the development of practice in that he must clear away inadequate theories, which are rendered out of date, so as to make further development of practice possible.

As long as the political condition of England was characterized by widespread formal inequalities, utilitarianism was an appropriate political doctrine. It was its very success, however, which rendered utilitarian social theory superfluous. The new period required a doctrine capable of moving beyond equality, so that it could be used to defend a positive interference with the living conditions of those parties in society which were not in a position to look after their own interests. Such a positive interference would provide the conditions needed for each individual agent to realize any specific capacities or talents he possessed.[29]

C. Green's Criticism of Utilitarian Social Theory

We shall now seek to come to a further understanding of Green's doctrine of positive freedom by considering the theoretical context in which he took a stand with this new term to be introduced into the political vocabulary of his time. For a full understanding of Green's doctrine it must be linked with his criticism of utilitarianism.[30] Rendered in its most general form, Green's criticism of this doctrine was that its simplistic presuppositions disregarded the essential nature of man and human activity. Proceeding from the view that any motive may be reduced to a calculus of the pleasure and pain involved in alternative modes of conduct contemplated, the utilitarian gives an intolerable simplification of human life.

A direct consequence following from this criticism is that utilitarianism is unfit as a moral theory. In the same way as was demonstrated in relation to so called 'natural ethics,'[31] utilitarian premises do not allow for moral activity properly so called. And, whereas he held a much less categorical opinion with respect to the merits of utilitarian political theory, Green

---

[29] *Works*, iii, p. 372.
[30] Criticism of utilitarianism was a force propelling and unifying idealism. See also P. Robbins, *The British Hegelians, 1875–1925*, New York, 1982, p. 47.
[31] See Chapter II, Section A.

also found a number of limitations inherent in the application of the utility criterion to political matters: it has a certain conservative bias, it is better suited to back electoral reforms than more substantial forms of social improvement, and it tends to focus on more readily quantifiable interests at the cost of other interests. The first limitation inherent in the workings of utilitarianism as a theory of reform was that it involved a structurally conservative bias. Green's point was that, as certain effects were more difficult to measure in terms of pleasure and pain, they were easily underrated in Bentham's hedonistic calculus. This argument applied in particular to cases in which common interests of the community at large had to be balanced against concrete interests of the individual. In these cases there was an inherent tendency to underrate the amount of public interest in favour of the individual interest which conflicted with the common good. Green envisaged such an inherent bias as a result purely of the fact that the public interest in these cases was less tangible than the concrete interests of a single individual involved.

The second point follows from this analysis. Eventually, utilitarianism failed even as a political theory, because it was better equipped to back reforms in the formal structure of the political system than to serve as a theoretical basis for more substantial forms of improvement of the 'condition of England'. Green's argument on this point is closely related to his earlier point on the working of the hedonist calculus. In his view, it is inherent in this mechanism that it will systematically tend to underrate effects which are by their nature more difficult to quantify. As a result the hedonist calculus will systematically belittle this kind of interest. In weighing the common good against various individual interests this will easily benefit the latter category.

Green's third point was that hedonism favours more readily quantifiable matters such as a person's preference for a certain candidate in an election. This sort of quantity is easily divided per individual person and for this reason the hedonist calculus will constitute an irrefutable argument for equal voting rights for all citizens. In these instances the logic of utilitarianism will invariably point towards a more egalitarian electoral system. However, in weighing different kinds of interests, which Green considered to be equally important, such as the introduction and extension of factory legislation, the relevant advantages of these legal measures are less easy to quantify.

Metaphysical Foundations of Green's Criticism of Utilitarianism

It was suggested earlier in this chapter that the noticeable difference in Green's assessment respectively of utilitarian political and moral theory may be understood in terms of the difference in their practical results. However, in order to gain a full understanding of Green's criticism of utilitarianism, it must be linked with the systematic feature of his philosophy. Previous chapters, it will be recalled, emphasized the intrinsic connection between his idealist metaphysics and each of the separate realms of his system of philosophy. In the same way as he construes his own system of philosophy on the basis of a certain kind of metaphysics he looks upon utilitarianism as hinging on a fixed set of first principles.

In Green's view there was a distinct link between these first principles, on the one hand, and the various separate theoretical realms covered by utilitarianism, on the other. Similarly, Green's criticism of the various doctrines belonging to the family of utilitarianism proceed on a criticism of their metaphysical assumptions. If we accept Green's argument that a certain metaphysical stand is inevitable, and that, as a consequence, every philosophical position necessarily rests on certain assumptions by way of first principles, it follows that utilitarianism and Green's idealism may be viewed as two systems of philosophy in their own right, which parallel one another in each of their separate domains: over against a theory of morality based on the general argument of utility, idealism puts its own doctrine of morality, just as the idealist doctrine of politics has its counterpart within utilitarianism. The two systems do not touch anywhere, though they do come very near in their political theory. In his lectures on *Political Obligation* Green observed, for example, that utilitarian political theory 'may be presented in a form in which it would scarcely be distinguishable from the doctrine just now stated.'[32]

On the basis of the view of the relationship of idealism and utilitarianism as two parallel systems of philosophy one could

---

[32]   *Political Obligation*, sect. 23.

explain the difference in Green's assessment of these two respective theoretical realms of utilitarianism by pointing to the difference in the nature of the two respective forms of human activity of which they seek to give a theoretical rendering. While intrinsically related, political and moral activity are yet clearly distinguished. The principal difference between these two forms of human activity is that moral duty is above all a matter of conscientious decision on the part of the individual moral agent, as opposed to political obligation which in principle does not take account of the motives behind people's actions. It follows from this that the latter form of obligation may, whereas the former, by its very nature, may *not* be enforced by political authority.

The principal reason for the success of the utilitarians in the field of political theory is that, from the point of view of political obligation, human activity is only regarded in terms of its outward conduct. In the field of theories of politics, people's motives are at best only indirectly relevant.

Green and Utilitarian Political Theory

According to Green, rights derive their rationale entirely from the fact that they constitute a necessary precondition to rendering moral activity possible.[33] Political activity and the institutions created to facilitate and structure it, such as rights enforced by the state authority, are ultimately to be justified on the ground that they constitute a kind of legal framework within which moral activity becomes possible. This constitutes an intrinsic link between any form of political activity and all instances of moral activity.

At the same time it will be remembered that there is also an important difference between moral duties and political obligation in the sense that the latter kind of commitment by its very nature does not set any specific qualifications as to the motive from which the act is done.

This difference in the nature of moral and political activity, which was reflected in an essential difference between ethical and political philosophy, may also be called on to explain the difference in Green's criticism of each of the utilitarian equivalents of these two realms of inquiry. According to his own positive doctrine, an agent's individual conscience constitutes an

[33] *Political Obligation*, sect. 25.

integral part of any ethical judgment properly so called, while conscience is by definition irrelevant from the perspective of political obligation. As utilitarianism cannot account for individual conscience, a utilitarian theory of morality must be doomed to failure on *a priori* grounds. Utilitarianism must therefore be taken to be an inadequate theoretical basis for any ethical theory.

However, since conscientious judgments do not form part of political obligation this same feature of utilitarianism need not preclude the possibility of a theory of politics based on the argument of utility. At the same time, however, utilitarianism did not grasp the ulterior reason of political life. It did not understand the deeper rationale of public activity and public institutions like the state and the system of rights structuring political life.

Later Utilitarians

Again, for an adequate understanding of Green's position on this point it should be kept in mind that his criticism of utilitarian social theory applies predominantly to its classical version as it was most authoritatively formulated by Jeremy Bentham. It may be said that Green found the arguments made by later representatives in the utilitarian tradition, such as J.S.Mill and Sidgwick, less erroneous than utilitarianism in its classical Benthamite version. An indication of this may be found in the fact that, with regard to these two latter theorists he goes to the trouble of discussing their arguments in detail in the course of his *Prolegomena*, an honour which is not bestowed upon the classical variant of utilitarianism. Carrying this point further, one might say that theorists like Mill and Sidgwick were prompted by essentially the same objections as Green held against classical Benthamite utilitarianism. The later utilitarians fail in that they do not move altogether outside the general theoretical system of utilitarianism. They just do not base themselves on an adequate metaphysics.

D. The Logic of Classical Liberal Political Theory

Liberal political thinking in England in the first half of the nineteenth century can roughly be divided into two categories, viz. the classical variant of utilitarianism as it was put forward by Bentham, and the political doctrine of the classical political economists, which for present purposes may be summed up in the term *laissez faire*. It was argued earlier in this chapter that Green's theoretical intervention in the contemporary political debate was to be situated against the dual background of an ever increasing volume of social legislation, on the one hand, and the incapacity of the current social theory to provide a compelling theoretical basis for these social reforms on the other. In order fully to elaborate this thesis it would be helpful to analyse the state of current social doctrines against which he thought it necessary to take a stand.

Such an elaboration of the social theory in vogue when Green started his academic career seems all the more opportune since classical Benthamite utilitarianism and *laissez faire*, while they share a number of common features, do not merely differ in intellectual origin, but are moreover fundamentally opposed to one another in terms of the 'logic' of their respective theories.

The Argument Based on Utility Does Not Imply Individual Liberty

As was pointed out, the psychology of classical Benthamite utilitarianism proceeds from a single basic criterion, viz the amount of utility to be expected from a certain contemplated act. 'Good' and 'bad' are rendered in terms of resulting quantities of utility which can be computed by means of hedonist calculus.

It follows that the argument based on utility is in principle neutral as to the question of what is to be taken as the most desirable extent of freedom in society to be allowed to the individual. As both criteria are fully independent, considerations based on either of them do not necessarily run parallel to one another and may occur in any combination. If, for example, we disapprove of a certain act on the ground that it does not contribute towards the greatest possible sum of happiness for the greatest number of people enjoying it, such a judgment does not tell us anything about its effects on the range of individual freedom of the agents concerned. Strictly speaking, Bentham's social theory does not carry any appreciation of individual freedom itself. For him, freedom is not of intrinsic worth. It is valuable only in so far as it produces pleasure. Freedom is desirable only as a means of increasing the volume of utility; and it is with reference to this ulterior standard that classical

Benthamite utilitarianism attaches value to individual freedom.

This conclusion leads to a further one. It follows that in
terms of the logic of classical Benthamite utilitarianism, law by
no means needs to be seen as a necessary evil. The fact that in
practice this is what classical Benthamite utilitarianism comes
down to is not so much inherent in its 'logic,' as a result of certain further implicit norms and tacit assumptions with which
Bentham clothes his theory.

Laissez Faire Closely Linked with Freedom

Taking a *laissez faire* position and attaching intrinsic worth to
individual freedom are far more intrinsically linked. While it
is true that — strictly speaking — *laissez faire* carries no normative implications for an assessment of individual freedom it
naturally tends to regard freedom as something desirable. As
a social doctrine it therefore carries an inherent bias against
state interference which it looks upon as interference in the
self-regulating mechanism of human interaction, and is consequently dismissed as counterproductive and objectionable.
Rather than attaching a normative value to individual freedom itself the argument based on *laissez faire* runs directly
counter to the idea of state interference which Green sought to
provide with an adequate theoretical defence.

It was argued that, in terms of its theoretical structure, classical Benthamite utilitarianism is capable of being employed
as a theoretical foundation on which to defend social legislation. It follows from this assessment of the logic of Bentham's
argument that the problem statement from which Green set
out to develop his innovation of the concept of freedom,
requires to be revised in the sense that there is no such thing as
a necessary restriction involved in the theoretical structure of
classical Benthamite utilitarianism that would prevent it from
being employed as an argument to support any form of social
legislation. There is nothing in terms of the logic of its theory
which forces us to conceive legislation and measures of government as a necessary evil.

But even if this were to prove a fully correct analysis of the
state of affairs of contemporary political theories prompting
Green's theoretical intervention, a further argument may be
levelled against classical Benthamite utilitarianism. This is
that it proceeds from a standard other than the actual one on

the basis of which it is to be decided whether some act or measure is or is not socially desirable. In other words, even if Green can be shown to be mistaken in his analysis of the 'logic' of utilitarian social philosophy it still remains for him to criticise theorists of Bentham's generation for unduly orienting themselves on the basis of the amount of pleasure and pain to be produced by a certain contemplated action or measure of state interference, whereas the real point at stake is the common good or the well-being of the community as a whole. At the same time, this is the only conceivable standard by reference to which one may judge the propriety of any such act or measure. Seen from this perspective it will be clear that any other criterion must be inferior.

While there is nothing in the theoretical structure of classical Benthamite utilitarianism on which to base such a view, all legislation, including social reform, assumes a negative character which will prevent it from ever developing beyond the level of a necessary evil or the lesser of two evils. This bias results from a number of Bentham's tacit assumptions and implicit norms. These assumptions and norms come to the fore in the manner in which the theory was applied in the earlier decades of the nineteenth century. While it thus follows in no way from his theoretical stand, there can be no doubt about the fact that Bentham looked upon legislation as a necessary evil. In this manner his theory assumed a certain bias in favour of a minimal extent of legislation, including social legislation. Viewed in this light Green's claim that classical Benthamite utilitarianism was less suited as a theoretical basis to support social legislation becomes intelligible.

As regards the argument based on *laissez faire*, the same conclusion was already drawn and we need only comment here on it briefly. The notion of *laissez faire* diametrically opposes the notion of state interference and as such Green would seem to have rightly taken it as an obstacle to an easy acceptance of a more active role to be played by the state in creating and sustaining the conditions for certain social desiderata.

E. The Professorial Lectures on Utilitarianism

So far we have been engaged in the present chapter in reconstructing the context in which Green's doctrine of positive freedom was intended to operate. We have spelled out the implications of the theoretical enterprise Green envisaged as well as the — largely implicit — presuppositions as to the relationship between theory and practice which Green can be shown to make. In the last paragraph it was argued that a number of these presuppositions are perhaps less evident than Green would like us to believe. It follows from this investigation that we would have good reason to query a number of Green's assumptions, which he would need in order to prove the practical relevance of his theoretical enterprise.

There can be no doubt, however, about the fact that Green actually did take his criticism of utilitarian social and political theory to have a bearing on the political practice of his age. Green's assessment of the practical relevance of his theory may be gathered from a number of hitherto unpublished manuscripts, which will be presented in this section.

A number of manuscript sources could be quoted here to show that Green was highly aware of the possible abuses to which any theory of politics is open. Perhaps the most explicit single statement to this effect is to be found in the following quotation, taken from a collection of miscellaneous lecture notes from Green's professorial period.

> Political parties [are] det[ermine]d by interest & situation, not by theory. They are always glad, however, to turn theories to acc[oun]t, & those who deal in theories sh[oul]d be on their guard ag[ain]st these being so used.[34]

The Practical Relevance of Political Theory

Green's first series of professorial lectures were delivered over the three terms of the academic year 1878–1879. The argument of these professorial lectures follows in broad outline the structure of the final two books of *Prolegomena*. In regard to his criticism of utilitarianism two arguments are adduced which demand attention. First it is demonstrated by means of a criticism of a number of details of the general argument based on utility that Green's own social theory is 'intrinsically truer'.[35] But he found it important to refute the pretensions of utilitarianism also on the point of its allegedly ready applicability. Having demonstrated the inadequacy of the utility criterion as

---

[34] Ms 'Notes A — E,' section D, p. 3.
[35] Professorial lectures, delivered in the Trinity Term of 1879, catalogued as Ms 20, 'On Utilitarianism,' p. 78. Together with Ms 24 this completes the text of the three series of professorial lectures entitled 'The Theory of Virtue,' which were delivered in the 1878-9 academic year.

a basis for a social theory, Green therefore goes on to argue that his own doctrine also forms 'a better guide to conduct' than any variety of utilitarian social theory whatever.[36] The principal objection which can be levelled against utilitarianism in practical terms is that it 'tends to become egoistic in application,' owing to the 'impossibility of carrying out a complete and impartial calculus of [the] pleasures to be expected fr[om] an act.'[37]

In order to present this part of Green's unpublished professorial lectures I propose to begin by reproducing a statement to bring out explicitly his view that the practical effects of a utilitarian social theory is likely to be more harmful when it is applied to questions of private morals.[38]

> This danger of deleterious consequences fr[om the] Util[itaria]n theory, so far as it takes pleasure on the whole to be [the] end by ref[erence] to wh[ich] Utility is to be tested, is likely to become more apparent as the theory comes to be applied more to questions of private conduct as distinct fr[om] questions of public policy & as the habit of asking for a rationale of our institutional judg[men]ts in regard to the former become more prevalent.[39]

In the professorial lectures Green makes two explicit points which may be linked to this argument: first, he gives an argument concerning the relevance of political theory in general for political practice; second, he specifies the reasons why utilitarianism eventually must fall short of an adequate political theory. As to the first point, he concludes:

> Just so far . . . as man's judgment comes to be affected by qu[estion]s in regard to the ultimate goal in political progress, truth in the theory of [the] ideal, as distinct fr[om] devotion to an ideal, becomes of practical importance.

Green's second point in this connection, the inadequacy of utilitarian political theory, is further elaborated in a number of specific conditions which must be taken to be indispensable for the effective appeal to an argument based on utility. By means of this method of argument Green seeks to explain the earlier successes of utilitarian social theory as well as its pres-

---

[36] Ms 20, p. 78.
[37] *Ibid.*
[38] In a modified form, this opinion also found its way to the published version of *Prolegomena*, sect. 324.
[39] Ms 20. All subsequent indented passages in the present section reproduce parts of this manuscript.

ent inadequacy. In order to make this last point, it suffices to show that the various conditions specified no longer hold.

The limits of possible political applications of utilitarianism are most urgently felt in connection with present pressing 'questions as to the laws and institutions of States & Churches.'

> In regard to questions of public policy also . . . issues may come to be raised wh[ich] will necessitate a more thorough consideration of w[ha]t is meant by [the] "greatest happiness of [the] greatest number" than practical Util[itaria]ns have given & will exhibit the inadequacy of [the] Hedonistic interpretation [of] it. So long as the obj[ec]t of pol[itical] progress c[oul]d be sufficiently described as [the] equality of all men before the law, or the removal of restraints wh[ich] were equally impediments to pleasure & to noble living on the part of those affected by [th]em, it did not much matter how [the] common good was conceived. It was enough to insist [that] it sh[oul]d really be *common* — the good of [the] greatest number. But now [that] equality before the law has been pretty well established in middle & western Europe; now [that] everyone is coming to be recognized as having a title to take part in the direction of [the] powers of society; further qu[estion]s arise as to [the] end to wh[ich] those powers sh[oul]d be directed . . . the difficulties wh[ich] reflecting & disinterested men feel in regard to the claims of [the] great causes & movements that affect modern society turn on questions as to the nature of the social good wh[ich] is to be sought for.

From this passage one of the conditions for the effective operation of the argument based on utility may be derived, a condition which does not occur either in the lectures on *Political Obligation* or *Prolegomena*. In order for utilitarian political theory to function properly it requires a certain degree of formal or juridical inequality. In view of the radical egalitarian implications of a political theory based on the principle of utility it is eminently suited as a theory of reform in such political conditions. But since inequality must be taken as a precondition for its effective use, it follows that utilitarianism, in a sense, is digging away the ground from under its own feet.

Political Culture in Britain and Germany

A further condition for the effective operation of a utilitarian theory of politics may be derived from the sequel to Green's argument. It appears from his treatment of utilitarianism in the professorial lectures that the successes utilitarian reformers had had so far in England were to an important extent to be attributed to the homogeneous nature of the British political culture. According to Green, England enjoyed such a solid constitutional tradition that a theory like utilitarianism could hardly have produced any adverse effects. It is for this reason, presumably, that he observes in regard to the above mentioned 'questions as to the laws and the institutions of States':

> In England these qu[estion]s are not yet br[ough]t into such distinct relief as elsewhere. There is at any rate some excuse for holding [that the] difference between L[iberals] & C[onservatives] is chiefly that betw[een] the Ins & Outs.

But in political systems lacking a strong constitutional tradition the case is altogether different. Apart from newly founded nations such as the United States,[40] Green is thinking of the political conditions in contemporary Germany, which, in his assessment, require a more substantial political theory than utilitarian concepts could provide. Applied to such a parliamentary practice, utilitarianism would, in Green's view, produce fatal results.

A comparison of England and contemporary Germany in respect of the applicability of a political theory based on the principle of utility gives the following picture:

> ... a cultivated German has to face a much deeper pol[itical] division − that between Liberalism, Ultramontanism & social Dem[ocra]cy, & [the] issues represented by these names are so far reaching that he can hardly decide betw[een] them on suff[icien]t grounds without considering [the] nature of [the] ultimate social good. It w[oul]d scarcely be true to say [that] each of these parties represents a diff[eren]t view of such good, but their claims can scarcely be measured without some decision ab[ou]t it.

In elaborating the question as to how the argument based on utility is employed by the various political parties in contemporary Germany, Green allows us an insight into the way in which he assesses the three chief continental political movements.

> The S[ocial] D[emocrat] pleads his cause in the name of [the] greatest happiness of [the] greatest numbers. He p[oint]s the way to an equalization of enjoyment as goal of social progress − to be attained by enlightenment as to [the] impediments to such equal[ity] & combined effort for their removal. The Catholic equally points to general pleasure as [the] end but to this as attainable truly by complete submission to [the] supposed commands

---

[40] *Political Obligation*, sect. 85.

of God conveyed thro[ugh] the Church — i.e. by complete abdica-
tion of the autonomy of the will. The Liberal looks to general 'culture' as the end & tho[ugh] the meaning of 'culture' is not very
definite, it seems to involve much, as commonly understood,
wh[ich] contributes rather to the balance of pain over pleasure,
than v[ice] v[ersa].

Apart from this little comparative study of the workings of the
parliamentary system in England and Germany at the time,
this passage provides us with a fuller insight into Green's
ideas on the relation of theory and practice. Generally speaking his argument is that utilitarianism can do less harm in England than in countries like Germany because of the more
homogeneous culture to be found in the former country. England's long constitutional tradition will act as a safeguard, so
to speak, preventing any political theory, including utilitarianism, from trespassing beyond certain boundaries. It sets
broad limits to all political activity. It forms the broad outline,
as it were, within which political life takes place and it keeps
any political theory from radical lapses.

We may conclude that, in his unpublished professorial lectures on utilitarianism, Green held some distinct and remarkable views on the relationship of theory and practice.
Ordinarily speaking, theory is taken to fulfil a certain prescriptive function in setting norms so as to direct practice. And, as
can be shown from the earlier reconstruction of the necessary
character of Green's theoretical enterprise, he seems to adhere
to this view, too. For, in order to render plausible this necessity, it would seem that one must attribute at least a minimal
prescriptive function to political theory. The argument set out
in the present section would rather seem to show the opposite;
or do we have to conclude that Green's views on this point are
coloured by a touch of British chauvinism?

Green's next step is to work out the reason why, in each of
the three cases mentioned, utilitarianism would not produce
the appropriate results. In the case of the continental equivalent of the liberal movement this fact is perhaps less obvious
since the concept of 'culture,' which German liberals made
their political end, at first sight seems compatible with the
results of a calculus of the pleasure and pain involved in the
various policy options.

We delude ourselves into thinking that more 'culture' means
more happiness because when we ask ourselves whether we
w[oul]d exchange the exp[erien]ce of the life of 'culture' with all

the pains of susceptible temperament, of unsuccessful effort, of baffled hopes wh[ich] it involves for that of contentment without culture, we cannot but answer *no*. But this does not show that it involves more pleasure on the whole even for those who do so prefer it, than others, who are not capable of preferring it, find from the life of uncultivated contentment.

The fact that utilitarianism actually seems capable of identifying the proper policy options may be explained by pointing out two 'unwarrantable assumptions' on which such a view can be shown to proceed. As is set out in a note overleaf, which Green added to the text, such a view takes for granted:

> (1) [that a] life of culture is preferred by those who seek it simply for [the] sake of [the] greater pleasure anticipated fr[om] it;

> (2) that their anticipation of greater pleasure fr[om] it is a proof [that] more pleasure is gained fr[om] it than fr[om] the life of uncultivated contentment. If having tried both, with *equal capacities for enjoying both*, they then preferred the former, & if the preference were det[ermine]d simply by [the] pl[easant] exp[erien]ce, then & then only the inference w[oul]d be valid.

These assumptions, Green goes on to say, are neither warranted nor are they ever considered by those who are guided in their political activity by the precepts of utilitarianism. For this reason Green considers himself to be justified in concluding that the applicability of utilitarian social theory, as it is being employed by liberals in Germany, is merely apparent. In addition, he repudiates the very idea that the ideal of 'culture' would always and automatically coincide with the pursuit of happiness.

> Still less does it show [that] the conditions favourable to [the] 'culture' of society — a culture of wh[ich] only the minority can ever partake — conduce [the] greatest happiness [e.g. = quantity of pleasure] of [the] greatest number.

Such are Green's conclusions as to the possible use of utilitarian concepts by the liberal movement in Germany. In view of Green's own political preferences it is little wonder that this exposition of liberal politics is somewhat more subtle and more differentiated than his assessment of the possible use of utilitarian social theory to support the Catholic ideal:

> On the whole it w[oul]d be difficult to dispute [that] a society, in approaching [the] Catholic ideal, w[oul]d exp[erien]ce more pleasure — when the balance with pain had been struck — than it w[oul]d in approaching any ideal wh[ich] those who resist

> Catholicism in the name of 'culture' have to offer. It does not fol-
> low [that the] Catholic ideal is the higher. On the contrary, if it
> offers general happiness thro[ugh] the means of a loss of autono-
> mous character, it is offering that which (if our theory is true) is of
> no moral value at all. But it becomes important for those who
> oppose Catholicism in the name of a diff[eren]t social ideal to con-
> sider what it is that is of real [ultimate] value in their ideal.

In order to assess the precise nature of each of these political
movements a deeper understanding of political activity is
needed than utilitarian concepts allow for. In working out the
specific points by which a utilitarian theory of politics would
produce something short of an adequate perspective on current political problems, Green again allows us an interesting
gloss on each of these three political positions, which he sees as
three partial views of the national political life in Germany.

> We cannot fairly estimate [the] tendency of social democracy,
> wh[ich] seems to sacrifice [the] possibility of disinterested
> ind[ividua]l initiative to [the] diffusion of enjoyments, without
> deciding whether [the] value of character is relative to pleasure,
> or v[ice] v[ersa]; [we cannot fairly estimate the tendency] of
> Catholicism without deciding whether [the] autonomy of [the]
> will wh[ich] it seems to suppress, is or is not of intrinsic value;
> [nor can we fairly estimate the tendency] of Liberalism [without
> deciding whether the] 'culture' wh[ich] it seeks to promote has
> real value as the condition of a higher develop[men]t of society —
> higher as measured by the [free] self-devotion to each other's per-
> fection of [the] ind[ividua]ls composing it.

We may conclude from these unpublished professorial lectures of Green's that he drew far more explicit conclusions
from the theoretical dispute with utilitarianism than might be
expected from the published version of this text. But, perhaps,
the reason for this noticeable difference between his position
on the practical relevance of social theories in his published
and his unpublished work should not be sought too far. One
may conjecture something along the following lines. In his
Prolegomena, which was composed with a view to publication,
Green must have been much more cautious about the possible
effects his theory might produce than in his lecture notes. It
would seem that the smaller setting in which he was lecturing
at Oxford tempted him to let himself go and to say what he
really thought without feeling restrained by considerations as
to the possible abuse of his doctrine. In his published work he
simply seems more wary.

F. Green and Mill[41]

At the outset of the present chapter it was suggested that Green's theoretical intervention in the debate as to the expediency of state interference to regulate the conditions of labour and to enforce certain sanitary standards and social reforms, could be interpreted as a reaction to a certain disparity which he conceived between current theory and practice. Hence, it was attempted to come to a fuller understanding of Green's theoretical enterprise by situating his political doctrine against the dual background of the new trend towards collectivism in public affairs and the inability of the current social theory to meet the new ideological needs resulting from these developments. Apart from a summary description of certain outstanding features of this period in English social history, we were predominantly engaged in exposing and analysing Green's criticism of classical Benthamite utilitarianism. In this concluding section I propose to consider the relationship between the theoretical enterprise Green envisaged and the work of a leading theorist of a later generation of utilitarians, John Stuart Mill.

Such a comparison of Mill and Green will serve various purposes. First, it will make clear that Green was not alone in his criticism of the classical version of utilitarianism. A second point which emerges from a comparison of Mill and Green concerns the central position of metaphysics in Green's theoretical enterprise. According to Green, Mill's failure to produce a coherent theory is to be attributed to the fact that he did not proceed from a more adequate scheme of things. In view of his metaphysical criticism of utilitarianism, it is appropriate to consider Green's social philosophy as an attempt to give a consistent rendering of the socialist leanings which are to be discerned in the later work of Mill. In this way Green can be viewed as the first theorist to have produced a compelling theory of the modern welfare state.

A further result which readily emerges from a comparison of Green and Mill is the conclusion that the transition from the classical utilitarian position to the idealist view is not as abrupt as might be suggested by their juxtaposition. Apart from certain distinctly utilitarian features which were already

---

[41] Nicholson also makes a comparison of Green and Mill (and H. Spencer), *The Political Philosophy of the British Idealists*, Study V.

observed in Green's political theory there are at least two significant aspects to be discerned in Mill, in which he may be
said to have anticipated the position later occupied by Green:
first, there is Mill's position on state interference, to which he
became more favourably disposed as years went by; and second, his views as to the intrinsic value of liberty. For these reasons, which will be elaborated below, it may be concluded that
Mill occupied a position which in many ways kept the middle
between Bentham and other classical representatives of utilitarianism, on the one hand, and idealist social theory, on the
other.

Mill's Revision of Benthamite Utilitarianism

In his admirable portrait of Victorian England, G.M. Young
suggested that Bentham was among the two most influential
persons of the age.[42] But just as Bentham had a profound
impact on the Victorian mind, so the ever increasing criticism
of his point of view may rightly be seen as a characteristic feature of the intellectual climate in England in the nineteenth
century. A comparison of Green and Mill on this point will
make clear that Green was not the only theorist to criticize the
harsh logic of Bentham's schemes for improvement. Mill
undertook a revision of classical Benthamite utilitarianism on
similar grounds.

The impact of Bentham's ideas on Mill's intellectual growth
is as well-known as the extraordinarily young age at which he
was educated by his father. Having started to read Greek by
the time he was three, he was taken through a programme of
classical literature, history, law and political economy. Eventually his father made him read Bentham's *Traité de Legislation*
at the age of fifteen so as to conclude his educational scheme.
'When I laid down the last volume of the *Traité*,' Mill later
recalled in his *Autobiography*,

> I had become a different being. The 'principle of utility' under-
> stood as Bentham understood it, and applied in the manner in
> which he applied it through these three volumes, fell exactly into
> its place as the keystone which held together the detached and
> fragmentary component parts of my knowledge and beliefs. It
> gave unity to my conceptions of things. I now had opinions; a
> creed, a doctrine, a philosophy; in one among the best senses of
> the word, a religion; the incalcation and diffusion of which could

[42]   G.M. Young, *Victorian England: Portrait of an Age*, Oxford, 1936, p. 157.

be made the principal outward purpose of a life. And I had a grand conception laid before me of changes to be effected in the condition of mankind through that doctrine.[43]

However, despite the close personal links with Bentham and the profound indoctrination with Benthamite ideas in his early years, Mill's own mature philosophy differed from classical utilitarianism on several important points. To an extent, these deviations from earlier versions of utilitarianism were prompted by motives similar to those already pointed out to situate Green's criticism of utilitarianism in its proper context. Like Green, Mill was whole-heartedly committed to social legislation to mitigate the destructive effects of industrialization and consequently he was more favourably disposed towards state interference to achieve these purposes than Bentham had been. Mill too sought to work out a social theory which would provide a more adequate theoretical defence of state interference. But Mill's attempts to improve on Bentham made him rather less consistent than the philosopher who once provided the 'keystone' to his early training.

Mill was profoundly moved by the sufferings of the poor. He had a deep understanding of the social problems of his times and was convinced enough a reformer to feel the need for increased state interference. As is well-known, each subsequent edition of his *Principles of Political Economy* became more socialist. In this respect, Mill, better than any other theorist of his generation, embodied the revision which came over English liberal thinking in the course of the nineteenth century. Whereas the earlier editions of his *Political Economy* may be reckoned one of the purest statements ever given of *laissez faire*, he moved sufficiently towards the idea of state interference in his subsequent editions for Fabians later to recognise him as an early kindred spirit. And, in his *Autobiography*, Mill ranged himself 'decidedly under the general designation of Socialists.'[44]

Mill thus stood in a position towards classical utilitarianism which in many ways resembled Green's. The chief difference between them was that Mill never moved altogether outside the theoretical framework of utilitarianism, owing to which, in Green's assessment, his attempts to come to a better theoretical defence of state interference were bound to fail. In Green's

---

[43] *Autobiography*, London, 1874, pp. 66–7.
[44] *Ibid.*, p. 231.

opinion, utilitarian social theory was prevented from a more adequate approach by its hedonist psychology.

On Liberty

A further point on which Mill dissented from the classical version of utilitarian social philosophy is to be found in his stand on liberty, as it was set out in his influential essay bearing that very title. In this essay, of which he himself already foresaw that it would constitute his most permanent contribution to philosophy,[45] he seeks to make clear that individual liberty is to be taken as of intrinsic value.

Superficially speaking, one could interpret Mill's essay as an attempt to rest his belief in the intrinsic value of individual liberty on a utilitarian footing. The two main categories of individual freedoms which he distinguishes are analysed as being contributive to the common good. Freedom of thought and discussion must be seen as conditions for the free interplay of opinions, which again forms the best guarantee for truth prevailing. Freedom to act upon one's opinion, by its very nature, must be subjected to certain restrictions; but, by itself, it is presented in *On Liberty* as functional to the progress of society. By means of 'experiments in living' on the part of certain gifted individuals the greater masses of the population could be given an example, so that they, too, would benefit.

All this would seem to suggest that *On Liberty* is, in fact, an exercise in the philosophy of utilitarianism. But whoever reads Mill's essay carefully will come to the conclusion that, while it may have been the outward purpose to point to such a utilitarian foundation of individual liberty, Mill's little book in fact takes an entirely new course, hitherto unknown to the utilitarian tradition.[46] As was already indicated in the preceding section of the present chapter, there is no intrinsic link between individual freedom and the standard of utility. If we want to read *On Liberty* as a utilitarian tract, we inevitably fall into contradictions. But, what comes out irrespective of any such interpretation is the importance and intrinsic value Mill places upon individual liberty. This may be illustrated by his argument on freedom of discussion. Mill is no doubt much concerned with the question of truth when he defends the

---

[45] *Ibid.*, p. 253.

[46] Cf. G. Himmelfarb, *On Liberty and Liberalism: the Case of John Stuart Mill*, New York, 1974.

fundamental right of freedom of discussion. But eventually he defines truth in terms of liberty.

It was asserted that in deviating from an earlier generation of utilitarians as to his view on the intrinsic value of liberty, Mill could be said to have 'anticipated' Green's later stand and this claim still requires to be elaborated. When we are pointing out a common feature of Mill and Green on this point, it must be understood that it is not so much in terms of their being more favourably disposed towards measures of state interference. This claim rather seeks to draw attention to a feature of Green's work which keeps him at all times within the liberal tradition. And this same feature is also found in Mill's thinking, distinguishing him from all other utilitarians. It may be questioned to what extent Green, as the author of a theory of positive freedom, can insist on this point. In fact, as was explained in Chapter Three, ultimately Green's statements with regard to the importance and the intrinsic value of 'negative' freedom must conflict with the general structure of the argument about the self-realization of each individual agent and the positive interferences this may require on the part of the state.[47]

Be this as it may, both Mill and Green are too wholeheartedly attached to individual liberty as an end in itself to renounce it for the sake of theoretical consistency. This is surely to their credit. It was the same fundamental belief in the intrinsic value of individual liberty which held Mill back from ever becoming an unqualified supporter of Bentham, that also kept Green from a more dogmatic form of socialism.

In connection with their common attachment to individual liberty, it is interesting to point out that Green, while he always was most critical of Mill's theoretical position, nevertheless highly esteemed Mill's virtuous character. In the first series of 'open' lectures, which he delivered in the framework of an arrangement between Balliol and some of the other Oxford colleges, he once described Mill's position as 'absurdly inconsistent'; while Mill's essay *Utilitarianism* was characterized as 'a most Protean book'.[48] But he also alluded to some inverse relationship of the theoretical and moral qualities of the utilitarian social theorist, as we learn from the notebook of one of the students attending, F.H. Bradley:

[47] See Chapter III, Section B.
[48] *Collected Works*, vol. v, p. 158.

> So to speak there are Virtuous & Vicious Utilitarians. The Virtu-
> ous are inconsistent; they say they hold Utility but they don't; for
> they recognize Duty.[49]

A similar conclusion with regard to Mill emerges from his article on 'Popular Philosophy,' published shortly afterwards,
where Green wrote:

> ... the modern English utilitarian is generally better than his logic.
> In defiance of Hume and Bentham, he distinguishes higher and
> lower pleasures by some other criterion than that of quantity, and
> takes as the object to which 'expediency' is relative a 'good of oth-
> ers,' which involves his own. He is not practically the worse for
> failing to perceive that to live for such an object is to live not for the
> attainment of any sum of agreeable sensations, but for the realisa-
> tion of an idea, of which the philosophy that starts from feeling
> can give no account.[50]

According to Green, Mill is led to his revision of classical
Benthamite utilitarianism by his strong moral intuitions,
which cause him in many cases to reject as unacceptable the
outcomes of Bentham's hedonist calculus. For Green, it is
Mill's moral intuition which makes him look in the right direction for a solution to the problem of the superficial nature of
Bentham's doctrine. Mill's only problem is that he does not
have an adequate theoretical framework to sanction his moral
intuitions, a lack which eventually will have deleterious
effects on practice, as was explained in an earlier section of this
chapter.

G. Conclusion

This chapter has sought to place the intervention which Green
intended by his concept of positive freedom in a twofold context. In addition to a brief survey of the main issues on the
political agenda of his times, we have especially focussed on
Green's ideas on the relationship of theory and practice.
Although, like Hegel, Green believes that moral and political
theories will always be too slow to actually provide direct
practical guidance, they nevertheless can have an important
indirect function. Inadequate theories can thus become obstacles to further reform. In Green's view this was precisely the
case with utilitarianism, the dominant philosophy of his times.

---

[49] *Ibid.*
[50] *Works*, iii, p. 124.

On the basis of his first series of professorial lectures his ideas were spelled out in some detail.

In the following chapter I shall briefly consider the impact of Green's political doctrine on the theory and practice of the modern welfare state, in the first place in England, but also beyond its borders. I will then review a number of criticisms of Green's doctrine, to see whether any of the arguments levelled against him may be met by drawing from the reconstruction of this doctrine in the framework of his theoretical system which was undertaken in earlier chapters. We shall then be in a position to assess the continued relevance of Green's argument to the present day.

Chapter V

Positive Freedom
Revisited

We saw that Green attached great importance to considerations concerning the practical impact of moral and political
theories, including his own. Given this pre-occupation of
Green's, it seems entirely appropriate to conclude the present
book by considering the implications which may be drawn
from the reconstruction of Green's doctrine of positive freedom, set out above, for our present understanding of politics
and political theory.

A central thesis developed in earlier chapters was that
Green's political theory only became known in an incomplete
form. The standard interpretation which became known as
'Green's theory of positive freedom' merely represents a partial and one-sided view of his thinking on this point. As was
explained in Chapter Three, this part of Green's political ideas
became known chiefly through his 1881 political speech to the
Leicester Liberal Association. Given the nature of this meeting
it can hardly surprise us that Green did not elaborate on the
metaphysical foundations of his doctrine. What he presented
in his speech on *Liberal Legislation* must be seen as a number of
conclusions resulting from a more extended argumentation. It
was in order to provide a better insight into Green's thinking
on this point that previous chapters attempted to reconstruct
Green's notion of positive freedom as an integral part of his
theoretical system by drawing from certain primary principles.

Although Green's political doctrine thus only became
known in an incomplete manner, it did not fail to have a profound impact on the development of the theory and practice of
the welfare state in late nineteenth- and twentieth-century
Britain. Building on the ideas of his speech on *Liberal Legislation*, later generations of theorists elaborated the positive

notion of freedom. Apart from direct pupils of Green like Bosanquet, Ritchie, and Muirhead, we may mention the states- man and philosopher Viscount Haldane, and social theorists like Hobhouse, Laski, and Ginsberg in this connection. While they were more remote from Green in a number of respects, this latter group nevertheless clearly belongs to those thinkers who adopted the positive notion of freedom.

This school of thought, commonly identified as the new lib- erals, was to dominate English political thinking until the second half of the twentieth century.[1] It was not until the 1950s that the movement of positive liberals lost its momentum and conceptual criticism was levelled against the notion of positive freedom itself. The general tenor of this criticism was that Green's doctrine, while it was enlightened in terms of its politi- cal aims, was in need of repudiation since it illegitimately sought to employ the term 'freedom' for these political ends. But — in the same way as positive liberalism itself — criticisms of this doctrine were based on a popular version and, there- fore, an incomplete rendering of Green's views on this point.

In order to bring out the relevance of Green's doctrine for our present thinking about politics we must first find out how the restatement of his doctrine stands up against the argu- ments of his posthumous critics. To accomplish this task we shall consider the chief arguments which have been levelled against the popular version of Green's doctrine and see to what extent they affect the revised statement of his doctrine developed in earlier chapters of the present book. I propose to concentrate on the two chief publications with which the con- ceptual criticism of the notion of positive freedom set in: Maurice Cranston's book *Freedom: A New Analysis*, which was first published in 1953 and reissued in 1967 (Section B); and Isaiah Berlin's inaugural lecture to the University of Oxford, which was entitled *Two Concepts of Liberty*, delivered and first published in 1958 and included in his collection *Four Essays on Liberty* in 1969 (Section C). In order to bridge the period between Green's death in 1882 and these criticisms in the 1950s

---

[1]   For an intellectual biography of this movement see Andrew Vincent and Ray- mond Plant, *Philosophy, Politics and Citizenship: the Life and Thought of the British Idealists*, pp. 43–93. This same topic is also covered by Matt Carter, *T.H. Green and the Development of Ethical Socialism*, Exeter, 2003, pp. 53 ff. On the relevance of the movement for the debate on liberalism and communitarianism see Avital Simhony and David Weinstein, ed., *The New Liberalism: Reconciling Lib- erty and Community*, Cambridge, 2001.

we will first undertake a brief survey of the direct influence Green's doctrine exercised on theory as well as practice.

A. Positive Freedom in Theory and Practice, 1882-1950

In the same way as theory and practice had been interwoven in Green's thinking, the impact of his doctrine of positive freedom was to be seen in the field of practical politics as well as in the development of welfare state theories in the late nineteenth and twentieth century.[2] In order to illustrate Green's influence in matters of practical politics, mention must be made of a group of politicians who, closely following Green's political ideas, effected a more direct application of Green's teachings than is ordinarily the case with a theory of politics. Men like H.H. Asquith, R.B. Haldane and Herbert Samuel had an important share in the great social reforms which may be said to mark the beginning of the modern welfare state in Britain.[3]

The first name to be mentioned in this connection is that of his disciple H.H. Asquith, who was to become Prime Minister of the 1908-1916 Liberal government. Asquith matriculated at Balliol in 1870 and was elected fellow of the College in 1874. He was reported soon to have become 'an ardent admirer of Green, though more, perhaps, with regard to his social and political ideas than to his metaphysics, which always remained something of a mystery to the politician.'[4] Asquith, who began his public career as Home Secretary in the Liberal governments of 1892-1894 and 1894-1895, based his election address of 1892 upon Green's positive notion of freedom. 'I am one of those,' he told his audience on that occasion,

> who believe that the collective action of the community may and ought to be employed positively as well as negatively; to raise as well as to level; to equalize opportunities no less than to curtail privileges; to make freedom of the individual a reality and not a pretence.[5]

---

[2]   For Green's impact on practical politics see also Andrew Vincent, 'T.H. Green: Citizenship as Political and Metaphysical' in David Boucher and Andrew Vincent, *British Idealism and Political Theory*, Edinburgh, 2000.

[3]   Sources for the following survey of Liberal politicians are derived from Nicholls, 'Positive Liberty, 1880–1914,' pp. 124 ff.

[4]   J.A. Spender and C. Asquith, *Life of the Earl of Oxford and Asquith*, London, 1932, vol. i, p. 36.

[5]   *Memories and Reflections of the Earl of Oxford and Asquith*, London, 1928, vol. i, p. 113.

This statement was made relatively early in his political career, but Asquith's later speeches show that he essentially maintained these views on liberty to the end of his life.[6]

Another Balliol man in the new generation of liberal politicians was Herbert Samuel, who studied at the college from 1889 to 1893 and consequently was fully exposed to Green's influence.[7] The author of a book on *Liberalism*, Samuel adopted the positive notion of freedom to work out its practical implications for the politics of his day, just as Green had done in his 1881 political speech at Leicester with regard to the then disputed issues of Liberal legislation. Samuel's principal argument in his book was that although self-reliance and self-help are legitimate liberal principles and important in their own right, this does not conflict with the quest for state-intervention. The extension of the law need not reduce the realm of freedom, but can enlarge it:

> ... to support a policy of State regulation in industry is quite consistent with a belief in liberty, and not merely consistent with it but rather to be regarded as its necessary consequence.[8]

The Liberal Governments from 1892-1895 were considerably influenced by the idea of positive liberty as advocated by Green. In order to conclude this survey of Green's impact on practical politics, mention may be made of a group of Liberals including Haldane who, at a later stage, went over to the Labour Party. While they thus parted from the Liberal Party, they claimed to retain a belief in liberty as the prime object in politics. They saw the policy of the Labour Party as the logical outcome of the ideas of positive liberty which they had held as Liberals.[9]

The Development of Welfare State Theories

Through his impact on this new generation of Liberal politicians Green's ideas found direct application in the earlier stages of the welfare state in Britain. However, in the course of the present survey we are primarily interested in Green's significance for the development of theoretical arguments, for-

---

[6]   Herbert, J.B., ed., *Speeches of the Earl of Oxford and Asquith*, London, 1928, p. 308.
[7]   Nicholson, *The Political Philosophy of the British Idealists*, Study V on state interference compares T.H. Green, J.S. Mill and H. Samuel.
[8]   *Liberalism: Its Principles and Proposals*, London, 1902, p. 28.
[9]   This is extensively documented in Carter, *T.H. Green and the Development of Ethical Socialism*.

mulated in support of the new kind of social legislation. Green's doctrine of positive freedom found an important later exponent in his pupil Bernard Bosanquet, who was, from a philosophical point of view, no doubt Green's most important disciple. Bosanquet studied at Balliol from 1866 to 1870, where we find his name in a list of attending students which Green wrote on the cover of a manuscript notebook which he used for one of his lecture courses.[10] In distinction from a number of other pupils of Green, who found their academic career hindered by the unorthodox philosophical positions they defended, Bosanquet got to the honours list without any problem. He gained first classes both in classical moderations and in *literae humaniores*. He was then elected a fellow of University College, where he taught philosophy and ancient history. This employment kept him in Oxford until 1881 when he went to live in London and played an active part in the work of the Charity Organisation Society. He was editor of the project to translate Lotze's *Logic* and his *Metaphysics*, an undertaking in which Green also participated. In 1886 Bosanquet was involved in the constitution of the London School of Ethics and Social Philosophy. An important part of Bosanquet's later publications grew out of his popular lecturing, including the book in which we are most interested in the course of a survey of the theoretical impact of Green's doctrine of positive freedom. This was *The Philosophical Theory of the State*, Bosanquet's chief writing in the field of social philosophy. It was first published in 1899 and was reissued several times during his life. In 1920 he added a longish preface to the third edition in which he sought to answer the devastating criticisms of earlier editions of the work, criticisms which were largely inspired by the events of 1914–1918. In various crucial passages of his book he acknowledges that his doctrine is closely related to Green's; so closely, in fact, that he feels the need to explain in the original preface the reasons why he thinks an independent exposition to be desirable.[11]

Bosanquet's argument regarding positive freedom proceeds from an appeal to intuition and experience. Any object of desire an agent may contemplate is, by definition, a product of his will. But we all know that not every desire we may enter-

---

[10] MS 10a.
[11] *The Philosophical Theory of the State*, fourth edition, London, 1923, p. viii; cf. p. 128.

tain is capable of producing permanent satisfaction. In this consideration Bosanquet finds a standard in terms of which he is able to criticize existing objects of will. Reference to this standard allows him to distinguish between any given set of objects of will according to their being adequate to its nature. Bosanquet's theory of political obligation is set out in line with this rationalist theory of the will, but his position on political obligation assumes far more extreme dimensions than the corresponding part of Green's political doctrine.

> Any system of institutions which represents to us, on the whole, the conditions essential to affirming such a will [i.e. an 'adequate' will, in the sense explained — B.W.], . . . has an imperative claim upon our loyalty and obedience as the embodiment of our liberty.[12]

This argument is consistent as far as it goes. But the real question becomes as to which conditions are to be held 'essential'; and whether a given system of institutions indeed fulfils them. Whereas Green's work constitutes an important improvement on Hegel in that he emphasised the individual as an end in itself, Bosanquet's deviations from Green seem to move him back in the direction where Green started. Bosanquet's more consistent position is secured at the cost of much of the attention for the individual which kept Green at all times within the liberal tradition.

Perhaps this is best illustrated from Bosanquet's treatment of force, an exposition which can hardly be called oblique. This much, at least, we must concede to Bosanquet. According to the argument of his *Philosophical Theory*, the use of force is inherent in the working of the state; it is not just a matter of a necessary evil, a temporary shortcoming which may be overcome in due course:

> . . . the force of the State proceeds essentially from its character of being our own mind extended, so to speak, beyond our immediate consciousness. ....
> The State is the fly-wheel of our life. Its system is constantly reminding us of duties, from sanitation to the incidents of trusteeship, which we have not the least desire to neglect, but which we are either too ignorant or too indolent to carry out apart from instruction and authoritative suggestion.[13]

It may be concluded from passages such as this that when Bosanquet used Rousseau's famous dictum that one could be

---

[12]   *Ibid.*, p. 139.
[13]   *Ibid.*, pp. 141–2.

'forced to be free,' this was not just a metaphor for self-discipline, as Green might have used the phrase. What Bosanquet had in mind was the force of the state exercised by the police.

It is hardly surprising that Bosanquet's interpretation of Green's doctrine solicited much criticism and the general hostility towards the Hegelian leanings of his work was further aroused by the anti-German sentiments accompanying the war of 1914–1918. The name which first comes first to mind in this connection is that of the social theorist L.T. Hobhouse. While he was much influenced by Green's social philosophy and has rightly been classified as the 'paradigm case' of positive liberalism,[14] he nevertheless ranks as one of the fiercest critics of what he called 'the metaphysical theory of the state'. This was the very title of a series of lectures delivered at the L.S.E. in the autumn of 1917. One of Hobhouse's primary aims in these lectures was to refute Bosanquet, whom he saw as Hegel's 'most modern and most faithful exponent'. Perhaps the volume which was afterwards published is nowadays better known for its preface than its actual contents. Hobhouse dedicated the work to his son, an R.A.F. pilot, who was fighting Germany. In the same way as Karl Popper, who at the time of the Second World War identified Hegel as the originator of Germany's warmindedness, Hobhouse pointed to Hegel as the root of all evil in 1914-1918. In his Preface the author describes how he had been annotating the *Phenomenology of Mind* in his garden overlooking London during the air raids of 1917.

> In the bombing of London I had just witnessed the visible and tangible outcome of a false and wicked doctrine, the foundations of which lay, as I believe, in the book before me.
> ... With that work began the most penetrating and subtle of all the intellectual influences which have sapped the rational humanitarianism of the eighteenth and nineteenth centuries, and in the Hegelian theory of the god-state all that I had witnessed lay implicit.[15]

Hobhouse's criticism of Green is otherwise relatively mild. Green is primarily reproached for having reverted to a metaphysical basis on which to erect his political theory.[16] His own

---

[14]   Nicholls, 'Positive Liberty, 1880–1914,' p. 117.
[15]   *The Metaphysical Theory of the State*, London, 1918, p. 6.
[16]   *Ibid.*, p. 122.

political ideas correspond to Green's in a number of respects, as he acknowledges on various occasions.[17] The 'principle of harmony,' in terms of which he seeks to characterize the relationship of individual and state, largely coincides with Green's position on this issue as set out in his *Political Obligation*. In his later *Elements of Social Justice*, Hobhouse seeks to distinguish this 'principle of harmony' from too extreme forms of individualism as well as from collectivism. Without discounting the fact that no individual could do without society, the reverse is equally true and Hobhouse warns against the danger of neglecting the individual when the social nature of man is being emphasized:

> ... the character of a social whole is as much in danger of being misunderstood when it is resolved into the component individuals as it is when conceived as separate from them, as though it were not made by them. The true organic theory is that the whole is just what is constituted by the co-operation of the parts ...[18]

When directing our attention more specifically to Hobhouse's conception of freedom, it may be observed that although he adopts each of the separate elements on which Green's definition of positive freedom rests, he yet proceeds from an ordinary, empirical notion of freedom and conceives it as the state of not being interfered with by others and the ability to do what one wants to do, whether good or evil. Proceeding from this point of view, it follows that, in regard to the individual agent, freedom may well be opposed to legal regulations. Hobhouse's point, however, is that there is no necessary antithesis between freedom and legislation when society is considered as a whole. This also provides Hobhouse with his criterion for state interference. According to him, the state legitimately intervenes in society when it thus increases the sum total of human freedom.

Green's emphasis on self-realization in Hobhouse's hand assumes the form of a plea for the development of individual character as the ultimate end of politics. This must be, at any rate, the aim of any liberalism properly so called. When liberalism tries to avoid laying down imperative legal regulations, this is not so much because it is indifferent to individual well-being and the full development of everyone's faculties. True liberalism is rather characterised by its understanding

[17]   *Ibid.*, p. 96.
[18]   *Ibid.*, p. 129.

that the growth of personality of the individual by its very nature cannot be prescribed. This impossibility compels governments to restrict themselves to providing the means needed to give full scope to everyone's character.[19]

B. Twentieth Century Conceptual Criticism of Green

In this section I shall discuss the implications which may be drawn from more recent literature for Green's doctrine of positive freedom. Generally speaking Green's posthumous critics justify and subscribe to his political motives and find no difficulty with the norms and policy options he seeks to support. Green is nevertheless reproached, implicitly or explicitly, for having employed the term freedom for his political purposes. The tenor of the criticism of Green's doctrine is that, whereas his recommendations were substantially right, he should not have used the term freedom in pursuit of these purposes. Characteristic in this connection is Berlin's comment on Green's political speech in the Introduction to his collection *Four Essays*:

> As a plea for justice, and a denunciation of the monstrous assumption that workmen were (in any sense that mattered to them) free agents in negotiating with employers in his time, Green's essay can scarcely be improved upon.
> ... Green's views were exceptionally enlightened ... Nevertheless, words are important, and a writer's opinions and purposes are not sufficient to render the use of a misleading terminology harmless either in theory or in practice.[20]

By seeking to redefine the term freedom Green induced a 'confusion of values' in the eyes of this twentieth century critic.[21] Another writer looks upon his work as 'half-obscuring, half-illuminating' and takes his doctrine as a 'many sided, suggestive, but diffuse attack' on the negative concept of freedom in which 'the force of Green's criticism is weakened by a misguided attempt to change the meaning of "liberty"'.[22] Freedom remains freedom irrespective of whether it is desirable in

---

[19] *Liberalism*, London, 1911, p. 143. Note the striking similarity with Green's argument, cf. *Political Obligation*, sect. 15.
[20] Berlin, *Four Essays on Liberty*, p. xlix note.
[21] *Ibid.*, pp. lvi, xlix and 133.
[22] Weinstein, 'The Concept of Liberty in Nineteenth Century British Philosophy,' p.150.

given circumstances, we may summarize the twentieth century criticism of Green; nothing is gained by conceptual confusion. Moreover, what Green has to say may easily be said
without all this terminological confusion.

In the opinion of the present writer, however, the arguments
of twentieth century theorists of freedom tend to neglect an
important point. In order to bring out the merits of the various
positions on freedom I want to outline a hypothetical discussion between Green and later theorists of freedom.[23] In order
to supply material for this discussion, I will begin by summa-
rizing the essentials of the theories of Cranston and Berlin; I
will then proceed to consider the implications to be drawn
from these two writers and establish the extent to which the
'genuine statement' of Green's doctrine set out in Chapter
Three throws a new light on these arguments.

Cranston's New Analysis

In reviewing the work of Cranston I will restrict myself to his
exposition about the meaning of freedom, which is the subject
of the first of the three parts of his book. In this initial part
Cranston sets out to undertake two things: first he aims at contributing to what he calls a lexicographical definition of freedom; second, he inventories a number of theories of freedom
from the history of political philosophy in order subsequently
to assess to what extent they may be considered as legitimate
descriptions of freedom.[24]

By a lexicographical definition Cranston intends all descriptions 'which report what words mean conventionally, what
people commonly mean when they use them'.[25] To establish
such a lexicographical definition of freedom he employs two
methods of argument. In addition to a piece of linguistic analysis he appeals to what may be seen as the authority *par excel-
lence* in disputes concerning the meaning of a word: the
dictionary. The chief conclusion of this part of his inquiry is

---

[23] One of the methological problems which we will encounter in the course of
such an enterprise is inherent in the attempt to survey the various interpreta-
tions of the concept of freedom which have been defended. Nicholson, *The
Political Philosophy of the British Idealists*, p. 131, compares the dichotomy
between positive and negative freedom to a Procrustean bed whereby a con-
fused debate is projected back into Green, who is subsequently charged with
being inconsistent and obscure.

[24] *Freedom: A New Analysis*, p. 28.

[25] *Ibid.*, p. 24.

that the term, as long as it is not further specified, does not carry more than a partial meaning. The only distinct common feature of all specific meanings, given to the term in everyday life speech, is that freedom is always a matter of absence of restraint. Distinct forms of freedom differ according to the kind of restraint which they imply. For the sake of clearness of our conversation, we should always make clear from which restraint or force we feel freed when we talk about freedom.

In connection with the second part of his investigation Cranston distinguishes between two kinds of definitions. In addition to lexicographical definitions he also distinguishes stipulative definitions, which are in a later stage further distinguished according to whether they are of a persuasive nature. Given that stipulative definitions are arbitrary by their very nature, it follows that only lexicographical definitions can be tested as to whether or not they are correct. 'True' and 'untrue' simply do not apply to stipulative definitions. This is not to say that this latter kind of definition is never appropriate: whenever a lexicographical definition is 'too vague' or 'too indefinite' a stipulative definition may be very useful.

This, then, provides the clue to the only sort of question which can appropriately be asked concerning stipulative definitions, i.e. whether they are useful or not. This criterion is subsequently operationalized in terms of whether any given stipulative definition helps to diminish the ambiguity of the conventional meaning of a word. In aid of his intended inventory of theories of freedom he then lays down two rules with which any sound stipulative definition needs to comply:

> 1. All *other* definitions should be repudiated, since the proliferation of different meanings for the same word must increase ambiguity, and thus aggravate the confusion which stipulation was intended to end.
>
> 2. A new meaning should not be stipulated for a word if another word has that meaning conventionally.[26]

These are to be seen as two minimal requirements which all stipulative definitions need to satisfy. Whenever a definition of freedom fails to meet either of these points, this constitutes a reason to reject it as unsound.

Cranston's method of investigating and assessing the various definitions of freedom can be summarized as follows. He

---

[26] *Ibid.*, p. 26.

begins by establishing whether any given definition must be seen as a lexicographical definition or a stipulative definition. If a lexicographical definition is concerned he goes on to inquire whether it is true or false; in the case of a stipulative definition he considers whether it satisfies the rules for sound stipulative definition.

From the history of political ideas Cranston singles out fourteen theories of freedom. The theories selected suggest a division into three categories: the notion of freedom as a faculty, freedom as government by reason, and enforceable rational freedom. The first mentioned notion of freedom, which is amongst others to be found in Locke, looks upon freedom as the ability to do something; according to the rational variant, which has Kant as its most typical representative, a man is free when he acts according to what reason dictates him; enforceable rational freedom, again, forms a subdivision of this same species and is distinguished by the fact that it allows freedom to be enforced whenever the individual agent has preferences or acts in a way which runs counter to what is best for him by rational standards.

Cranston proceeds to classify all definitions depicting freedom as some faculty or other, as lexicographical definitions and since they all differ from his own earlier findings on this point, he is in a position to reject all the instances of this type of conception of freedom. This fate befalls, amongst others, Hobbes and Locke. Theories of rational and enforceable rational freedom, on the other hand, involve descriptions of freedom which clearly belong to the category of stipulative definitions. It follows that they can only be tested by reference to the two rules for sound stipulative definition, quoted above. None of the theories thus investigated passes this test.

Cranston's contribution to a lexicographical definition of freedom and his inquiry into the various theories of freedom both aim at establishing something like the 'factual' meaning of the word freedom or its 'descriptive meaning'. In the course of his first enterprise he seeks to provide a better understanding of the factual meaning given to the term in common speech. Similarly, in his inquiry into the various theories of freedom, he classifies and assesses the factual meaning denoted by the term. In addition to this — but entirely separated from this former kind of inquiry — Cranston comments in passing on a fundamentally different sort of meaning, which he terms the emotive meaning of words. This refers to the outspokenly emotive connotation which some words have; apart from carrying a purely factual meaning, these words also reflect the attitude of the speaker with respect to its descriptive content. These attitudes are conveyed together with the descriptive meaning of the word. Cranston's chief conclusion with respect to this point is that freedom carries an almost invariably laudatory emotive meaning. It is, unmistakably, an 'hurrah word'.

Emotive and Descriptive Meaning

With respect to the relationship between the emotive and the descriptive meaning of words Cranston relies predominantly on Stevenson's *Ethics and Language*, an early contribution to analytical political philosophy. One of Stevenson's central arguments was that the emotive meaning of words may in some cases get its own momentum, acquiring a status more or less independent of its descriptive meaning. This may be explained as follows. We are all familiar with the fact that the meaning of a word is not fixed once and forever: in due course it may gradually adopt a different meaning. One of the new insights pointed out by Stevenson is that, in the course of such a process of change, the emotive and descriptive meaning of such a word may shift with respect to one another. In this way it may happen that the descriptive meaning, which a certain word denotes at a certain point in time, gradually changes while its emotive meaning remains the same, or vice versa. Stevenson describes this phenomenon in terms of a certain 'inertia of meaning': it is as if something of the original laudatory connotation of the word remains even though its factual meaning has already changed.

Cranston is well aware of the intrinsic connection of the emotive and the descriptive meaning of a word. Yet, when it comes to his analysis of freedom, he seems to have dropped this idea of an intrinsic connection altogether. This is, at all events, what emerges from the conclusion which he draws from his inquiry into the meaning of freedom:

> 'freedom' ... has a strong laudatory emotive meaning for English-speaking peoples, whether in political or more general use ... while the descriptive meaning of 'freedom' ... varies, the emotive meaning tends, nevertheless, to be constant.[27]

---

[27] *Ibid.*, p. 15.

However, such a stringent and absolute distinction between emotive and descriptive meaning presupposes an untenable interpretation of the first kind of meaning. We may safely assume that the emotive meaning of a word is not God-given. A more plausible genesis would seem to be that it somehow reflects a certain evaluation of the content of the term on the part of the speaker. Such a reading would suggest an intrinsic relationship between the emotive and descriptive meaning of a word, and that feature certainly sets limits to the range within which such mutual shifts in the position of the two kinds of meaning can occur.

Cranston's conclusions may be situated in a wider context by pointing out that the sharp distinction which he draws between the emotive and descriptive meaning of words largely corresponds to the positivist notion that norms and facts belong to two altogether different logical categories and should consequently be kept strictly separate. The idea was practically unchallenged at the time when Cranston wrote his book and in this sense he may be seen as a child of his time. In later years, however, the notion of some fundamental division between norms and facts became the subject of devastating criticisms.

The questionable status of the dichotomy between facts and values has been set out meritoriously in Hannah Pitkin's chapter on judgment in her book on the significance of Wittgenstein for our thinking about politics.[28] According to Pitkin the dichotomy between norms and facts is a familiar and widely accepted idea which is but too often — and usually uncritically — accepted. In particular, it is common to assume that by means of these two categories it would be possible to make an exhaustive and yet meaningful classification of all the propositions and statements about the world. It is this very assumption which Pitkin questions.

While it is no doubt a widely accepted idea, it is yet less self-evident than has sometimes been assumed. In the first place there are many propositions which simply cannot be grouped under either of the categories, at least not without considerable distortion. Moreover, it is not sensible to try to divide the world at all costs into norms and facts. Pitkin suggests that one might just as well try to divide all commodities in the market-

---

[28] Hannah Pitkin, *Wittgenstein and Justice: on the Significance of Ludwig Wittgenstein for Social and Political Thought*, Berkeley, California, 1972.

place into herring and fruit. While a strict division into norms and facts may at times appear illuminating, it is very often quite the contrary since a good deal of important and relevant distinctions are blurred in the attempt.

Instead of fixing our attention on the pointless division into norms and facts it would be better to take into account that there are many kinds of activity in which we may be involved in our everyday life and that each of these separate activities has its own rules in terms of which that activity is being done. Similarly, the kinds of argument and the sort of events which will be taken as relevant to the *discourse* belonging to that activity, equally depend on these defining rules. In this manner ethics, aesthetics, politics and scientific activity are separate domains constituted by a set of defining rules: seen from this point of view, taking part in political activity becomes a matter of learning and applying the rules governing that activity. And, the other way round, it is only by referring to those rules that one can establish whether or not someone is taking part in a certain activity. This is not to say that data or insights, which are seen as relevant by all the people practicing a certain kind of activity, cannot change over time. It simply is part of the defining characteristics of such an activity that there are certain rules in terms of which may be established what kind of data will be taken to constitute sufficient evidence.

Given that every field has its own criteria of validity and rationality, it is obviously less meaningful to try to group all these separate realms of human activity into two large heaps. This fundamental criticism of the notion that norm and fact need to be kept strictly separated would seem to dig away the ground under what I have presented here as one of the two pillars of Cranston's analysis. The more recent criticism of positivism also points in the direction of a less extreme opposition between the emotive and descriptive meaning of words. Freedom is no neutral, non-committal term and the question as to its factual meaning can only be answered in connection with its evaluative meaning.

Lexicographical and Stipulative Definitions

A second comment on Cranston's inquiry into the various theories of freedom may be made with regard to the way in which he writes about stipulative definitions. His inquiry proceeds on the assumption that there is only one kind of description of freedom, to which the question as to whether it is correct or not properly applies, and that is a lexicographical definition. Such a definition, reporting on the way a word is used in common speech may be right or wrong. Descriptions which have a different aim are by definition of an arbitrary nature and consequently do not allow for a conclusion as to whether they are correct.

Given the great proliferation of meanings attributed to the term freedom, it would seem tempting to establish what actually is its correct meaning and which of the rival descriptions is correct. However, by Cranston's standards, such an enterprise would be bound to fail from the very beginning. According to him, the said 'philosophical' theories, by their very nature, cannot be tested as to their validity. For, this would be like asking whether a stipulative definition is correct, a question which, given its arbitrary nature, is meaningless.

Cranston rightly points to a certain arbitrary element in the nature of stipulative definitions. Yet, in my opinion, he exaggerates this point when he tests the selected concepts of freedom merely in terms of their being unequivocal. In a formal sense, it may be said that everyone is free to produce his own definition, but it will be obvious that whenever this assumes too idiosyncratic a form nobody would understand it. There is no such thing as a private language.

This objection suggests a less extreme interpretation of stipulative definition. We may concede to Cranston that there is an arbitrary element in this activity, but that does not make it into an entirely arbitrary thing. And, for the same reason, it becomes possible and useful to determine whether a definition of freedom is appropriate, irrespective of the fact of whether it happens to be a stipulative definition.

We have seen that Cranston uses just two criteria for sound stipulative definition and, although neither of these is unreasonable, it is by no means obvious that they form a sufficient set of conditions for the stipulation of meaning. In the first place Cranston requires an unequivocal meaning: his 'repudiation' criterion demands that every term may carry one meaning only. This requirement is presented as a simple operationalization of the quest for *clarity*. However, an unequivocal meaning appears to me to be an insufficiently specific criterion. It is at once too broad and too narrow. Meaning and sense cannot invariably be situated in individual words. Meaning appears in the context of language. The requirement that every individual word should have a distinct, well-defined and uniform meaning unjustifiedly excludes certain more complex — but for that reason no less real — concepts. To establish the meaning of a word one needs to turn to its 'grammar,' the rules governing its use. In this respect Cranston's quest for an unequivocal meaning may thus be taken as too stringent a criterion, which also disqualifies a number of meaningful definitions. Again, in a different respect Cranston's criterion is too broad. On the basis of his assumptions any stipulation would be appropriate as long as the speaker avoids all different meanings and does not stipulate that new term to denote an already existing meaning. This provision allows for the most idiosyncratic stipulations.

Language is not a private matter. If at least I want to make myself understood by others, I will have to make sensible stipulations which implies that there must somehow be an intelligible connection between the current meaning of a word and its newly stipulated meaning. I may decide that a certain term has an insufficiently specific meaning in everyday life speech and thus is unfit for my purposes. In such a case I may attempt to improve upon the clarity of the discussion by defining the meaning of the term more precisely through a stipulative definition. Such a fencing off of the meaning does leave an intelligible connection with its meaning in ordinary speech.

Persuasion

Once it is established that none of the investigated theories of rational and enforceable rational freedom meets the necessary criteria for sound stipulative definition, Cranston suggests that they might be seen as persuasive definitions. Such a rhetorical device intends to replace the current descriptive meaning of a word with a new content which the author or speaker presents as a more appropriate rendering of the term. It is distinguished from stipulative definitions in general by its intention to persuade a certain audience that the newly stipulated meaning of the term is its correct meaning. This last feature of persuasive definition allows Cranston relatively easily to demonstrate the illogical character of persuasive definitions: for, as a stipulative definition, a persuasive definition simply cannot make a claim to validity.

While this would seem to be a fatal inconsistency in the structure of persuasive definition Cranston does not draw any consequences from his reasoning. At this point he chooses to leave the material to 'speak for itself'. But even without further elaboration the implications of his argument are obvious: in his hands theories of rational and enforceable rational freedom acquire the status of pure fabrications, arising from the brain of imaginative writers and it is crystal clear to him that these theories have nothing to do with 'the meaning of freedom'; the only thing which still needs explaining is as to how these doctrines nevertheless proved capable of persuading so many people.

In this section I shall restrict myself to setting out my chief objections to Cranston's dealing with the concept of freedom in general, objections which also bear on the hypothetical conclusions concerning Green's doctrine. These objections are twofold. First, Cranston's method of argument reflects an untenable view of language and the part words have to play in it. His formal test of stipulative definition in fact presupposes that everyone is free to attach his own meaning to a word. This point of criticism may first be brought to bear on his interpretation of stipulative definition; in turn this works through in the distinction between lexicographical and stipulative definition.

This latter distinction, as we saw, forms an essential part in his argumentation. As a second point of criticism, it may be said that Cranston's argument on the meaning of freedom neglects the specific nature of political concepts, like freedom. This readily emerges when we point at a tacit assumption of Cranston's contribution to a lexicographical definition of freedom. Cranston's method of argument tacitly assumes that the meaning of freedom may be established empirically, in the same way as one goes about determining the meaning of words like 'table' or 'chair'. But this assumption is less evident than Cranston apparently thinks. It would seem to me that he has sought to cut short with one stroke the perennial discussion about the most appropriate meaning of freedom by investigating such a neutral looking subject as the factual meaning of the word. This project is then carried out by establishing its meaning in everyday life speech. For, an obvious corollary of the appeal to something like the factual meaning, or lexicographical definition of a word is that all different meanings of that word are wrong and tend to mislead the public. Moreover it is inconceivable that the term freedom would have been able to provoke such a longstanding discussion, if the debate could have been concluded by an appeal to its factual meaning. In my view, in its politically relevant sense, the question as to the factual meaning of freedom is a question which penetrates to the essence of political theory. Its meaning never is simple or unproblematic.

C. Berlin's Two Concepts of Liberty

In 1958, 80 years after Green made preparations for his public lecture on the occasion of his being appointed to the Whyte's professorship, Oxford University heard an inaugural address voicing a substantial criticism of his conception of freedom. This was Isaiah Berlin's *Two Concepts of Liberty*, delivered when he was appointed to the Chichele chair. With this speech, which soon established itself as a classic text in political theory, the discussion on the meaning of freedom provoked by Green's redefinition seemed for the time being to be settled in favour of the negative conception of freedom.

In his lecture, Berlin suggested grouping all current notions of freedom around two archetypes, respectively indicated as negative and positive freedom. Negative freedom is then defined as a certain area within which an individual can act unhampered by others and do what he wants. Positive freedom is described as self-mastery, the situation in which one can direct one's own life. An important thesis Berlin develops is that, although the two do not start at great logical distance, these two conceptions of freedom went through such an historical development that they came to mean two entirely opposed, even incompatible attitudes to life. In its negative rendering, freedom always remained connected with its original, proper meaning whereas positive theories of freedom in fact often involved repression of the individual.

On various occasions Berlin stressed the empirical nature of this thesis. In his Introduction to *Four Essays* he says for instance that he does not mean to imply that positive theories of freedom necessarily result in an authoritarian doctrine which would lead to and legitimise brutal repression in the name of freedom. Berlin's point is primarily a matter of factual observation, which he then seeks to render intelligible in terms of a sketch of the development of the positive notion of freedom which, starting from a genuinely liberal notion, proceeded to its opposite. Central to Berlin's analysis on this point is a metaphysical theory of the self, whereby the self is no longer conceived as a empirical entity, but is divided into a 'higher' or 'true' self and a 'lower' self. This latter term is subsequently identified with one's ordinary, empirical life whereas the higher self is identified with all sorts of 'forms of life wider than the empirical spatio-temporal existence of the finite individual'.[29] By means of this construction it becomes possible to force individuals and to repress them in the name of freedom.

Proceeding from such a division of the self into two distinct components various historical instances of positive theories of freedom have been formulated in terms of which all sorts of claims could be made which, in Berlin's assessment, no longer have anything to do with freedom. In the first place, Berlin discusses in this connection doctrines of 'self-abnegation,' i.e. theories which aim at sublimating unrealisable ideals or desires, a psychological mechanism which is commonly known as 'sour grapes'. Secondly, Berlin discusses what he calls the 'positive doctrine of liberation by reason'.[30] According to this doctrine individual agents merely have one fundamental aim which is 'rational self-direction'. All ends which individuals gifted with reason could conceivably have, form part of one comprehensive rational order. It follows that conflicts about norms can only originate from a lack of rational faculties on the part of the individual involved. Seen in this perspective such conflicts may in principle be solved and will automatically disappear when all those involved grow sufficiently rational. When everyone eventually has become an entirely rational agent, people will by their own inclination abide by rational laws which are identical for everyone. In this way all members of a community are at once bound by the law and yet completely free (in the positive sense, as set out by Berlin).

Berlin's criticism of the positive doctrine of rational freedom constitutes the most substantial issue of his lecture and it has a clear bearing on Green's theory. However, in order to bring out the rich variety of insights, recommendations and conclusions, as they can be derived from his lecture, we have to con-

---

[29] Berlin, *Four Essays on Liberty*, p. xlv; cf. Cranston makes essentially the same point when he observes that the said theorists employ 'a more rarified self,' *Freedom: A New Analysis*, p. 23.

[30] Berlin, *Four Essays on Liberty*, p. 144.

sider his criticism of this specific point as part of a more general thesis.

The main important general recommendation Berlin makes in his essay may be rendered as a plea against conceptual confusion. Berlin is fully aware of the normative character of political terms like freedom and he is fully alive to the fact that this category of words cannot invariably be pinned down to a well-defined factual meaning, owing to the part these words play in political argumentation. However, this feature of political terms does not justify any undue ambiguity of their factual meaning. While admitting the peculiar nature of the relationship of evaluative and descriptive elements in the meaning of political concepts, Berlin nevertheless repudiates the conceptual confusion which came over many doctrines and expositions on freedom. His criticism as to this point may be summarized in three, partly overlapping points:

1. confusion of the various distinct political and ethical norms;

2. confusion, in particular, of the positive and negative conceptions of freedom; as well as

3. confusion of freedom and the conditions for its effective use.

In the Introduction to *Four Essays* moreover he singles out for criticism the identification of freedom with its actual exercise, as can be seen in the work of Fromm. All these forms of conceptual confusion with regard to freedom seem to be prompted by the fact that freedom – by itself – is almost invariably looked upon as something desirable. Its laudatory nature makes the term much called for and it is this intensive appeal to freedom which gave rise to the extensive conceptual confusion.

According to Berlin the inflation of the meaning of freedom, which is thus brought about, is nevertheless inappropriate and he provides a decisive argument in support of his opinion. To admit the intrinsic importance and the value of individual freedom is one thing, but this does not imply that it should be pursued in every situation at all costs. Freedom is not the only end of life; it is just one end among many others, each of which may have its own intrinsic value. To stamp individual freedom as an end in itself does not make it into an ideal which can claim priority over other ideals. It is this mistaken reasoning which has provoked many undue attempts to change the meaning of the term freedom. Here, as elsewhere, the making of the diagnosis already points the way to the remedy; to acknowledge the pluriform nature of human values is to recognise that the meaning of freedom should not unduly be extended so as to turn the concept into a *summum bonum*; it is equally unnecessary, according to such a point of view, to discount the desirable character of freedom or any other human value. Berlin advocated a pluralistic system of values in which often a choice will have to be made between conflicting ideals, each of which may be counted as of intrinsic value. If we do not allow ourselves to be restricted by a number of monistic assumptions, such a pluralistic system of values is the only tenable position left to us and Berlin even reckons the necessity of choosing between conflicting values to be one of the fundamental characteristics of the human condition.

Monism and Pluralism

A discussion on the concept of freedom between Green and Berlin may be rendered in terms of a number of separate points. First there is Berlin's criticism of what may be called the monistic fallacy. This presupposition, which does not allow of proof or disproof was already touched upon in the course of an earlier exposition of Berlin's criticism of what he characterised as positive doctrines of rational freedom. As to this point Berlin argued that many political thinkers tacitly assume that all political and moral values will eventually fit into some comprehensive, harmonious order. Berlin's point is that whenever this assumption would be appear to be unwarranted, people would necessarily have to choose between a number of ends of life, all of which may be of intrinsic value. Such a choice would not be made easier by the fact that each of these separate values may equally present absolute claims.

This point involves both a fundamental creed of Berlin's and a theoretical argument. Berlin's criticism of monism is central to his pluralism. He is not only convinced of the possibility that different human values, each of which may appear to have an absolute title, will come into conflict, he is also painfully aware that many of these values actually are mutually exclusive. His conviction both supports the importance he attaches to individual freedom and gives an undeniably tragic note to his conception of man. From a theoretical perspective his point of view must be reckoned to be superior to the position of the authors he criticizes since he points out an assumption which is demonstrably made by others without their being aware of it.

Berlin's criticism of monism fully applies to Green. And, in the case of the author of the *Prolegomena*, this is not even a matter of tacit assumption. In his book Green explicitly avows the ethical monism to which Berlin draws attention. It is made explicit, for instance, when Green states that 'There is no such thing really as a conflict of duties.'[31] Green holds this opinion without fully being aware of the eventually incompatible nature of this line of argument with the more voluntaristic elements which are equally to be discerned in his ethical theory. Chapter Two argued that this rationalistic assumption in fact takes away the basis of any ethics properly so called; when duties eventually cannot be in conflict, all ethical questions could – at least in principle – be resolved by providing a better insight into the circumstances of the case.

It must equally be pointed out that this is not to be reckoned an accidental passage or a slip of Green's pen. This opposition runs through Green's entire moral philosophy: the conflict between a rationalistic and a more voluntaristic line of argument leads Green to his remarkable claim that there is a proportional relationship between the goodness of someone's character and intentions, on the one hand, and the moral value of the results of his act, on the other. While the lines of argument are eventually incompatible, Green is capable of sustaining the two alongside one another by referring to the idea of omniscience. As to this point, too, the apparent discrepancies between intentions and results are explained away by an appeal to our insufficient understanding of all relevant circumstances; a full understanding, as would be required to see the proportional relationship between intention and effect of our activity, simply is not within the reach of ordinary mortal souls.

Proceeding from a rationalistic foundation Green creates room for a voluntaristic ethics by means of his argument concerning the imperfect understanding of man. At all events, it was not until a relatively late stage that Green became aware of the implication that in such a way ethical questions are reduced to the technical problem of an adequate insight. In my reading of Green, this detail about his philosophical develop-

[31] *Prolegomena*, sect. 324.

ment helps to explain a good deal of the otherwise inexplicable and, at any rate, remarkable turnings and twistings in the argument of the *Prolegomena*.

Green, Berlin, and the Status of Political Principles

If we are to discuss something like a dispute between Green and Berlin as to the status of political principles it must be made clear at the outset that this is, above all, a difference in emphasis between the arguments of Green and Berlin on this point. Political norms and values have a nature of their own. They are governed by their own rules and laws. This provides the vocabulary of politics with a number of specific characteristics, resulting from the task it is to accomplish. For this reason specific political concepts cannot be pinned down by something like a precise 'factual' meaning. According to his inaugural address, Berlin subscribed to this point about the nature and status of political norms and ideals.[32] However this acknowledgement does not commit one to the view that no distinction could be made between various political norms: freedom is not equality, or justice etc.

Berlin reproaches Green for having mixed up a number of things which ought to have been kept separate. Green's doctrine of positive freedom involves an unnecessary confusion of − amongst other values − absence of restraint and equality; equal opportunity for all members of the community to give full scope to their natural gifts, etc. This conclusion simply follows from the terms in which Berlin chooses to describe this fallacy and these terms apply indeed to an important extent to Green's theory:

> ... nothing is gained by a confusion of terms ... a sacrifice is not an increase in what is being sacrificed, namely freedom, however great the moral need or the compensation for it. Everything is what it is: liberty is liberty, not equality or fairness or justice or culture, or human happiness or a quiet conscience.[33]

One kind of defence which could conceivably be made of this point is by viewing his doctrine in the light of the political values current in his age. In view of the political norms of his age it would have been futile for Green to argue that individual freedom is not always equally desirable.

---

[32] Berlin, *Four Essays on Liberty*, p. 158.
[33] *Ibid.*, p. 125.

However, I think that, in his crusade against conceptual confusion, Berlin allows himself to be carried to the other extreme.[34] In spite of his own confirmation that this is not to be carried too far,[35] I think he is nevertheless trying too hard to pin down some factual meaning of freedom. Where Berlin feels he is in a position to make statements about the correct meaning of 'freedom,' and challenges certain other meanings attributed to the term, I cannot but conclude that he must assume some kind or other 'essence' of freedom. Failing this it would be difficult to see on which grounds he could claim priority for freedom in the negative sense.[36] Nor would it be possible, in that case, to claim that any genuine concept of freedom must always involve an element of his version of negative freedom.[37]

Political ideals are not all the same. Freedom is not equality. Yet, emphasizing something like the factual meaning of freedom tends to neglect the peculiar character of political norms and values, a character which, in the absence of a better term, I will provisionally refer to as their 'visionary' nature.[38] By this predicate I refer to the fact that terms in the vocabulary of politics have a part to play in the constitution of a certain practical conception on the part of the members of a community concerning what is politically expedient and desirable. This will be worked out in the following section in which a rejoinder to his twentieth-century critics will be given on Green's behalf.

A Further Criticism

Berlin's inaugural address raised a good deal of discussion and caused a genuine revival of the debate on the meaning of freedom. One of the attempts made on the occasion of Berlin's lecture to create a certain order in the wide variety of shades and nuances in the meaning which various authors had sought to attribute to the term freedom was that undertaken by W.L. Weinstein, like Green a staff member of Balliol. According to Weinstein, Green's positive doctrine of freedom

[34] It is not only Green's rendering of 'positive freedom' which occasions Berlin's criticism, he also opposes the use of the term 'freedom' by 'liberation movements,' originating from an increasing national consciousness.
[35] Berlin, *Four Essays on Liberty*, p. 158.
[36] Explicitly on p. lvi, amongst other places.
[37] See, for example, p. 161.
[38] This is chosen with reference to the title of Sheldon Wolin, *Politics and Vision*, Boston, 1960.

draws attention to a number of important points and provides a fundamental criticism of certain blind spots which are characteristic of champions of negative freedom. However, in Weinstein's opinion these criticisms are weakened, as it were, since Green presents them in the form of a 'misguided attempt to redefine the *meaning* of freedom itself'. According to Weinstein, the doctrine of positive freedom should not be taken as a statement concerning the meaning of freedom as much as belonging to an altogether different logical category, i.e. an argument concerning the *criteria* which make freedom an end worthy of pursuit.

In order to create a common ground in the babel of tongues about the concept of freedom, Weinstein suggested that all arguments concerning freedom should distinguish carefully between two kinds of questions. The first is as to the 'purpose or value of being free'; whereas the second inquires into the appropriate extent of freedom allowed to the individual.[39] This distinction is important since, as Weinstein argues, an answer to the former does not have a direct bearing on the latter question: it sets 'only broad limits' within which such a criterion for the proper extent of individual freedom must be found. The question as to why freedom is important cannot be answered without considering the conditions for its effective use. Weinstein criticises Green and many of his later interpreters for having packed into one notion a multitude of desirable things, thereby neglecting the distinction pointed out. He offers a clear analysis of the three distinct elements on which rests Green's transition from the negative to the positive concept of freedom. He then goes on to present self-realization as a 'fourth element' of Green's concept of positive freedom. Apparently this is seen as something *alongside* the three separate points distinguished earlier in his essay by which he analyses the distinction between negative and positive freedom as it is to be found in his *Liberal Legislation*. Now, in the reconstruction of the doctrine of positive freedom in the framework of Green's system of philosophy, as was given in Chapter Three, I hope to have pointed out sufficiently clearly that, for Green, positive freedom is in fact intended to serve as an equivalent to the sum of conditions rendering a man's self-realization possible. Self-realization cannot be reduced to one

[39] Weinstein, 'The Concept of Liberty in Nineteenth Century English Political Thought,' p. 146.

of the elements involved in positive freedom. Rather, it should be taken as identical to freedom in the positive sense, or, at any rate it should be seen as an attempt to give a non-teleological equivalent to the notion of self-realization so as to be effectively employed in arguments about the appropriate extent of state interference in society and the proper relationship of these legal regulations and individual responsibilities.

Self-realization is not so much one of the elements of positive freedom as positive freedom itself; the three elements discerned by Weinstein all form part of the process of self-realization of the individual agent. When an individual pursues an ideal of self-realization this already qualifies his activities. Thus, while on the one hand it would be impossible to say beforehand what exactly his ideal self consists in, there are nevertheless certain limits set to this process. These limits follow from the structure of all moral activity. The three concrete qualifications, which — according to Green — are involved in positive freedom, all have this *a priori* status. They do not restrict the freedom of the will, but are inherent in the structure of all moral activity.

D. A Rejoinder to Twentieth-Century Criticism of Green

In so far as they have a bearing on Green's theory of positive freedom, the arguments of twentieth-century theorists of freedom rest on an essential misapprehension of what Green intended to accomplish with his theoretical enterprise. When brought to bear on Green's position, arguments derived from the work of these later authors look upon his theoretical enterprise as if he was merely seeking to give a new meaning to the concept of freedom by means of a persuasive definition. Green does not stop at what he thinks is a more appropriate meaning of freedom. Apart from stipulating a new meaning Green also provides a number of *reasons why* his sense of freedom is more appropriate. Later theorists, all of whom explicitly or implicitly criticize Green's enterprise, entirely neglect this part of Green's argument.

What Green sought to accomplish with his doctrine of positive freedom touches upon the essence of political theory. Green provided his contemporaries with a conception of a desirable organization of society in terms of which certain matters could be justified which so far — i.e. on the basis of existing political ideals — could not be defended. The element of persuasion in his vision of positive freedom is a feature which his enterprise has in common with all other political doctrines. For, by its very nature, political theory aims at persuading people. Green provided his audience with a conception of political activity in terms of which the policy he sought to support could be justified, a function which earlier political doctrines could not perform.

Earlier in this chapter it was already indicated that most of Green's critics based themselves on his *Liberal Legislation*. Given this source, it is not surprising that the conceptual link with the orthodox negative meaning of freedom eluded them. To bring out this conceptual link of positive and negative freedom, Green's doctrine of freedom must be situated in the context of his philosophy of consciousness; in particular it must be taken in connection with the notion of a process of 'self-assertion of reason' in terms of which the progress of human consciousness may be understood as a process of development in the direction of an ever-unfolding, ever-deepening reason, or an ever-continuing rationalisation of the world. The conceptual continuity of positive and negative freedom readily emerges by situating the two concepts of freedom as two subsequent stages in this process.

The Status of Political Principles

It will be clear that the posthumous critics of this theoretical enterprise of Green's proceed from a number of presuppositions concerning the nature and status of the concept of freedom, which differ considerably from Green's assumptions. Even a perceptive thinker like Berlin appeals to something like the factual status of the concept when he seeks to make out what freedom *is*, i.e. absence of restraint.[40] By dealing with the concept of freedom in this manner it is turned into a factual entity, comparable with 'table' or 'chair'. It is only on the basis of such an assumption that an investigation into the correct meaning of the word may be undertaken. And, once such an investigation is attempted, it is obvious that an appeal to the factual meaning of the word constitutes the strongest possible argument. If it is a matter of empirically determining the

---

[40]   Berlin, *Four Essays on Liberty*, p. lvi.

meaning of the word, there remains little, if anything, to be discussed once this is done.

However, if I am correct with my reading of Green, freedom differs in a fundamental sense from empirical concepts. As an evaluative concept it occupies an important place in the vocabulary of the discourse and the theory of politics. In view of its unmistakably laudatory connotation, 'freedom' must count as an evaluative as much as a descriptive concept.

In a summary form Green's argument may be reduced to his pointing out a logical continuity of the accepted, orthodox meaning of freedom and the positive notion which he seeks to introduce. This continuity cannot be apprehended as long as 'freedom' is conceived as a merely empirical concept. Green's claim to a certain conceptual continuity of the positive and negative notions of freedom presupposes a peculiar status of the concept of freedom. Freedom should not be looked upon as a merely descriptive concept; it is a term which apart from its descriptive meaning also has what I would like to call — with a reference to Wolin — a visionary meaning or function. With this term I refer to the fact that, like other terms in the vocabulary of politics 'freedom' is fit to play a part in the image by which the political theorist seeks to convey his message to his audience. This may be explained as follows. The laudatory connotation which a word may carry at a given point in time is not entirely separated from the practical conception underlying people's activity. As set out in Chapter Two the notion of a certain practical conception forms the foundation of Green's moral psychology. Green argues that all human activity proceeds from practical conceptions, i.e. representations of some desired state of affairs directing one's activity. These value judgments, which are invariably involved in the laudatory meaning of words (such as freedom), enter into the constitution of these practical conceptions. In other words: by conceiving the laudatory meaning of a word as something which can be established in separation from its factual meaning one tends to neglect the peculiar nature of words from the vocabulary of politics. In the remainder of this section I shall briefly comment on this point.

Intersubjectivity and the Conveyance of Values

Green's intervention in the practical situation in nineteenth-century England constituted a pure example of the activity of a political thinker. By means of providing a new perspective on the current state of affairs he sought to resolve a problem which so far had been an obstacle to a justification of more advanced forms of state interference in society. To accomplish this task Green had to demonstrate that the conception of a just organization of society he advanced was indeed valuable and desirable. His political philosophy served to convince his contemporaries that the value judgments involved in his vision of a just society constituted a valid political ideal. By means of his political theory he sought to persuade his audience to share this value judgment.

Such an enterprise can be attempted in various ways. First of all, a value judgment may be conveyed to others by means of an appeal to moral intuitions. Value judgments are sometimes simply stated and in certain cases this simply works. Political theory is distinguished from this sort of conveyance of norms and values by the fact that, characteristically, it seeks to persuade people by giving *reasons why* something must be seen as a good cause.

It is true that in providing such reasons, one always and necessarily proceeds from certain presuppositions. If only one goes sufficiently far back in the chain of reasoning, one will always find certain normative assumptions. The reasoned positions of political theory also rest on certain normative assumptions which it would be futile to discuss. In the absence of agreement as to those assumptions, a political discourse would be impossible.

Political theory properly so called distinguishes itself from a mere positing of normative judgments in that it provides reasons to support these judgments. There are, it is true, limits to the degree in which one can argue about value judgments, but this does not render it impossible. In this respect there is an obvious parallel with argumentation in the field of aesthetics. In aesthetics, too, it is not always possible to draw sharp distinctions, less so, in any event, than is the case with judgments on matters of fact. But that is not to say that 'everything goes' in aesthetics.

Political theories characteristically consist in giving reasons by which certain value judgments concerning the organization of society may be supported. In general terms, a political theory is better, or 'stronger,' according as it provides better arguments. And, other things being equal, providing reasons is a more sophisticated procedure than merely stating value judgments. In the realm of political theory 'x is a good thing because . . . ' is better than 'x is good.'

Green's doctrine of positive freedom provides this kind of reasons and by reproaching him for conceptual confusion his critics entirely neglect this feature of his doctrine. These criticisms of Green fail to consider what is the most important part of Green's argument, the part, namely, which makes his enterprise into a compelling political theory. Had Green merely given a new rendering of the concept of freedom, his work would have been merely expedient in view of the political and social conditions in nineteenth century England, but, as was in fact argued by Weinstein, it would have lacked a philosophical basis.[41]

E. On Political Theory

Political theory intends to give a vision in terms of which certain factual circumstances may be made politically relevant. Characteristically, such an intellectual enterprise aims at persuading a certain community that a certain organization of society is desirable. Each political theory properly so called proceeds on certain normative ideas about the most desirable order of things. These norms and values the theorist seeks to convey to his audience. Given this need to convince his audience and to persuade them into sharing these values the theorist usually cannot restrict himself to mere statements. To convince his audience he will have to work up a line of reasoning in such a way that the opinions he holds will result as its logical conclusion.

As a next step in ascertaining the nature of political theory I must point to the peculiar nature of value judgments. Assertions about values are not objective in the way factual judgments are, but neither are they entirely subjective. As was already mentioned, the status of value judgments is best compared to that of aesthetical judgments. They should be situated somewhere in between subjective and objective matters. With regard to both kinds of judgment it is possible, in principle, to convince others by stating reasons. In this respect morals and aesthetics have a common feature and the same may be said

---

[41] Weinstein, 'The Concept of Liberty in Nineteenth Century English Political Thought,' pp. 153-4.

about political norms: in a political discourse it is also possible
to convince others, by giving relevant arguments, that certain
values are superior to others and that they therefore deserve to
be adopted and cherished.

Eventually, there is only one criterion for the persuasion of
other people, and that is effectiveness. When you succeed in
persuading others into accepting your values, your mode of
persuasion is effective. This may well be the case if these values immediately appeal to human intuition. In those cases
these norms and values do not need any further foundation.
Most of the time, however, persuading other people will take
place by means of an appeal to reason, the faculty which all
human beings share. In the search for a universal standard in
terms of which value judgments may be compared and
asserted, reason is, of course, pre-eminently suited.

In line with these observations, I want to suggest the following model in terms of which all political philosophy may be
understood. This model looks upon political theory as consisting of a set of norms and ideals and an appeal to the rational
faculties of man. In the context of political theory the said
norms and ideals are presented as the result of a certain train of
reasoning. Ordinarily, it is only in this manner that others can
be persuaded to accept a certain position; I would like to suggest that we can only properly speak about a political theory
when such a theoretical construction consists of a certain train
of reasoning, in addition to a given normative position (which
is, it seems to me, a *sine qua non* for political theory).

Political Theory, Persuasion, and Human Understanding

The activity of the political theorist may also be characterized
by saying that he seeks to convince his audience of the desirability of a certain order of things by offering them a vision
representing such an order. When a theorist favours a certain
organization of society he can convey the conception of such
an order of things by depicting a sketch in which various factual circumstances and presently existing forces in society are
harmoniously worked up.

In what manner exactly does this way of persuading by
means of depicting such a vision take place? All human understanding operates by interpreting experiences in terms of a
certain prior conceptual scheme. A similar pattern may be discerned in perceiving things: in this kind of mental activity sen-

suous impressions are related to a certain prior concept and thus being interpreted as a distinct object.

Given that all thinking operates by means of concepts it would be impossible to test whether concepts are adequate by referring to the reality 'behind' these concepts. We cannot rid ourselves of our own scheme of things, we are entirely dependent on it. The corollary of this is that the only conceivable test as to whether concepts are adequate would be a comparison of rival ways of conceptualising the world, as a result of which one could conclude that a given conceptual scheme represents reality in a better way than other modes of conceptualisation. Some interpretative schemes are found to produce more satisfactory results than others. The only way to make ourselves independent of the concepts in terms of which we conceive reality is by avoiding a one-sided reliance on one single conceptual scheme; this may be accomplished by continuously scrutinising our practical conceptions and representations concerning what is desirable and expedient. In this way, our individual preferences are continuously being updated, but at the collective level, too, the conceptions as to what is politically expedient will be subject to perennial revision.

At this point, the significance of political theory may be explained. For it is up to the political theorist to provide new visions wherever existing modes of conceptualisation fall short of providing a theoretical framework capable of supporting a certain type of policy as is required by certain groups in society. Faced with political demands which call for policies that cannot be defended within the framework of existing models of society, people will have to revert to political theory once more and set up more adequate theoretical constructions.

Concepts forming part of the vocabulary of the discourse and the theory of politics have a persuasive function. In order to grasp the nature of this persuasive function, it is helpful to take account of the fact that all human understanding operates by means of concepts. Whenever we claim to understand something we relate a certain experience to an already established conceptual scheme. The precise nature of this experience of course constitutes a difficult problem for this theory of human understanding, but fortunately, this is not a problem which we need to resolve to achieve our present purposes. In the course of this exposition we only need to take account of the fact that, as human understanding necessarily operates in terms of concepts, we cannot do without these conceptual-isations about the world. In Green's terminology these indi-vidual concepts are seen as clusters of relations between objects of experience. Perhaps the most convincing illustration of this mental activity of relating experience to a prior concep-tual scheme is to be found in the case of perception. Perceiving an object involves the interpreting of certain sensuous impulses in terms of a certain concept. This may either be con-ceived prior to the act of perception, as the result of earlier observations and conceptualisations; or a new concept may be coined to cover a phenomenon which cannot be interpreted in terms of concepts based on earlier experience. According to the idealist theory of cognition, there is an essentially analo-gous mechanism operative in the more abstract forms of human understanding.

A certain conceptual scheme is a precondition of our under-standing. It would be futile to attempt to work out what our understanding would be like without these concepts. Since all our thinking inevitably employs certain concepts there arises a special problem when we want to establish whether these con-cepts are adequate. Such an investigation in fact seeks to find out the extent to which our conceptions correspond to reality as it 'really' is, i.e. independent of the formative activity of our mind. However, such a comparison is impossible, if only because the second term of the equation is beyond our cogni-tion. As our thinking inevitably makes use of concepts, the only way to assess whether they are 'adequate' is to compare them to alternative conceptualisations.

Concepts play a central part in both the theoretical and the practical mode of mind, but in the course of the present exposi-tion, we are primarily interested in the latter. In practical con-sciousness man presents to himself certain preferences or objects of will. It is by means of these representations that man sets his aims, to be achieved by his activity. The important point here is that political activity equally employs such repre-sentations of an expedient order of things which is capable of directing our practical activity. In fact, there are at least two ways in which concepts are essential to political experience. First, they enter into the constitution of the ends of our activity. Second, they are equally necessary to render factual circum-stances politically relevant. It is only on the basis of conceptions of things that we are capable to think about political matters.

Political theory forms an essential element in this process because it provides us with new ways of looking at things in terms of which we can conceive and give shape to political reality. Green's theory of freedom performs such a function. His doctrine forms part of the long tradition of political philosophy in that it provides a new vision for a situation which otherwise would have constituted a substantial theoretical obstacle to social reform. Earlier English liberal political theory looked upon freedom as the absence of restraint. The corollary of this conception of freedom was that the case for state interference in society could not be made in an unqualified manner. Proceeding on this rendering of freedom, the best case to be made for the kind of protective measures Green sought to defend was by depicting these measures as the lesser evil. It is clear that this point of view was less suited to serve as a theoretical basis on which to defend state interference in society. Green's doctrine of positive freedom provided a perspective in which state interference and individual freedom were no longer to be seen as two mutually exclusive things. On the basis of this new vision, both entities could be conceived as two forces working in the same direction.

F. Conclusion

By way of conclusion we may return to the question raised at the beginning of this chapter as to whether Green's doctrine stands up against the arguments levelled against him by his posthumous critics. Regarding this point, it must first of all be concluded that his theory of positive freedom goes beyond a mere persuasive definition. Green seeks to persuade by giving reasons supporting his point of view. These reasons are derived from an analysis of the structure of human consciousness. On the basis of this analysis he is able to situate the political ideal of freedom and explain it as the result of a certain stage in the development of human consciousness. This enables him to incorporate in a comprehensive theory the established fact that people look upon absence of restraint as a condition which is by itself something desirable and worthy of pursuit. And, by thus incorporating negative freedom, he is at once in a position to indicate its proper limits. Freedom, as absence of restraint, is no God-given value. It cannot make any

absolute claims which demand to be pursued in all circumstances and at all costs. Whenever it runs counter to the
ulterior standard, by reference to which it derives its value, it is
obvious that it cannot prevail as a political principle.

However, in the light of the arguments of later theorists of
freedom one might wonder why Green thought it appropriate
to call his political ideal by the name of 'freedom'. Why did he
think it necessary to present his political ideal as a form of freedom? We may go about answering this question in two ways.
The first is to point out that Green's theoretical enterprise
should be understood against the background of certain ideological needs of his age. In general terms this kind of answer
centres on the fact that freedom was looked upon as such an
important value that it would be most inopportune to leave
this argument to his political opponents. But, this line of argument would at best justify Green's opinions by situating them
in his time and any possible significance of his work for our
own thinking about politics would thereby at once be
excluded.

But a stronger claim can be made on behalf of Green's doctrine. Such an approach does not merely seek to explain
Green's move in terms of the ideological climate in which it
originated but to pay particular attention to the points in
which he shows a more profound insight than later theorists.
Concepts like freedom and other political ideals have a common feature in that, apart from a factual meaning they also
have a strong evaluative meaning. Along with this evaluative
meaning there is a distinctive motivating element to be discerned in these terms. Each evaluative meaning reflects a
value judgment concerning its conceptual contents on the part
of the speaker whereby this is at once stamped as something
which is by itself desirable, or just the reverse. This is not so
much a mechanistic connection; not every laudatory assessment of freedom necessarily implies that its factual contents
must for that reason be pursued at all costs. A laudatory connotation of a word does not produce an invariable commitment to pursue its factual contents. Perhaps one might say that
by describing a certain condition as freedom it acquires a certain credit, among other valuable things which are fit to be
objects of human pursuit. By describing something as freedom
one indicates that it is, *prima facie*, desirable. A laudatory connotation of a word does not mean that it should invariably be

strived for. On the other hand, this connection does imply that to establish what, in a given context, freedom consists in, is not entirely non-committal. For that reason I think it to be positively misleading to attempt to establish something like the 'descriptive' meaning of a word like freedom in separation from its evaluative meaning.

Green, more than any of the critics discussed, showed himself to be aware of this point. Even in the argument of his political speech at Leicester clues to this effect can be found, although these are partly distorted by ideological motives, as I will briefly indicate. On this occasion Green advanced the thesis that 'freedom, rightly understood, is the greatest of blessings; . . . its attainment is the true end of all our efforts as citizens.'[42] In this manner he already links the factual condition, which is referred to as 'freedom,' and its evaluation in a judgment concerning the desirability of such a state of affairs. Since he found freedom too powerful an argument to leave to his political opponents, he said in fact: freedom is rightly conceived of as a supreme value; but for that very reason it cannot merely denote absence of restraint. Green's argument in *Liberal Legislation* may be reduced to the following if-then statement: if you accept liberty as a politically expedient ideal, it cannot possibly consist in merely formal terms. Or, conversely, if conceived in these formal terms, liberty can never constitute a supreme good, for the conception of such a supreme good can only be expressed in a positive description.

The first point of permanent value which Green provides is therefore as to the politico-visionary function of the concept of freedom, a characteristic which it has in common with other concepts of the vocabulary and the theory of politics. A second observation to be made with regard to Green's theoretical enterprise, centres on his appeal to intuitions which people actually have about freedom. Part of his argumentation is founded on the real sense of freedom which people may experience in cases in which, according to the orthodox notion, their freedom is just being restricted. One of the arguments which Green makes in his first series of professorial lectures to justify his own use of the term freedom is that negative or 'juridical' freedom is not invariably looked upon as positive, or even relevant, while, on the other hand, it may well be that a restriction of the number of options open can produce a

[42] *Works*, iii, p. 370.

greater feeling of freedom.[43] Green illustrated his thesis with a reference to liquor traffic, a topic in which we know he was much involved. To take just one commonplace example: when one has nothing to do, a certain structuring of one's daily programme may well be taken as a liberation, even though it in fact involves a restriction of the things one can do. In my opinion, Green's appeal to people's actual intuitions constitutes a powerful argument in support of his presenting as a form of freedom a political ideal which we now would rather call social justice.

A further argument for Green to present this political ideal as a form of freedom is that, proceeding on the idealist theory of human consciousness, these two political ideals can be conceptually linked. Both principles can be interpreted as products of a certain stage in the development of human consciousness. Idealist philosophy of consciousness takes society itself as a product of the development of the individual self-conscious agent. This process of development, we saw, inevitably results in the mutual dependence of the members of a community, and eventually this will produce a mutual recognition of one another as being equally gifted with reason on the part of all members of that community; this, again, forms the basis of all rights and legal entitlements.

According to the idealist philosophy of consciousness, the ideal of negative freedom corresponds to this very stage in social development. The self-same dialectical mechanism which produced the ideal of freedom as absence of restraint, will eventually replace it by a social conception of freedom.

---

[43]   Cf. Chapter III, Section B.

Bibliography

Abbott, E. and L. Campbell, *The Life and Letters of Benjamin Jowett*, 2 vols, London: John Murray, 1897.

Acton, H.B., 'Idealism' in *The Encyclopaedia of Philosophy*, ed. Paul Edwards, London, Macmillan, 1967.

Aristotle, *Nicomachean Ethics*, translated by J.A.K. Thomson, Harmondsworth, Middlesex, 1976.

Asquith, H.H., *Memories and Reflections of the Earl of Oxford and Asquith*, 2 vols, London, 1928.

Barker, E., *Political Thought in England 1848-1914*, Oxford, 1951.

Berlin, I., *Four Essays on Liberty*, Oxford, 1969.

Bosanquet, B., *The Philosophical Theory of the State*, fourth edition, London, 1923;

— *The Principle of Individuality and Value*, London, 1912.

Boucher, D., and A. Vincent, *British Idealism and Political Theory*, Edinburgh, 2000.

Bradley, F.H., *Ethical Studies*, London, 1876.

Brink, D.O., 'Self-love and Altruism,' *Social Philosophy & Policy*, 14 (1997), pp. 122-57;

— *Perfectionism and the Common Good: Themes in the Philosophy of T.H.Green*, Oxford, 2003

Brooks, T., 'T.H.Green's Theory of Punishment,' *History of Political Thought*, 24 (2003), pp. 685-701.

Cacoullos, A.R., *Thomas Hill Green: Philosopher of Rights*, New York, 1974.

Caird, E., *A Critical Account of the Philosophy of Kant*, Glasgow, 1877;

— *Hegel*, Edinburgh , 1883;

— *The Critical Philosophy of Immanuel Kant*, 2 vols, Glasgow, 1889.

Carter, M., *T.H.Green and the Development of Ethical Socialism*, Exeter, 2003.

Clarke, P., *Liberals and Social Democrats*, Cambridge, 1978.

Collingwood, R.G., *An Autobiography*, Oxford, 1939.

Collini, S., *Liberalism and Sociology: L.T. Hobhouse and political argument in England 1880-1914*, Cambridge, 1979.

Cranston, M., *John Locke: A Biography*, London 1957;

— *Freedom: A New Analysis*, London, 1953.

Dimova-Cookson, M., *T.H. Green's Moral and Political Philosophy: A Phenomenological Perspective*, Basingstoke, 2001;

— 'A New Scheme of Positive and Negative Freedom: Reconstruct-
ing T.H.Green on Freedom,' *Political Theory*, 31 (2003), pp. 508-32.
Ensor, R.C.K., *England 1870-1914*, Oxford, 1936.
Entrèves, A.P. de, *The Medieval Contribution to Political Thought*,
London, 1939.
Fairbrother, W.H., *The Philosophy of T.H. Green*, London, 1896.
Freeden, M., *The New Liberalism: An Ideology of Social Reform*, Oxford,
1978;
— *Liberalism Divided: A Study in British Political Thought 1914-1939*,
Oxford, 1986.
Gaus, G.F., *The Modern Liberal Theory of Man*, London, 1983;
— 'Green, Bosanquet and the Philosophy of Coherence' in C.L.Ten,
ed., *The Routledge History of Philosophy, vol. vii: The Nineteenth
Century*, London, 1998.
Ginsberg, M., *Law and Opinion in England in the Twentieth Century*,
London, 1959.
Green, T.H., *Prolegomena to Ethics*, ed. A.C. Bradley, Oxford, 1883;
— *The Works of Thomas Hill Green*, 3 vols, ed. R.L. Nettleship, London,
1885-8;
— *Collected Works of T.H. Green*, ed. Peter Nicholson, 5 vols, Bristol,
1997;
— *Lectures on the Principles of Political Obligation and other writings*, ed.
Paul Harris and John Morrow, Cambridge, 1986;
— *Prolegomena to Ethics*, ed. David O.Brink, Oxford, 2003.
Grosskurth, P., *John Addington Symonds: a Biography*, London, 1964.
Halévy, E., *A History of the English People in the Nineteenth Century*, 6
vols, London, 1949-54;
— *The Growth of Philosophical Radicalism*, London, 1928.
Hayek, F.A., *John Stuart Mill and Harriet Taylor*, London, 1951.
Hegel, G.W.F., *Phänomenologie des Geistes*, Bamberg, 1807;
— *Wissenschaft der Logik*, 3 vols, Nürnberg, 1812-16;
— *Werke. Volständige Ausgabe durch einen Verein von Freunden des
Verewigten*, 18 vols, Berlin, 1832-45;
— *Philosophische Propädeutik* in *Werke*, vol. 18, ed. K. Rosenkranz,
Berlin, 1840;
— *Briefe von und an Hegel*, 4 vols, ed. J. Hoffmeister, Hamburg,
1952-60;
— *The Philosophical Propaedeutic*, translated by A.V. Miller, ed.
Michael George and Andrew Vincent, Oxford, 1986.
Herbert, J.B., ed., *Speeches of the Earl of Oxford and Asquith*, London,
1928.
Himmelfarb, G., *On Liberty and Liberalism: the Case of John Stuart Mill*,
New York, 1974.
Hobhouse, L.T., *Democracy and Reaction*, London, 1904;
— *Liberalism*, London, 1911;
— *The Metaphysical Theory of the State*, London, 1918;
— *Elements of Social Justice*, London, 1922.
Hurka, T., *Perfectionism*, New York, 1993.

Hylton, P., *Russell, Idealism, and the Emergence of Analytic Philosophy*, Oxford, 1990.

Irwin, T., 'Morality and Personality: Kant and Green' in A. Wood, ed., *Self and Nature*, Ithaca, 1984.

Kant, I., *Kritik der Reinen Vernunft* (1781, 2nd ed. 1787), Frankfurt, 1968.

Lamont, W.D., *Introduction to Green's Moral Philosophy*, London, 1934.

Laski, H.J., *Authority in the Modern State*, New York, 1918;
– *A Grammar of Politics*, London, 1925;
– *Liberty in the Modern State*, London, 1930.

Lasson, G., *Hegel-Archiv*, 3 vols, Leipzig, 1912-17.

Lindsay, A.D., *Kant*, London, 1934.

Locke, J., *Essay Concerning Human Understanding* (1690), London, 1961;
– *Two Treatises of Government* (1689), ed. P. Laslett, Cambridge, 1960.

MacCunn, J., *Six Radical Thinkers*, London, 1907.

Mill, J.S., *Principles of Political Economy* (1848), London, 1871;
– *On Liberty* (1859), Harmondsworth, Middlesex, 1974;
– *Autobiography* (1873), London, 1874.

Milne, A.J.M., *The Social Philosophy of English Idealism*, London, 1962.

Muirhead, J.H., *The Service of the State*, London, 1908;
– *Coleridge as Philosopher*, London, 1930;
– *The Platonic Tradition in Anglo-Saxon Philosophy*, London, 1931.

Newman, J.H., *The Idea of a University*, ed. C.F. Harrold, London, 1947.

Nicholls, D., 'Positive Liberty, 1880-1914,' *American Political Science Review*, 56 (1962), pp. 114-28.

Nicholson, P., *The Political Philosophy of the British Idealists*, Cambridge, 1990.

Packe, M. St. John, *The Life of John Stuart Mill*, London, 1954.

Passmore, J., *A Hundred Years of Philosophy*, London, 1957.

Pitkin, H., *Wittgenstein and Justice: on the Significance of Ludwig Wittgenstein for Social and Political Thought*, Berkeley, California, 1972.

Pucelle, J., *L'idealisme en Angleterre. De Coleridge à Bradley*, Neuchâtel, 1957;
– *La Nature et L'esprit dans la philosophie de T.H. Green*, 2 vols, Louvain, 1960-5.

Quinton, A., *Absolute Idealism*, London, 1972.

Richter, M., *The Politics of Conscience: T.H. Green and his Age*, London, 1964.

Ritchie, D.G., *The Principles of State Interference*, London, 1891.

Robbins, P., *The British Hegelians, 1875-1925*, New York, 1982.

Rodman, J.R., 'Introduction' in *The Political Theory of T.H. Green: Selected Writings*, ed. J.R.Rodman, New York, 1964;
– Review of A.R. Cacoullos, *Thomas Hill Green: Philosopher of Rights, Political Theory*, 4 (1976), pp. 142-5.

Samuel, H., *Liberalism: Its Principles and Proposals*, London, 1902;
– *Memoirs*, London, 1945.

Seth, A., and R.B. Haldane, ed., *Essays in Philosophical Criticism*, London, 1883.

Sidgwick, A., and E.M. Sidgwick, *Henry Sidgwick: A Memoir*, London, 1906.

Sidgwick, H., *The Methods of Ethics*, London, 1874;
— *The Principles of Political Economy*, London, 1883;
— *The Elements of Politics*, London, 1891;
— 'The Philosophy of T.H. Green,' *Mind*, 10 (1901), pp. 18-29;
— *Lectures on the Ethics of T.H. Green, H. Spencer and J. Martineau*, London, 1902.

Simhony, A., 'T.H. Green's Theory of the Morally Justified Society,' *History of Political Thought*, 10 (1989), pp. 481–98;
— 'Idealist Organicism: Beyond Holism and Individualism,' *History of Political Thought*, 12 (1991), pp. 515-35;
— 'On Forcing Individuals to be Free: T.H. Green's Liberal Theory of Positive Freedom,' *Political Studies*, 39 (1991), pp. 303-20;
— 'Beyond Negative and Positive Freedom: T.H. Green's View of Freedom,' *Political Theory*, 21 (1993), pp. 28-54.
— 'T.H.Green: The Common Good Society,' *History of Political Thought*, 14 (1993), pp. 225-47;
— 'Was T.H.Green a Utilitarian?,' *Utilitas*, 7 (1995), pp. 121-44.

Simhony, A., and D. Weinstein, ed., *The New Liberalism: Reconciling Liberty and Community*, Cambridge, 2001.

Skorupski, J., *English Language Philosophy 1750 to 1945*, Oxford, 1993.

Smith, C.A., *A Critical Study of T.H. Green's Theory of Political Obligation*, Ph. D. thesis, London: L.S.E., 1977;
— 'T.H.Green's Philosophical Manuscripts: an Annotated Catalogue,' *Idealistic Studies*, 9 (1978), pp. 178-83.

Soper, A. (O.S.B.), *T.H. Green as Theologian*, London, 1972.

Spender, J.A. and C. Asquith, *Life of the Earl of Oxford and Asquith*, 2 vols, London, 1932.

Stevenson, C.L., *Ethics and Language*, New Haven, 1960.

Taylor, C.., 'What is Wrong with Negative Liberty' in Alan Ryan, ed., *The Idea of Freedom*, Oxford, 1979.

Thomas, G., *The Moral Philosophy of T.H.Green*, Oxford, 1987.

Thomson, D., *England in the Nineteenth Century*, Harmondsworth, Middlesex, 1950.

Tyler, C., *Thomas Hill Green (1836-1882) and the Philosophical Foundations of Politics,* Lewiston, 1997;
— 'T.H.Green, Advanced Liberalism and the Reform Question 1865-1976,' *History of European Ideas*, 29 (2003), pp. 437-458.

Vincent, A.W., 'In Memoriam Thomas Hill Green,' report of the T.H. Green centenary conference, *Bulletin of the Hegel Society of Great Britain*, no. 6 (autumn/winter 1982), pp. 4-8;
— 'T.H. Green and the Religion of Citizenship' in Vincent, ed., *The Philosophy of T.H. Green*, Aldershot, 1986;

— 'T.H.Green: Citizenship as Political and Metaphysical' in David Boucher and Andrew Vincent, *British Idealism and Political Theory*, Edinburgh, 2000.

— , ed., *The Philosophy of T.H. Green*, Aldershot, 1986.

Vincent, A.W. and R. Plant, *Philosophy, Politics and Citizenship: The Life and Thought of the British Idealists*, Oxford, 1984.

Walsh, W.H., 'Thomas Hill Green,' in *The Encyclopaedia of Philosophy*, ed. Paul Edwards, London, 1967.

Ward, Mrs Humphry, *Robert Elsmere*, London, 1888.

Weinstein, W.L., 'The Concept of Liberty in Nineteenth Century English Political Thought,' *Political Studies*, 13 (1965), pp. 145-62.

Wolin, S.S., *Politics and Vision: Continuity and Innovation in Western Political Thought*, Boston, 1960.

Woodward, E.L., *The Age of Reform, 1815-1870*, Oxford, 1938.

Young, G.M., *Victorian England: Portrait of an Age*, Oxford, 1936.

Index